MURRAY HUBBARD is a journalist who has worked for 40 years in print media in Australia. He completed his cadetship at the *Melbourne Sun News Pictorial* in 1973 and later worked for *The Age* in Melbourne, the *Townsville Bulletin* after a sea-change, and then at the *Gold Coast Sun*. While at the *Gold Coast Sun* he was a three-time finalist for investigative reporting in the Walkley awards, was awarded the Golden Quill in the Gold Coast Media Awards and a three time winner of the Queensland Country Press award for Individual Journalistic Excellence.

Murray was the Sun's motoring editor from 1996 to 2008. His first book, *The Search for Harold Lasseter*, was published in 1993 by Angus & Robertson. He later researched with Ray Connor, and wrote the manuscript which was turned into the multi-award winning *The Day of the Roses*, a Ch.10 TV mini-series and Telemovie. This was an investigative doco-drama of events in Sydney that led to the January 18, 1977 Granville Rail Disaster. He lives in Brisbane with wife Shelly.

The Steering Wheel October 1916

CAR WARS DOWN UNDER

The untold story of Australia's first land speed record

MURRAY HUBBARD

ETT IMPRINT

Exile Bay

for Tatum J. Golden

First published by ETT Imprint, Exile Bay NSW, Australia 2021

ETT IMPRINT
PO Box R1906
Royal Exchange NSW 1225 Australia

ISBN 978-1-922473-89-9 (pbk)
ISBN 978-1-922473-90-5 (ebk)

Text design by Hanna Gotlieb
Cover design by George Hubbard
Internal photographs design by Tom Thompson

CONTENTS

1

The Eagers, The Sphinx and John North Willys

It was a Brisbane business founded on entrepreneurialism. Edward Eager did things differently from everyone else. He wrote his own rules. Every company department was similar to competitors, but the execution, or way they operated, was guided by EG Eager's hands. The motivation to be different led Edward Eager to drive a Willys Overland to Egypt's Great Pyramids in January 1911.

After driving through soft sands from Cairo, he stopped his Willys car at the Sphinx, barely out of the shadow of the Cheops', Egypt's largest pyramid. No automobile had ever parked here; others defeated by the moving sands of the camel-friendly Sahara Desert. A few cars had reached halfway; the two Overlands went all the way. This symbolism became a company mantra: a father-to-son trait. Don't do things by half.

Frederick Zina Eager was his father's son: Edward G Eager's only child. Together they laid the foundation for a car sales empire that not only survived but thrived: World War I, the Great Depression, World War II and every other hiccup, recession and trauma that can bring a business to its knees. All failed to dent Eager's car business, a game that is more volatile than most. EG Eager & Son was founded in Brisbane in 1912.

Dressed in his best suit, fashionable rounded collared shirt and neatly knotted tie, Edward Eager stood tall and proud behind his Overland parked in front of the Sphinx. An impressive figure, he was handsome with a strong chin and piercing brown eyes complementing his slightly olive skin. Mrs Dora Eager was seated on the tonneau of a second Overland. Others in the party were scattered about the two vehicles, the cars' canvas ragtops folded down, under the broken gaze of the Sphinx, it's nose and face shattered by wind and rain, and possibly earthquakes.

To create history, you need not only to achieve but show the world what you achieved. A party member clambered to a stone edifice east of the monument and framed the magnificent Sphinx in the camera lens, overlooking the two Overland cars and passengers. Sometime in the future the photograph would come in useful. On the left of the image is a tall, dark figure wearing a turban: Mr Gabriel of Gabriel Bros. Alexandria, recently appointed by Eager as Willys Overland agent in Egypt. The Sahara sands lap at Cairo like an incoming sea and are about as far as you can get from Wauseon, near Toledo, Ohio, a city perhaps is best known for scales manufacture.

Edward and Frederick Eager were born in Wauseon, 50 kilometres west-south-west of Toledo, Edward in 1864 and Frederick on December 7, 1887. Edward was involved in the bicycle business when a young man until the formation of the American Bicycle Company, which in time would dominate the two-wheel industry. He was someone with a good head on his shoulders, intelligent, innovative and wise with a go-get-it attitude. He loved a good cigar.

Edward Eager started the first motor garage in Toledo in 1900. Two years later, he was snapped up by Goodyear Tyre and Rubber Company, making two trips to Europe to investigate rubber production processes. To this time horse-and-cart buggies used iron and steel rims over timber. Both were forerunners of the motor car wheel. Both would need rubber to progress handling, safety and comfort levels. Like many Americans, Edward Eager was fascinated by a new type of transport: the motorised buggy. The automobile.

The Goodyear trip in 1902 opened his eyes to the possibility of starting nationwide automobile sales businesses. He dealt in tyres, automobiles and bicycles until 1909, barely a year after Henry Ford presented the world with the first Model T - judged the car of the century because it revolutionised mass production. In 1909 the Ford Motor Company entered Edward Eager's life. He joined the company with his first task to head overseas and report trade prospects in Africa and

Australasia. As part of the Ford trips, he travelled extensively in Asia, Australia, Africa and Europe.

His links with Ford ceased soon after. What he had learned at Ford was a significant influence on Edward Eager's career and working life. He learned valuable lessons through his involvement with the bicycle business. He had not only seen the bicycle boom of the 1880s and '90s, but he had also been part of it as a bicycle retailer. The bike business owed three things to its success: a public that wanted cheap, convenient transport, mass production and a wide network of outlets retailing the machines. In real terms, the US bicycle business was a stop gap between the horse- -and-buggy era and the automobile. But, like the horse, it had limitations as a convenient means of transport.

It did achieve the principle of mass manufacture and mass marketing with a linked network of retail outlets. It was a blueprint for the automobile business. Many bicycle factories became car factories, and bicycle retailers added the automobile to showroom floors, increasing the public's transport options. After 20 years in the bike trade, Edward Eager understood the business well. With a world overview of the motor trade fresh in his mind, thanks to Goodyear and Henry Ford, he returned to the US to discover a new automobile manufacturer on his front doorstep.

John North Willys was manufacturing cars called the Willys Overland, and the manufacturing plant was in Toledo, Ohio. The stars were aligned. The 1909 trips for Ford gave Eager an insight into greenfield markets: the vast continents of Africa and Australia, with massive distances between cities and towns. It was prime territory for the horseless carriage. His future was linked with Willys when in 1910 the super-salesman Willys offered Edward Eager the down-under rights to sell Willys Overland cars in Australia and New Zealand.

The following year Eager introduced Willys Overland and Hupmobile to Australia and Africa. During a business visit to Cairo, North Africa, in 1911, Eager accompanied his local agent, Mr Gabriel, on their venture to the Sphinx, a pivotal point for Edward Eager and son Frederick. Overland cars were not only made in his adopted hometown, but they were world-class. They could go where others could not. They were reliable and capable. Eager's education in all aspects of the motor industry was impeccable. Key influences were two of the car industry's greats, having worked directly for Henry Ford and John North Willys and the Goodyear company. While Ford's history is well known, Willys was a bit of a mystery.

John North Willys was born in upstate New York in Canandaigua, a pretty town at the northern end of one of the finger lakes that carries the same name. In winter, a cold place when the snow forms off the freezing winds that glide across Lake Ontario through Rochester and down the terrain formed by enormous glaciers that carved out the finger lakes. Canandaigua is about two hours' drive east of Buffalo and Niagara Falls.

Willys, like Eager, saw an opportunity in bicycles and did very well. In 1899 all that changed. On a visit to Cleveland, Ohio, on the southern shore of Lake Erie, he saw his first automobile in action. This contraption, he figured, would replace not just the bicycle, but the horse and buggy, maybe even trains. Willys, aged 27, with shops across the US, was selling $US500,000 of bikes a year. He paid $US800 for a Pierce automobile, made by bicycle maker George Pierce, from the factory in Buffalo and went into the car business. Using the Pierce as a demonstrator and with an agreement as an agent, he started selling Pierce automobiles. None in 1900 and two in 1901.

This inauspicious beginning was invaluable, not just for Willys, but anyone who would associate themselves with him. Most people would have given up and returned to what they did best: selling bicycles. But Willys believed the future was the automobile. He had no doubts. He took on a Rambler franchise in 1902. His sales of both makes jumped to eight cars in 1902 and 20 in 1903. As time passed, the automobile gained credibility with those who, for generations, relied on a horse and buggy. It was then, as now, a status symbol. Now the status is in the badge. Then it was merely riding in a carriage not under tow by a horse or horses.

Willys heard of a company owned by Standard Wheel that had acquired a car built by Claude Cox. It was called the Overland. Willys was well acquainted with Standard Wheel, which enjoyed an excellent reputation. He decided to dump Pierce along with Rambler and make Overland his single source of cars. In 1904 Willys world was shattered. An explosion in the factory left the directors of Standard Wheel disillusioned with the car industry. Claude Cox bought the company for a song, modernised the factory, and re-started production, with David M Perry's finance. Willys was back on track. He was in his element with an almost unlimited supply of cars, and as fast as vehicles arrived, he had them sold through his network of bicycle shops, now sharing the limelight with automobiles. The Overland Company was, like many others, underfunded. A brief recession hurt Perry, who could no longer fund the company. Production ceased.

Willys was in a bind with no supply chain. In 1906 he sent a cheque for $US10,000 to Overland to keep cars coming. It was to no avail and supply dried up. November saw John North Willys board a train to the Indianapolis factory. There had to be something he could do! He found 45 cars on the assembly line, unpaid workers, and a bank account short on funds to meet weekly wages.

Willys toured the factory on a Saturday. Everything was in place, equipment and components. Workers were all that was required. That meant money. In life, reputation means everything, and by Monday afternoon John Willys had raised $US3500 from friends. This amount was a substantial kitty to rake up at short notice. Willys knew what he was doing and was enough to suggest he could repay Overland creditors $US80,000.

Willys had the gift of the gab. He was a salesman. He was able to convince creditors that if he could get the company going again, they might see a return of their funds. They had no choice. In no time the production line was restarted, workers paid, and Overland cars shipped. Willys sold all 46 cars produced in 1907. Production ramped up to 465 Overlands in 1908, and Willys again sold the lot.

The tail was wagging the dog. Willys bought the Overland company, renamed it Willys Overland, and built a new factory in 1908, to realise before completion the demand for automobiles meant the factory was already outdated. He looked about to buy another going concern and settled on Marion Car Company in Ohio in early 1909. The company came complete with an automotive genius called Harry M. Stutz. Unfortunately for Willys, Stutz had plans and left the company to follow his dream of owning a car company. Thus, the incredible Stutz cars were born.

Out of left field came another opportunity. The Pope Motors factory in Toledo went on the market, and Willys bought it for $US285,000. It was a large, modern factory set up for automotive car production. Toledo was now the home of Edward Eager who in 1900 set up shop in selling automobiles. It was the only car showroom in Toledo, 80km southwest of Detroit.

With Eager the only car yard in town and Willys building automobiles, the pair would inevitably cross paths. The Toledo factory became the jewel in the crown of Willy's empire. John Willys was a shrewd businessman and sold off surplus equipment to pay off most of his initial outlay of $US285,000.

With Willys happy to look after sales in the United States, Eager secured the rights to import and sell Willys Overland in the Southern hemisphere. It was a massive market with huge potential. Australia beckoned. It was a large landmass with an English-speaking population. Eager recognised the parallels with the US. Besides, he was well-schooled in the US. car business. Eager knew the Henry Ford story. He knew John Willys. He knew Goodyear. He understood what made a good newspaper story. All Edward Eager had to do now was put that knowledge into practice.

There was one other person likely to have an impact on Edward and Fred Eager. Bern 'Barney' Eli Oldfield. Oldfield, like the Eagers, was born in Wauseon. The town was founded in 1854 as a railroad stop. When the first loco and carriages steamed through it had 15 inhabitants. Edward Eager was born ten years later, and the population had grown to more than 350. It wasn't significant.

Oldfield was the first man to drive a car at 60 miles an hour. 'Who do you think you are, Barney Oldfield?' was the standard rebuke when lead-footed drivers were at it in the US. While Edward Eager was selling cars in Toledo after 1900, his Wauseon-born neighbour, Barney Oldfield was racing them. Oldfield quickly took on legendary status. On dirt circuits, he mastered the art of sliding cars around corners.

Most drivers in this era drove around circuits. Oldfield pioneered the art of speed driving on dirt, putting the cars into deliberate oversteer, taking corners as fast as possible, then tweaking the steering wheel to correct the slide, and power out of bends. In one race Oldfield took on then-champion, Alexander Winton, and won by half a mile in a five-mile sprint. Not bad for a lad from little 'ol Wauseon. Henry Ford sold Oldfield the car, one of two test racers he built and subsequently turned over to Oldfield for $US800.

There were lessons in the era that shaped the business mind of Edward Eager. He noted how racing success brought fame for Oldfield and more sales for Ford. Newspapers could not get enough of the racers, their daring and the phenomenal speeds the automobile could attain. Yet, this particular lesson he was tardy to put into operation in Australia. First, he needed to put his toe in the warm down-under water.

"In the year 1909 I saw that conditions were ripe for a good American car that would stand the road conditions throughout Australasia and could be sold at a fair price to bring it within reach of people of moderate means," he told the *Australian Motorist* in September 1911.

"Upon my return to the States the Willys-Overland Company had purchased the largest and finest equipped motor concern then in the USA. The factory had never made anything under $US5000 cars, in Toledo, Ohio, this being my native city. I investigated the leading makes on the market carefully, taking the advice of ten of my motor expert friends, who are in the business, with a view to selecting a car which embodied all the features for Australian conditions, both as to price and quality."

Manufacturers offered other car makes to Eager "but the special features of the Overland, especially its cylinders cast separately, five-bearing crankshaft, three-point suspension, thermo syphon, dual magneto ignition, crucible steel housing for differential gears, with the reputation they had already attained in its two years of existence, having placed it in the front rank," he said.

"I selected the Overland as being the most suitable for Australian conditions." Eager was influenced in his car choice by friends in the US, who sold cars other than Overland. "I made arrangements with the Overland Company to take up their cars for Australasia."

Eager purchased a new Overland off the production line for a demonstration vehicle running the car 'in' around Toledo while awaiting passage to Australia. He booked himself, and his car, aboard a ship to Australia via New York and New Zealand.

"I arrived first in Auckland. It was not long before the merits of the Overland asserted themselves." His order book was soon overflowing. In Auckland, he took orders for 80 Overlands and 40 Hupmobiles from the Overland dealer, and 100 Overlands and 40 Hupmobiles from the Farmers' Co-Operative Society in Christchurch on the South Island.

He sailed across the Tasman and in Tasmania signed up Messrs A G Webster & Son for 100 Hupmobiles and 10 Overlands. "I proceeded to Sydney, where I closed the Willys Overland agency for New South Wales with the Cooperative Motor Society of Sydney - then booked an order for 100 Overlands and the Hupmobile, with I Phizackerly, with a contract for 65, including Queensland.

"I then brought my car to Victoria and immediately placed the agency with the Melbourne Motor Garage and received an immediate order for 25 Overlands and 25 Hups."

Buoyed by success, Eager crossed the border into South Australia where he made a small contract, soon after transferred to Murray Aunger, who ordered 50 cars.

Eager left his demonstration car in Australia and returned to Toledo with record orders bursting from his briefcase. He spent a month in the factory, increasing his knowledge of Overland product. Willys added Africa and Asia to Eager's territory at the end of the month. "I shipped my sample cars to Egypt, where I readily placed the agency with Gabriel Bros, Alexandria and Cairo.

"From Egypt I went around the East, across to Africa; four cars were waiting in Durban. I had no trouble in placing an order for 50 cars in Johannesburg, and another agency in Cape Town, covering the agency for that territory."

Eager sailed from Cape Town to Hobart, travelled through New Zealand and back to Melbourne. "I found every agent had far exceeded the contracts, and agents have, every one, doubled their orders for the coming season. In fact, my return visit has been one triumphal procession, far exceeding my most sanguine expectations, and I now return to the United States with the largest order for cars that has ever come out of Australia and New Zealand."

Sunshine Motor Cars purchased the well-known Melbourne Motor Garage and intended to 'push' Overland cars throughout Victoria. For Edward Eager, sales more than cemented his decision to move to Australia. It was a bright, young, enthusiastic nation. It reminded him of his homeland, only more laid back. If the US was a land of opportunity, Australia was its younger sibling.

In 1912 Edward Eager relinquished his African interests to concentrate on Australia and New Zealand. Unlike most other makers' representatives who chose Melbourne or Sydney as a base, he selected Brisbane as his Southern Hemisphere headquarters. Frederick turned 24 and had come under his father's enthusiastic spell. World travels, the accumulation of wealth, photographs of his father in front of the legendary Sphinx, all were an irresistible attraction for a son who shared his father's intellect and entrepreneurial personality.

They also shared a love of cars: driving and exploring. In 1912 Edward Eager hung an EG Eager & Son shingle on their modest shop front in Adelaide Street, Brisbane. There were just three of them in the business, including Wally Webb, an engineer and mechanic who handled the work-shop. Inside Edward's office there was another sign, made of cardboard, that read: 'And when the Great Scorer comes to write against your name, he'll write, not that you won or lost, but how you played the game.'

As a team in the highly competitive and brutal car business, they would take on the challenge of selling Willys Overland cars. The competition was fierce. And they were Americans, in probably Australia's most parochial city. Their nationality, however, was not the gap they placed between themselves and the competition. Another trait filled that void. Pre-World War I Australia was a far different place than the Australia we see today. And we are not talking of development of the man-made Australia. With our mostly British heritage, we were a young nation. The Anzac legend was yet to be born.

We were not so much insecure, as immature: a wild colonial bunch, but naïve in the ways of business, American style. We were conservative as a group. In business, we were not forthright. Snake-oil sellers were few and far between. People bought products, more than salespeople 'selling' them. We didn't hard sell, and deals were often sealed with a firm handshake. The two Americans decided to put down roots and start their car business in this ultra-conservative, home-on-the-farm culture. Two men whose optimism and enthusiasm knew no bounds. Men who understood the American ethos of sell, sell, sell ... and then sell some more. And they knew how to sell and market their cars, so people would want to buy. Men who used their personalities to stamp their names on the car busi-ness, as no one else could. In addition to having the Overland agency Eager also had the rights to Hupmobile. Eagers move to Brisbane was not made lightly. The path they took was the road less travelled. Not everyone appreciated foreigners in sub-tropical Brisbane. Some dealers were locals, born-and-bred Queenslanders. Old school.

The STEERING WHEEL

VOL. I.   FEBRUARY, 1915.   No. 5.

The First and only Cars to go right to the very base of the Sphinx.

2

Alec Fraser Jewell
– the need for speed

The Willys Company and the Eagers were not the only ones to launch their automobile careers from the humble bicycle seat. Around 1880 in Ballarat, Victoria, a baby was born who would go on achieve great success as a cyclist and car speedster.

He would cross paths with Fred Z Eager on Christmas Day 1916. One of them would become Australia's fastest man on four wheels by setting the first Australian land speed record. This baby was Alec Fraser Jewell. (aka Alex Jewell and Alexander Jewell)

Fred Eager and Alec Jewell came from vastly different sides of the tracks. Eager was an only child and capitalised on his father's entrepreneurship. Some could argue he was born with a silver spoon in his mouth, but that would be a grossly unfair appraisal of Fred Eager's career.

Jewell came from a family of battlers. He was one of seven children, and as tough as you need to be growing up in Ballarat in the latter part of the 19th century. He had it more challenging than most. His father, Edward, died the year Alec was born. Alexandrina, his mother, was left to bring up her flock single-handed. Alec was youngest of the Jewell clan. Schooling finished, Alec started work, aged about 14, with Phoenix Foundry Co in Ballarat and finished his time with Mitchell & Co, brass founders and engineers.

With older brothers, Don and Tom, already accomplished cyclists, Alec also took up the sport. Like eldest brother Don, he was good at it. Extremely good. However, it seemed there was a better life elsewhere for those who could pedal hard. In 1898 the three brothers moved to Perth, Western Australia. In March that year, local media reported an event at the Association Cricket Ground, where a 'first-class programme of cycle races was planned.'

The St. Patrick's sports committee put up a large amount of prize money with the result 'all the cracks', including Healey and Stotter, will 'compete.' And there was a newcomer too: "Alex Jewell, a new arrival from the Eastern colonies, will make his first appearance in Western Australia." It was the first time Alex Jewell's name made Perth print. It would not be the last.

In his first year, Alec Jewell won the Colony of West Australia 25-mile road race, which made him an instant sports star and darling of the West Australian media's cycling columns. Alec Jewell and brother Tom worked for Armstrong Cycle Agency, Alec as a mechanic and Tom as a painter. A fourth brother, Edward, also competed.

Bike races, then, as now, are no place for the faint-hearted. Put three brothers in one race and tactics will play a hand in the result. Prizemoney was at stake as well as many a side-bet. By 1899 Alec Jewell had settled into his new surroundings and was training hard for the new season. He was a big man, powerfully built, tipping the scales at 12st 7lb, with a chiseled face that had determination written all over it. Tom won the Western Australia 50-mile race, giving the brothers a high profile in Perth. Road racing was all the rage in the West.

The 1899 season was a year of consolidation for Western Australian cycling after finance problems dogged the sport. For Alec Jewell, his goal was to retain his crown as 25-mile champion of the Colony. The race was between the Victoria Park Hotel and a half-way point on the road to Albany. As races go, it was no picnic. The road was in poor condition and under repair. Loose metal had been freshly laid in soft patches. There were 11 competitors sent away by the starter, Mr PW Harrison, shortly after 3pm on a fine Saturday afternoon.

The pace was a cracker from the start. The leading riders rotated the lead and quickly created a gap to the rest, lagging further behind. At the turn-around point, 12.5 miles out, the front bunch included WC Best, Alec and Tom Jewell, J Coultas and NFP Salomons, who turned together for the homeward journey. To this point, many of the riders had fallen as a result of the loose metal. But, within the leading group, there was a camaraderie.

"Best had several mishaps," reported the *West Australian*, but with true sportsmanship, his opponents, with one exception, waited for him to remount." "Subsequently the rider who created the exception collapsed and was left by his rivals. Coultas met with an accident and sustained some nasty cuts on his face on the return journey. His shoulder was also injured."

The newspaper reported Coultas was leading when the accident occurred, and while watching his opponents 'ran into a strip of loose metal.' "Fortunately, none of the others participated in the fall, though T Jewell had a narrow escape." With Coultas out of the way, the Jewell brothers and Best fought out the race at a breakneck speed. Alec Jewell pulled away in a final thrust and finished 18 seconds in front of brother Tom with Best finishing just a length behind.

Salomons was a little more than 50 seconds behind Tom Jewell while one unfortunate, Ward, failed to finish as his bike hit a dog just 50 yards from the finish line. It was a remarkable effort for Alec Jewell, and the win ensured his high profile would only grow. If he wanted publicity, he was about to get it in barrow loads from an unexpected quarter.

The *West Australian* headline was captivating: Serious Charge Against Racing Cyclists.

"During the progress of the 25 miles' road cycling championship on Saturday last several falls, attributed to the patches of loose metal on the course, were sustained by different competitors. J Coultas, one of the riders, was one of the unfortunate numbers. Some surprise was occasioned in wheeling circles yesterday when a warrant was issued for the arrest of Alec Jewell, Tom Jewell and Edward Jewell, three brothers who were also competitors in the event."

The Jewell brothers appeared before two Justices of the Peace, Messrs WJ Holmes and RH Barratt, charged with assaulting Coultas during the race with intent to do grievous bodily harm. The brothers were granted bail pending a court hearing the following day. The police charges arose after Coultas wrote to Western Australia's Council of the League of Wheelmen, protesting against the three brothers for 'wilfully and maliciously assaulting' him in the race and also 'using obscene and threatening language before and during the progress of the race.'

The police charges were the first laid against Alec Jewell in the West, but not the last. The ensuing court case provided an insight into the internal workings of road racing and the tricky tactics involved. It had all the intrigue of the Tour de France. The police case Coultas v Jewell Brothers for assault fascinated the Colony of West Australia and made news across the nation. The story led the main news page in the *West Australian* during the court case and was the talk of the town. The previous day James Coultas had given evidence along with several corroborating witnesses as part of the prosecution case.

"Coultas shows a black eye and the remains of several abrasions," reported the *West Australian*. "The black eye, he alleged, was sustained by a blow rendered by Alec Jewell, one of his opponents in the 25-miles road championship of the Colony run Saturday last. "The abrasions, he alleged, were caused by Jewell bringing about his fall on a heap of metal. Other allegations of attempts to bring about his downfall in the race, and of general ill-using him were made against the three brothers Jewell."

In road races, riders take turns to lead the pack or set the pace. It's a shared burden, and etiquette demands it be equally split among the riders. Even before the race, it was a topic of conversation. Edward Smith, who worked at Armstrong's Cycle Agency., along with Alec and Tom Jewell, said on the morning of the race Coultas was in the cycle shop with his machine to have his pedal adjusted.

"After he left, Tom Jewell said to his brother, Coultas will have to do a bit of pacing this afternoon." Smith said Alec Jewell replied, "If he doesn't and gets behind me, I'll break his ... neck." The journalist commented, it was optional with racing men whether they took their turn at pacing, "but it was generally done."

Bad blood existed between Alec Jewell and James Coultas. The starter, PW Harrison, an architect, said Coultas kept the other riders waiting on the mark, and some of them complained about the delay. "Alec Jewell used abusive language to Coultas for keeping him waiting," said Harrison.

Harrison was then cross-examined and stated he had a good deal of road racing experience and had not known of a black eye sustained through a fall from a machine.

Alfred W Bishop, who was at the finish line, then gave evidence. When Alec Jewell came in, he asked him 'where he shook Jimmy (James Coultas) off, and Jewell replied that Coultas fell. Bishop had told Jewell, "You seemed to be rising at loggerheads at Canning." Bishop said he remembered telling a detective that Jewell told him 'Coultas was a pest to him all the way, and he had to push him away a couple of times.'

Cross-examined, Bishop said when the competitors passed him at Canning T Jewell was pacing with Alec Jewell and Coultas hanging on to him about a yard apart. There was a good deal of 'bustling' in a scratch race. John Harris, a farmer at Canning, told the court he did not see Coultas fall but saw him lying on the ground. He then saw two men 10 yards away but did not notice who they were. Cyclist trainer John Brownlie gave evidence that he was in the dressing-room before the event when someone asked a question - he did not know who - about 'How much would it take to bring Coultas down?'

That concluded the prosecution case by Mr Ewing for the crown. It was now the defence's turn led by Mr Vynor, on behalf of the Jewell brothers. In opening the defence case, Mr Vynor stated the prosecution's allegations would be contradicted. He said some of the actions alleged against Alec Jewell were next to impossible and the fall was the fault of Coultas himself. The Jewells did not contribute to the fall, but Coultas, trying to pull off on to a good piece of land to catch up the race leaders, ran on to a heap of metal and fell. Mr Vynor told the court on the way out there was a good deal of 'bustling', which was caused through Coultas persistently endeavouring to cut in between the first and second riders and take advantage of the pacing, which he was not going to share.

He told the court the proper place for the settlement of such a case was before the governing body of cycling, not before the courts. "The magistrate (Mr Panton) stated the League of Wheelmen should have sorted the matter out. It was now Alec Jewell's turn to defend himself. After being sworn in, he told the court there was no arrangement to block Coultas, and each were out to win. There was absolutely no truth in the statement he struck Coultas. He admitted all through the race there was a good deal of 'bustling' and the pace was a cracker from the start with Wyatt for a couple of miles before Best paced to Canning. The speed was such that it shook off six of the riders. Jewell himself paced for a while then asked for someone else to take over, and Salomons took the lead.

At this stage, a herd of cattle crossed the road, and Best fell. Jewell said he called in distinct tones 'We'll all wait for him' and all but Coultas slowed. Coultas 'cleared out'. Jewell took off after Coultas who, when he saw he could not get away, slowed and the others overtook them. This action set the tone for the rest of the race. The *West Australian* reported Jewell's evidence in detail. "At the jarrah (West Australian timber) blocks witness (Alec Jewell) was riding next to the pacer. Coultas came up on the left-hand side of Jewell and tried to bore him on to the blocks of the narrow 'pad' upon which Jewell was riding. To save himself from falling on the unrideable blocks, Jewell put his hand on Coultas' shoulder, saying 'You don't run me on the blocks, Coultas'.

Jewell said all the riders but Coultas took pace and as each change was made Coultas tried to cut in on the front man's wheel, causing great danger. A mile-and-a-half from the turning point on the homeward journey he heard his brother call out that he had lost his pedal. Coultas came up by his side and bored him on to the side of the road, causing him to run over some bricks. From Jewell's evidence, it was apparent the race had degenerated into a last-man-standing affair. "Pacing alternately, nothing further occurred, with the exception that Coultas was continually bumping in front of the second man trying to get the pace," said Jewell.

Eight miles from home Alec Jewell spotted a small track at the side of a sandy stretch that constituted the road. Those at the front missed seeing the 'pad' and Jewell soon found himself 10 yards ahead of the pack. Best was the only other rider near him, just at his rear. Jewell said the allegations that he threatened to bring Coultas down or break his neck were 'absolutely false.' He said he did not hear of the Coultas fall until after the race.

Mr Vyner: Did T.Jewell say to Coultas, 'You b......, we've got you cut off now' and then tell you (Alec Jewell) 'Go like h-'

Witness (Alec Jewell) emphatically: No! My brother Tom never swears (Laughter).

His Worship: Witness (Alec Jewell) I would not try to prove too much. It is asking me to believe too much that a cyclist of 15 years' standing never swears (Laughter).

Jewell: It's a fact, all the same.

Mr Vyner: When you got back did you have talk with a man named Bishop

Jewell: I'm not sure; there were so many people there eager to congratulate the winner.

Mr Vyner: You won.

Jewell: Yes

Jewell was then questioned about discussions in the workshop before the race and denied words to the effect he would break Coultas' neck unless he paced.

Mr Ewing: Are you like your brother - never swear?

Jewell: No, I'm not an angel. (Laughter)

Mr Ewing: You did not use any bad language to Coultas?

Jewell: No

Mr Ewing: Then, after all the annoyance from Coultas, you did not abuse him?

Jewell: No.

Mr Ewing: Then, you're a near angel after all?

Jewell: I am.

Mr Ewing: Oh! Just now you said you weren't (Laughter)

Jewell: I said that I was not an angel. Now I say I'm near one. You are not far away from me, you know. (Loud laughter).

This dialogue gives an interesting insight into Alec Jewell's personality. He was unfazed by the court proceedings and was able to keep one step ahead of the crown prosecutor, without appearing arrogant. It also reveals he could think on his feet and respond without jeopardising his case. His ability to make the courtroom crowd laugh, endeared him to those present. He was taking on the aura of an atypical Aussie larrikin. This trait would serve him well for later indiscretions.

Next to take the stand was Edward Jewell. He told the court the road was in a terrible condition and many of the riders fell. One of them, Ward, was still getting around with the assistance of a walking stick. He saw no blows struck. He said crossing the Canning Bridge he was in front and no one came near him. The allegation he bumped Coultas against the (bridge) railing was false.

Last of the brothers, Thomas Jewell, an enameller at Armstrong's Cycle Agency, took the stand and denied the charges against him. When Coultas fell, he said he was close to him, while Alec Jewell and Best were 40 to 50 yards off. Another competitor, William Best, said he did most of the pacing during the day and had two falls going out to the turning point. "No matter who was following the pacer, Coultas always tried to 'chip in', thereby endangering the other riders," said Best.

He saw no blows struck during the race and did not see Coultas fall, as he was around 20 yards in front at the time and Alec Jewell was ahead of him. "It was absolutely impossible for Alec Jewell to have brought Coultas down," he said. "We were sprinting at the time." Best said at the end of the race while being massaged another rider, Salomons commented that Coultas caused his accident. E Powell, a checker at a turning point, said Coultas did not have a black eye at that stage.

On the home journey, he found Coultas lying on the roadside, helping him on to his machine, and pushing him home to Perth. Coultas told him that Edward and Thomas Jewell had hit him during the race and that Alec Jewell had not touched him.

"Coultas was the cause of all this because he always cut in after the first man," said Mr Parker, a witness. He said, had any of the riders been of an 'excitable nature' he would not have been surprised to see Coultas knocked off his machine, because of the manner in which he tried to 'bustle' the others, and refused to take his fair share of pacing.

When Coultas and Tom Jewell were together, Alec Jewell and Best were 30 to 40 yards ahead. The court adjourned for the day. The following morning the courtroom was packed for the decision by the magistrate, Mr AS Roe. He said evidence was totally contradictory and was in no mood to hear more arguments by counsel on either side. He commented the case could have been heard a lot faster if the evidence given regarding how the riders had interfered with each other had not been presented - evidence that should have been put before the appropriate governing body of cycling.

The magistrate found the allegations by Coultas were uncorroborated by anyone and totally unsupported.

"Of all the witnesses called not one of them could say that he saw a blow struck." He said he was quite satisfied the Jewells had made up their minds to help each other in the race. He said it was not in question Coultas had sustained a very severe fall indeed, which was probably when he suffered the black eye. He said the most serious charge was of boring Coultas into the side of the bridge.

"Travelling at a rate of 20 miles per hour as these riders were said to be if one of them were to run against the railing, he would stand a big chance of being killed." In the end, the magistrate dismissed all charges based on a lack of corroboration and unmistakable evidence. However, it was clear Coultas had been trying to get in behind the pacer, thus endangering the other competitors.

However, he would say the race had not run on fair and square lines, and that Alec Jewell had not been too choice in his language. Reading between the lines of the judgment the magistrate, in the absence of any witness to corroborate Coultas' evidence, had no choice but to dismiss the charges. Yet, it seems, the race ran in a way that favoured Alec Jewell to win, hence his comment that the Jewell brothers had decided to assist each other. There appears no doubt Coultas upset all other riders with his tactics of cutting in on the second rider while refusing to take his turn as the paceman.

It is not out of the realms of possibility the Jewell brothers assaulted Coultas, but with all riders either turning a blind eye to the retribution by the Jewells and then denying seeing anything in the hearing. This was Alec Jewell's first - but not his only - court hearing on assault charges in Western Australia.

As Christmas 1899 approached cycling broadened its appeal by moving into night-time competition. Sporting organisations had recognised the possibility of using electric lights to have cricket competitions. On December 13, an Electric Light Meeting was held in Perth's illuminated Cricket Association Ground, and Alex Jewell was again in the newspapers. Jewell and one other rider were severely injured and remained unconscious for some time during the five-mile race after four riders fell. There were no broken bones, but the other rider was 'particularly badly injured', according to newspaper reports on December 14.

Two weeks later, the day before New Year's Eve, Alec Jewell was again in the wars, this time at Fremantle in the final of the Mile Handicap. Entering the last lap of the race there was the 'usual' dust-up, a rider touched the wheel of the bike in front and swerved into the fence. JW Beck lay on the track and Jewell, riding in the middle of the pack, ran over him, resulting in Jewell and his bike crashing into the asphalt. Both riders received treatment at the scene, and Jewell was administered an 'opiate' to relieve pain. Jewell was taken to hospital suffering broken ribs, while Beck had several stitches inserted into a deep head wound. For Jewell, the rough and tumble of road racing, and cycling in general, was his passport to more extraordinary things.

A public profile lifted a man's chances of opportunities to get ahead, and by late 1890s Alec Jewell was a household name in Perth. Perth's first motorist is Mr W Brookman, who in 1897, imported a Benz. Three years later Perth still had one car, several motorcycles and a motor tricycle. However, this modest list was added to shortly after the turn of the century when Alex Jewell converted a De Dion Quad motorcycle into a small car.

According to reports in the *Perth Daily News*, the De Dion needed "much persuasion to keep going, and Jewell always saw to it that he took along a sturdy passenger with him, to help push."

"Then Dr McWilliams bought a Baby Gladiator car, its performance, however, belied its name as it invariably lost heart at the sight of a hill."

Back in the day, one of Perth's great road races was the Beverley-to-Perth aka The Beverley, conducted from 1897. Underlining the importance of the race it concluded at Government House, and the Governor, (in 1897) Sir Gerald Smith acted as judge. In the race's history, at least for the first 38 years, there had been only one back marker come through the field to take honours in the race that takes more than 8½ hours to complete. That rider was Alec Jewell and the year 1901. This win cemented Alec Jewell's name in the history books. To this day it still gets referred to with reverence whenever the history of the Beverley comes up in conversation.

"History was made … when Alex Jewell, starting from the back mark defeated all other starters to win the race. Never since has a man from-scratch won the event …," stated the *West Australian* in a 1935 feature outlining the race's history.

"In winning the race, Jewell caught the leader, Williams (handicap 55 minutes) at Midland Junction, and, after a stern, hard, struggle shook him off over the last mile," states the *West Australian*.

This win speaks volumes for Jewell's fitness, tenacity and stamina in what was a gruelling event over 116 miles (187km) of rough, turn-of-the-century roads. Jewell had a strong incentive to win. The rider with the fastest time in the Beverley race won a trip to Melbourne to compete in the 1901 Melbourne-to-Warrnambool race. He finished the Melbourne-Warrnambool race in around 20th spot, in the middle of the field.

Alec Jewell was an Australian motoring pioneer. In October 1902 he ran a depot in Market Street, Fremantle, where he met with a journalist from Perth's *Sunday Times*. Jewell had just returned from a 2.5 horse-power motorcycle trip to Perth and back, an each-way trip of around 25 minutes. Jewell was working for a company that would supply motor cars to the West. He said the company was preparing to supply motors of every description, driven either by oil, steam or electric power and "the public should not be surprised if that an early date they should see buses driven by motor power."

That company was the American Motor Car Co, which Jewell was now managing along with working in tandem with his other business, selling Massey Harris cycles ... which at the time were taking all before them in the hands of Western Australia's top racing cyclists. A week later Alec Jewell took out honours in the 25-mile State Championship of cycling, beating his nearest opponent by just the length of a bike in one hour and nine minutes. He won the race in 1898, 1900 and 1902, running second in 1899 and 1901.

In Western Australia it was noted as a remarkable record in road racing, cementing his name as a West Aussie champion. Just a few days later he again made headlines when a supplier took him to Perth Local Court for 3 pounds and 3 shillings for unpaid goods supplied. After hearing the evidence, the magistrate made a judgment against Jewell for the full amount, plus costs. The year 1904 started badly for the cycling champion when he was charged with breaching the Customs Act by possessing two bicycles on which duty was unpaid. Jewell allegedly bought the bikes aboard the steamer Haversham Grange without paying duty.

Jewell's defence was that he purchased the bikes from a third person who told him he had paid duty. This excuse did not wash with the Magistrate, Mr Fairbairn, stating Jewell should have procured a receipt. He fined Jewell five pounds. Jewell's roller-coaster life snowballed when charged with breaching local by-laws by driving at night in a motor car without a light, and with having driven the car to the danger of the public. He was fined 5 shillings on the first charge and 15 shillings on the second, plus costs, after a court appearance on June 4, 1904.

In September, 1904 he was again in the headlines for all the wrong reasons. The *Perth Daily News* reported that Alexander Jewell, a well-known cyclist, was charged with having driven a motor car at a furious pace in the street - the second time he was charged with this offence. He was fined 40 shillings, with costs when he appeared at City Police Court.

In early 1905 Alexander Jewell again made headlines. Along with jockey John Long police charged the car salesman with robbery with violence towards gold prospector, Patrick Lawrence O'Dwyer, in Perth's Kings Park. The court case makes for fascinating reading and made head-lines across Australia. As Alec Jewell was about to discover, one of the problems with fame is that the exemplary achievements may be reported by media and just as quickly, deeds from the dark side.

The pair were charged with having stolen 15 pounds from O'Dwyer with actual violence and further having assaulted O'Dwyer with an attempt to steal. O'Dwyer came to Perth from Kalgoorlie, west of Perth, in August 1904 and was frequenting many hotels, making up for lost time on the rich diggings.

On the day in question, he took 10 pounds out of his bank and visited Perth's Metropole Hotel where he met Jewell and Long in the bar and 'had a few drinks.' They then went to Her Majesty's Hotel and had some more drinks. O'Dwyer had never been in a car, so Jewell suggested they go to Subiaco, where Jewell had a motor car. On the way, they told their taxi driver to call in at the Melbourne Hotel.

After leaving Subiaco in the car with Jewell at the wheel, they called in at the Subiaco Hotel and had more drinks there. From there they drove towards Fremantle and had a few drinks at the Brighton Hotel. After this hotel, O'Dwyer said he remembered nothing. O'Dwyer had a habit, when drunk, of giving valuables to hotel licensees and then picking up the cash or items when he was sober. When he met Jewell and Long he had 16 pounds, a watch and a silver-mounted walking stick.

It turned out later O'Dwyer had left his watch with a publican on the day and previously had lost mining scrip, later found in the safe at the Criterion Hotel. The majority of drinks at the five hotels visited by the trio were paid for by O'Dwyer. Police attended Kings Park at midnight on the night in question and found O'Dwyer on the ground groaning. He stated he been taken there by two men in a motor car and robbed of a silver watch and about 15 pounds.

One witness told the court he was driving through Kings Park with a lady friend when he saw three men grappling, and one of those was Alex Jewell, who held another man around the neck while the third men had the same man around the waist. He parked his car and went back and saw Jewell kneeling on, or beside two men lying on the ground. One of those men was O'Dwyer. All three men appeared to be drunk, he said. Case dismissed with the magistrate stating the prosecution did not supply enough evidence to support a conviction.

3

Brisbane's car industry 1912

It was a balmy Brisbane that greeted Edward Eager in March 1912. His regional groundwork, setting up agencies in most Australian capital cities and New Zealand in 1910 and 1911, was completed. Now was the time to set up his own business, using Queensland's capital, Brisbane, as the base. He found an office at Evers Bros' Queen Street Garage, at Petrie's Bight, near what is now the northern side of Brisbane's famous Story Bridge. He felt right at home. Evers was the appointed Overland dealers in Brisbane and also parked Hupmobile vehicles on the small showroom floor.

On April 20, 1912 - just six days after the world's worst maritime disaster, the Titanic sinking -- Eager tagged an Evers' advertisement for Overland in the *Brisbane Courier*. The message was simple and to the point: 'Agents wanted in every district of Queensland. EG EAGER, Representing the Willys Overland Company, Toledo, Ohio.'

Why Eager chose Brisbane ahead of Sydney or Melbourne is not known. Perhaps it could have been a desire to live in a warm climate after being raised in Ohio's icy winter breath. If he expected an easy draw or warm welcome for Overland, he was mistaken.

Canada Cycle and Motor Agency (Queensland) is well entrenched with the Studebaker agency and Talbot and Renault. CCM had branches in Brisbane, Rockhampton, Charters Towers, and Lismore in northern New South Wales. There were sub-agencies in Longreach, Blackall, Toowoomba, Maryborough, Bundaberg, Townsville, and Warwick. CCM's distribution network was in place. Eager was still to start his. EG Eager & Son would become direct rivals of CCM.

Behind CCM was the Ipswich-born AV Dodwell. He received his business training with a large mercantile and pastoral company in Brisbane. Like so many others who came into the automobile business, he started with bicycles.

In 1897 he entered the two-wheeler business as Queensland manager for the Massey Harris Company. Later on, when the amalgamation of various companies took place in Canada to link bicycles and cars, he was appointed Queensland manager for the Canada Cycle and Motor Company --- with his role to develop the automobile side of the business.

In 1905, as the automobile was starting to take off as a reputable form of transport, he purchased Canada Cycle and Motor and floated it. Dodwell is known as 'AVD' and regarded as being highly competitive in anything he attempted. He did not like second best and was a no-nonsense businessman. He kept his hair cut short and wore a healthy moustache, drooped slightly on either side. He was powerfully built, of average height.

Alexander Vaughan Dodwell had the same passion for Studebaker that Edward Eager had for Willys. Like Eager, who was the first to import Willys, Dodwell was the first to import Studebaker into Australia. Dodwell had one thing over Eager. He was well connected. The general manager of the *Brisbane Courier*, C H Briggs, who later became a director of Queensland Newspapers Pty Ltd, recommended Dodwell to the Australian manager of Massey Harris Company that eventually led to CCM. This connection would later prove beneficial when Dodwell wanted publicity in his battles with Eager. Dodwell was a part of the Brisbane 'establishment'.

The Queensland Motor Agency Ltd, Brisbane, was also part of the furniture with the ubiquitous Model T Ford. Like Eagers and CCM, the agency was led by a super-competitive individual. Its managing director, G W Whatmore, was elected an alderman of the Brisbane City Council in 1919 and came from the bicycle business in the purest sense. He was the amateur cycling champion of New South Wales and moved to Brisbane around the same time as Edward Eager, around 1912. "The history of George W Whatmore is the history of the 'Fords' success in Queensland." reported *The Steering Wheel* magazine in a short bio of Whatmore in 1915.

Whatmore took control of the Queensland Motor Agency in July 1913, when the June sales figures totalled five Model Ts. By March 1914, sales had rocketed to 47 cars. Whatmore knew how to run big business. He was formerly a New South Wales public servant administering the Forest Department.

"Five years ago, chafing under the limit of scope, he decided to cut for the tall timber," stated *The Steering Wheel.*

Whatmore resigned and became Melbourne Motor Garage manager and later of the Sunshine Motor Cars Property Limited. It was while he was with Melbourne Motor Garage, he met Edward Eager, Overland representative in Australia. Melbourne Motor Group, under Whatmore, became Edward Eager's first agent to take Overland cars in Australia. He also became a firm friend of the Eager family.

"When the world was younger, Mr Whatmore was an amateur cyclist and sculler of considerable prowess," wrote *The Steering Wheel.* "He was the first cyclist to ride the full journey from Brisbane to Adelaide, some 2000 miles, in 21 days. As far as Sydney, he was accompanied by Mr L H Isles, then Queensland's amateur cycling champion. Part of the journey was accomplished on the old type of high bicycle (perhaps a penny farthing), fitted with solid tyres."

When Geo Whatmore retired to concentrate on selling Ford, he was the holder of no less than 120 prizes, including the 50 guineas Milbrook Cup, and with it, the Amateur Cycling Championship of Australia. He was a man with many strings to his large bow. He formed the first motorboat club in Australia, built Australia's first hydroplane, and was an accom-plished Shakespearean actor and scholar. In Brisbane, he made 'Gee Whiz' a 26ft stepless hydroplane, equipped with an eight-cylinder, 150hp Daimler engine, capable of 34mph.

On four wheels, he was a devoted Ford man. You could purchase from Queensland Motor Agency a 20hp two-seater Torpedo runabout Model T Ford – in black, of course – for $460 (230 pounds). Or a five-seater 20hp touring car for $500 (250 pounds).

Equipment included the fold-down hood, folding windscreen, speedometer, headlights and generator, side lamps, tail lamps, pump, jack, Ford kit of tools, and let's not forget the horn. Queensland Motor Agency were also agents for Crossley, Bianchi, and Metallurgique cars. They, too, were advertising for 'sound and enterprising agents in districts where Ford is not represented.'

There is nothing new in dealerships having multiple brands on the lot.

In George Street, Brisbane United Motors sold Maxwells, in Queen Street, Howard Motor and Cycle Co Ltd sold Cadillac, Karrier, Wolseley, Belsize and KRIT cars, Triumph and New Hudson motorcycles and Rover bicycles, while further down Queen Street, W F Turk & Co, electrical engineers and motor importers, sold Mitchell cars and RCH. Brisbane's would-be motorists could not complain about a lack of choice for car brands.

In announcing the RCH cars, Turk told Brisbane, 'Mr. R C HUPP has resigned his position as managing director of the Hupmobile Motor Co. and is devoting all his time to the manufacture of his own car. The vast experience and knowledge of colonial conditions gained by him during the many years he has been manufacturing cars have made it possible to manufacture the best car, at a reasonable price, ever offered to the public. You may be sure that he has included all the good features worth adopting from other cars in addition to the many original ones when designing the RCH.'

This statement gives some clue to the volatile nature of the motor industry in its infancy. It was not so much musical chairs, but musical cars as entrepreneurs and engineers, particularly in the US, swapped companies or went out independently. In Adelaide Street, the McGhie Motor Co Ltd had just acquired the English Sunbeam cars, 'Holder of 15 World's Records and twice winner of the Royal Automobile Club's Gold Medal for best performance in monthly trials.' It also marketed the smaller Delage car, as well as the larger Hudson. It was a hectic time to be a Brisbane business.

Edward Eager did not let his feet touch the ground after arriving in Brisbane. By the end of April, he announced agents in Charleville, Rockhampton, Winton, Townsville, and Toowoomba and stated he was still looking for more agencies in areas not represented. By June 1912, Edward Eager appears to have become frustrated at Evers' bland advertising for the Overland. Their ads were matter-of-fact based on the car's mechanical output, rather than the driving experience, ownership benefits, and the company behind the vehicle.

This was old school for Edward Eager. On June 19, Edward Eager penned his *Courier* advertisement based on his intimate knowledge of the product, the company, and its future. He cut right to the chase in the first sentence. "There are more Overland cars being bought today than any other similar type of car produced."

While Ford had its 20hp Model-T set in steel-reinforced concrete, Overland had 30hp, 35hp, and 45hp cars in its stable; therefore, Ford was not a 'direct' competitor. Eager continued: 'We average five sales to the other makers' one. Have you ever stopped to figure this out? Has the full force of this significant fact been brought home to you? Do you imagine we are selling more merely because we are making more? 'We are marketing the greatest number of cars purely and simply because we can give more for the dollar than any other manufacturer in the business.' For the staid Brisbane establishment, Eager's advertisement was bold and out there.

He had not finished: 'The greatest number of people today who are buying high grade, popular-priced cars are choosing the Overland. Figures prove this. Does it not occur to your sense of reasoning that this vast majority of shrewd buyers CANNOT be wrong? The unparalleled value in this car has moved the motor buying public of every civilised country under the sun. The response is world-wide. What better guide can you have as to how to get the best and most for the least amount of money? Its purchase gives you more actual car value for less actual money than you can get from any other manufacturer in the world. Model 59 is a thirty horsepower, five-passenger touring car. It is big, handsome, powerful, comfortable, and efficient. It will give you years of service.

"According to the run of market prices, it is a 425 pounds ($850) car for 355 pounds ($710). In order to get this much value for $355, you must buy an Overland '59' or pay at least 425 pounds for some other make. Which shall it be? See our dealer below and decide early."

Edward Eager's confronting style was at odds with ads run by other agencies. It was a hard sell, designed to make the prospective purchaser weigh options before deciding which car to select. This advertising style was more aggressive than Australians had seen before, particularly in Brisbane, noted for its laid back, sub-tropical way of life. Eager's brashness was not only borne of his business experience in his birthplace 'the land of opportunity' but also of confidence in his product. He knew John North Willys personally. He spent months in the Toledo factory, getting to know and understand its manufacture and construction, and saw what extras came included and why.

He tested Willys Overland cars on the streets of Ohio and probably a Willys' test-track. He had driven Overland cars in Egypt, South Africa, the US, New Zealand, over much of Australia's east coast and, in recent times, all over his adopted state of Queensland as he set up agencies.

There was little he did not know about the Willys product and what was coming in the pipeline out of Toledo. Edward Eager probably knew more about his product than any other Australian automobile agent. While Edward Eager was extolling Overland's benefits, the choice of cars in Brisbane expanded almost weekly as more and more brands sought agencies.

McGhie Motor Co added 'The indomitable Itala ...The car of Kings, used by Royalty all over the Continent' while The Town and Country Motor Co announced the 'noiseless' Napier, the proved best car, the British 'Reliable Star' and the Empire 'Twenty-Five.'

At Petrie's Bight, King's Garage launched the Sampson '35' for $950, 'complete with hood and windscreen.' With so many new businesses competing for sales, there was always conflict — tit-for-tat sales talk, jealousies, rivalries, stunts aimed at creating publicity.

The biggest show in town every August is the annual Royal Exhibition, known affectionately throughout Queensland as the Ekka. On August 16, 1912, the Ekka and a stunt combined to make headlines. Not only a race but a contest of car and aircraft at Eagle Farm Racecourse on the outskirts of the Brisbane CBD. Several thousand spectators gathered in anticipation.

The *Brisbane Courier* recorded the event under the headline Aeroplane v Motor Car. "The aviation display by 'Wizard' Stone at Eagle Farm Race-course ... yesterday attracted a mass of spectators who, including those who occupied a free view from outside the fences, probably numbered from 7000 to 10,000 people. The interest was further increased by the announcement that there would be a race between the aeroplane and a motor car, and the double event was fixed for 11.30am.

"Among those who attended was His Excellency the Governor (Sir William McGregor) and the Right Hon. James Bryce."

"The motor car was a 'Cadillac' 1912 model lent by the Howard Motor Co, Ltd, and on this occasion driven by Mr. Arthur Hobbs."

'Wizard' Stone taxied the aircraft onto the track and checked the engine was at operating temperature. Helpers held the plane in place while he raced the engine. "About eight minutes past the hour 'Wizard' Stone gave the signal to let go, and the aeroplane skimmed along the surface, rose gracefully skyward, the whole assemblage cheering enthusiastically."

"At an altitude of a couple of hundred feet, the aviator turned, and the so-called race was begun. Circumstances beyond their control compelled the competitors to go in opposite directions.

"The motor car, putting on full speed, dashed around the course at a very high rate of speed --- some of the calculators putting it down at about a mile in 1.27 minutes and others at somewhat less.

"Mr. Hobbs piloted the Cadillac splendidly," stated the *Courier*. "While he followed his course, 'Wizard' Stone navigated his He circled in steady, bird-like flight across the grass enclosure, and, after remaining in the air for six to seven minutes, descended to the earth, alighting easily and without the slightest mishap."

As for the race, it resolved itself into a spectacle rather than a competition. "Mr. J Howard, the managing director of the Howard Motor and Cycle Co Ltd, who was present, received not a few congratulations on the performance of the Cadillac, and Mr Hobbs upon his plucky and skillful driving."

While these five minutes of fun appears innocuous, it holds special significance from several aspects. Firstly, it was one of the first reports in the *Brisbane Courier* to highlight a local motoring event. It showed that motoring could be seen as news and take its place in the local daily paper's early pages.

Secondly, the PR and marketing value for the Howard Motor Co and its much-vaunted Cadillac was unprecedented. This was better publicity than any paid advertisement could ever achieve. It was not the dealer or the maker saying the Caddy had an outstanding performance, but by independent observers reported by the newspaper.

There was a lesson in the exercise for all Brisbane car dealers. Lastly, but most importantly, it highlighted one of the most significant drawbacks to the car in its early years, not just Brisbane, but Australia. The reason the 'contest' took place at Eagle Farm was not only its proximity to Brisbane and the timing of the Ekka. Another more over-riding reason was there was nowhere else but a horse racing track that cars could even come close to full speed around Brisbane. Even the racetrack did not allow a flat-to-the-board, top speed. There were corners to negotiate, which was why Mr Hobbs received congratulations on his 'plucky and skilful driving'.

Anyone can drive fast or flat out in a straight line, but in Australia, in 1912 no roads are flat enough to attempt the high speeds of which cars were capable. The streets were mainly gravel and still traversed by horse and buggy. During the wet season or after rain, they became quagmires and, when dry, set as hard as sandstone as deep, rutted tracks. No place to speed, let alone get out of first or second gear.

In the Eagle Farm race between plane and car, the Cadillac covered a mile in 1 minute and 27 seconds, or about 40 miles per hour. Brought back to kilometres an hour, this is about 60 kilometres an hour and well below the Caddy's top speed. For any attempt at an Australian land speed record, a long, dead-flat road would be essential. In the same *Courier* of August 17, 1912, Canada Cycle and Motor were at pains to promote the Talbot as a car for the colonies.

There was sound logic for the Talbot ad. The Ekka attracted massive crowds from throughout the state. For many on the land and in the small country towns and cities, the Ekka was not just an annual event, but their yearly chance to go to the big smoke. A pilgrimage. Blokes would buy farm equipment, pumps, and stationary engines, the women would visit Brisbane's department stores, and the children would spend their days at the Ekka. On August 16, 1912, a Friday record, 27,000 people attended the show. The previous Wednesday, 57,000 people crammed into the venue, topping the record of 52,000 set on the first Saturday of the Jubilee Show in 1909. The show was, and is, a big deal in Brisbane. The Ekka is a Queensland institution. With the fledgling car industry extolling cars' virtues over the horse and buggy, farmers and out-of-towners had more than cattle judging on their minds.

There were enough cars on Queensland roads in 1912 to create a have-and-have-not mentality. But, if you were in the market for an automobile, which one to choose? Dealers were all advertising; they, whichever brand, were the 'best.' This led to confusion in the buyers' minds. Money was also a factor. You could buy a block of beachfront land for 60 or 70 pounds. A car would cost around 300 pounds. It was a far more significant decision than motorists make today. For first-time motorists, this increased pressure to make the correct decision.

Those who already owned a car knew what to look for. If they were happy with a particular brand, most likely they would trade-in on the same make. The Automobile Club of Australia started to conduct various types of car trials from around 1906. These included hill climbs, reliability trials, petrol consumption trials, speed contests.

When CCM took out an advertisement in the *Brisbane Courier*, it pointed to no less than 41 car trials, Australian and international, won by 'The Invincible Talbot' cars between 1906 and 1912. The advertisement's aim was clear: to convince Brisbane Ekka visitors the Talbot could handle anything they could dish out to it, not just in Brisbane, but in the harsh and lonely sticks of the state's outback.

Others tried a different tack to entice buyers from the bush. "The Hudson '33' for the Bush and the West" clamoured one advertisement from McGhie Motor Co.

"The man in the country is placing himself at a distinct disadvantage without the Hudson '33' Car, and, at the same time, is denying himself the greatest blessing that has come his way for centuries. "He can live a fuller life than the man who hasn't a car, besides conferring upon his family innumerable facilities for healthy enjoyment."

The advertisement did not just target visitors from the country, but city folk also.

"The man with a Hudson '33' gets to his business early in the morning, quickly, cleanly, with the sparkle of sunshine and fresh air in his blood and veins. He can take up his business problems with a clearer vision and greater energy than the man who is worried by the rush and jam of crowded trams and trains. After the day's work, a brisk drive home banishes weariness and worry from the brain."

At the time of writing, 2021, given Brisbane's traffic problems, this is perhaps an idiom that Brisbane's public transport system could use, or for that matter, Sydney or Melbourne.

Dalgety and Company in George Street, in November 1912, announced it had procured Buick, Rover, Daimler, Austin, and F/N car agencies as well as Halley and Lace commercial vehicles. By December 1912, the industry recognised it was not enough to sell cars, but there was an opportunity for vertical integration of the motor sales industry.

Canada Cycle and Motor was one of the first to capitalise on the new opportunity and announced 'a complete repairing plant in Queensland ... first-class staff and can undertake repairs of any description to any make of car. We have our own Body Builders, Blacksmiths, Trimmers, and Painters and can give estimates for any class of Body Work required.'

Four years later, the CCM garage built a Studebaker race car that would compete in Australia's first attempt at a national land speed record. And in a matter of months, it would cause Edward Eager a marketing nightmare. Then, as now, the automobile industry had issues. Among these were reliability, tyre wear, and, not surprisingly, the cost of fuel.

When reports emerged that the prestigious 30hp 1912 Cadillac was heavy on fuel and tyres, the Howard Motor Company was forced into damage control and took out a full-page advertisement to refute the claims. The ad consisted of half-page testimonials from around 70 Queensland Caddy owners – who had forked out $1200 each – with Howard's offering anyone interested the opportunity to view 'the originals of the above ... at our office for the asking.'

Typical of the testimonials was, 'I have averaged from 17 to 19 miles to the gallon. Of course, you are aware that my car is not by any means a town carriage and that I have taken it over many of the worst roads in the vicinity of Brisbane, including several trips to Southport and Mount Mee.'

In September, Edward Eager re-ran an advertisement, pushing the 30hp Overland and talking up the $850 value for just $710 for the five-seater. "And it is a fact that no other maker in the business can build this car and sell it at this price without losing money," he said. "This is due to our enormous manufacturing facilities – the largest in the world. "The manufacturer who turns out but 5000 cars must have greater production costs for each car than we who make 20,000 cars."

The problem for all makers was that Henry Ford's Model T outproduced them all and still had the market cornered with no significant improvements, despite being four years old. Unlike many of the 1912 models, such as Studebaker, Overland, and Cadillac, all had electric self-starting; Model T owners were still using a hand crank. Despite the lack of changes to the car, Ford had plenty of surprises for competitors in the coming years. They were not alone in that.

15 H.P. "STANDARD," To Seat Five Persons.

ALEC JEWELL Motor Co. Pty. Ltd.
675-677 ELIZABETH STREET, MELBOURNE.

Alec Jewell's catalogue for the first Motor Exhibition in August 1912.

4

Jewell returns to Melbourne

Declared bankrupt, Alec Jewell returned to Melbourne in early 1907 and took a position as a travelling representative for Massey-Harris Motor and Cycle Company.

He again made headlines, this time after a brush with death. In May 1907, Alec spent a week in Renmark, South Australia, as a base for his job as a rep for Massey-Harris and decided on a two-day trip to Mildura and back in Victoria. Business completed, he left Mildura mid-morning bound for Renmark, but instead of taking the shortest way, the mail route in New South Wales, he elected to stay south of the Murray River in Victoria.

He was going along well on the open plains for the first 75 miles on his motorcycle that tipped the scales at 220lb. Tyre troubles started soon after, and he lost a lot of time before coming to Lindsay Creek - about 20 miles from Renmark. Despite the proximity to the town, this is wild, dune country and rarely visited.

He found the heavy bike all but useless in the drifting sand, so he left the track and headed off through the mallee scrub.

"The travelling here was better, but darkness set in, and had to camp for the night," he told the *Renmark Pioneer* newspaper.

"I set off at daylight next morning and soon struck a boundary fence between Victoria and South Australia. There is a good, cleared track along the fence, which I followed south."

He missed vital tracks due to high undergrowth and ran out of petrol. He left the bike and, as he was parched, decided to look for water. By noon he was worried, his predicament was serious. He decided to return to Lindsay Creek - he did not know it, but the creek was 40 miles away.

"I kept going until dusk and again made the best of mother earth for a bed, starting off again at daybreak. I was tired, thirsty and hungry. That day I shall never forget. I trudged mile after mile, up and down hills and through scrub, my clothes torn and my thirst growing almost unbearable. I was hardly able to put one foot after the other," he told a reporter.

"At about five o'clock I expected to go mad, and I couldn't last the night without water. But before lying down for the last time I made a final desperate effort and caught a glimpse of the big trees on the riverbank, four miles away."

Jewell said he was torn with sensations of doubt and fear and hope and gave a silent prayer for strength. He reached the Lindsay River at dusk, tired and exhausted.

"I can't tell you how wonderful was the sensation experienced as I washed out my mouth, took a small drink and taking off what was left of my clothes and let myself slip into the cool water."

He found a track that ran alongside the river and followed it for two miles before spotting a house on the other side of the river. He could not talk but beckoned a man, Mr H Bland, a boundary rider, who rowed across and took him back to the home. It was a close call which Jewell never forgot.

"I am somewhat noted for stamina, having won the 116 miles Beverley-to-Perth road race from scratch ... but my strength and stamina were never put to so severe a test as on this occasion. I hope never again to have to go through the same awful experience."

With the assistance of another local, Mr R Sandford, they set off to locate his bike on Sunday, finding it below Beardy gate, well south of Renmark. Mr Sandford also remarked that Jewell had come within two miles of a dam. The bike recovered. It was re-fuelled, and Jewell set off for Renmark, worse for wear but glad to be alive.

He moved on from selling and maintaining bicycles and demonstrating cars to potential customers, to the natural progression: exclusively selling automobiles, and he started work for Canada Cycle and Motor Company. His territory included Victoria and Tasmania. When Alfred Deakin was in-between terms as Prime Minister of Australia (He was the member for Ballarat – Alec Jewell's hometown) and as it happened, Jewell was on business in Tasmania at the same time Mr Deakin visited the island state on the campaign trail.

Jewell made a public offer of his car to transport Mr Deakin and Senator Keating from Queenstown in the west of the state, where they were addressing a public meeting, across to Hobart, the state capital. Jewell was media-savvy and the offer generated high-profile local publicity for himself, and his new employer, CCM Melbourne. It's unknown if the past, and future, Prime Minister took up the offer.

Back in Melbourne a few months later he joined Kellow Motor Co, and when customers entered the showroom, Alec would turn on the charm, show them a car, and offer a demonstration ride around Melbourne.

Most of the city roads had paving, but road surfaces deteriorated as soon as you left the CBD. Horse and buggy were still the primary method of transport, as well as trams and bicycles. For some reason - most likely a better job offer, including a car - he left Kellows to take up a position with Acme Motor and Engineering, at 355 Lonsdale Street, Melbourne.

An article in the *Australian Motorist* shows he left Kellows on good terms and was a popular employee. On April 13, 1910, the Kellow company held a 'smoke night' with prizes handed out from a recent staff picnic. On hand was Mr C B Kellow himself, who expressed great satisfaction with all staff. The *Australian Motorist* reported:

"It was a jolly gathering, and everybody seemed to be in the best of spirits, as evinced by the hearty greeting and humorous interjections given to the prize-winners. Mr Coleman proved a first-class chairman, and Mr Alex Jewell was in great nick, this being possibly his final flutter, as, by the time this appears in print, we believe he has joined the ranks of the benedicts." This was a dig at Jewell for doing a 'Benedict Arnold' and being a 'traitor' to his employer.

That Jewell worked for Kellow Motor Co was not surprising. Charles Brown Kellow and Alec F Jewell had a lot in common. They probably met and competed against each other in cycling events in the 1890s, before Jewell moved to Western Australia in 1898.

Charles Kellow was an Australian champion cyclist, winning many races, including the 1896 Austral Cup which finished at the Melbourne Cricket Ground. The rough-and-tumble of road races, together with the need to formulate tactics, was excellent training for business. The similarities did not end there. Kellow at one stage, with H B James, held the world record for distance covered in a motor car in 24 hours.

Jewell was no doubt inspired by Kellow to go into business. Kellow ran a car importing company started in 1907. On a darker side, the two men also shared a commonality in court appearances. Both had speeding fines, had, or would, knock over a pedestrian near a tram - Kellow's J-walker coming away unscathed. Kellow had been drinking alcohol just before the crash in the Melbourne CBD.

Kellow also faced court over alleged attempts to avoid paying duty on imported cars around the time Jewell was in his employ. While at Kellow Motor Co, Alec Jewell sold Talbot, Renault, Minerva, Rolls-Royce, Standard, Willys Overland and Albion vehicles. Jewell left Kellows and moved to Acme Motor & Engineering Co, agents for the American 'Regal' cars.

While working at Acme, something odd happened to Alec Jewell. He was the victim of a car related incident in which his Acme-supplied vehicle was stolen. Alec was living in the Rose of South Yarra Hotel in Toorak Road, where the vehicle was 'stabled'. What followed was not much short of an episode from keystone cops.

Rupert Le Vere, also lived at the 'Rose' and got up early one morning and took three drams of brandy for a cold. Thus sustained, he went down to the 'car house' and started experimenting on Alec Jewell's work car. He pushed it backwards and forwards and finally got it out of the garage.

The engine fired and the car took off while he was at the back pushing. He jumped into the car from behind and grabbed hold of the wheel. "He could not stop it," the court was told. "But he managed to steer it round the street corners.

"At Balaclava it stopped, and he thought it was for want of petrol."

He rang the hotel and left a message for Jewell that he would look after the car until he came for it. Mr Le Vere was remanded to the jail hospital for a week for medical examination, as his behaviour in court had 'excited comment'.

In July 1910 Alex Jewell again graced the inside of a courthouse. This time on the charge of driving in a manner dangerous to the public on

May 30, 1910. He appeared before Mr Cohen, a magistrate, and JPs Brinsmead, Hattam and Holmes. It was the opening day of the Prahran-Malvern tramway and the arresting officer's job was to keep the crowd off the tram tracks.

The officer told the court Jewell was driving a car with three passengers when it came around the corner at a rate of 12mph and pulled up abruptly among people, only six yards from the tram shed gates. People had trouble escaping from the car's path. The *Melbourne Argus* reported the court case.

"There was an accident, and I saw a lady being attended to by a doctor," said Sgt McGillicuddy.

"On a clear road 12 miles an hour would not be fast, but in the circumstances, the defendant should have almost crawled around the corner."

Constable John Thompson said he narrowly escaped being knocked down by the car. He put his hands up to stop it, to no avail.

Jewell's lawyer told the court the accident had nothing to do with the charge. He said when Jewell's car stopped, a lady and two men, who had been invited to the celebration, stepped out of Jewell's car. They were about to enter the tram shed when a tramcar came out, and the back of the tram swung around a corner and struck the lady on the legs.

It was Alex Jewell's turn in the box. He said his car was not capable, with four passengers, running up and down hills at 12mph and there were no people on the tram track when he turned the corner. He said he drove along the loose metal at a walking pace, the engine in second gear, limiting the car to 4 to 5mph. He denied the constable put out his hand to stop the vehicle.

One of his passengers, Arthur Foyer, stated he was nervous and told Jewell to slow the pace down – which Jewell did, to a fast walking pace, and the tram track was clear.

Mr Cohen said there was a doubt in the bench's minds and they were giving the defendant the benefit, dismissing the case. Alex Jewell's ability to mesmerise courts by muddying the evidence continued.

Jewell fronted the court later in the year, this time on a charge of speeding. He gave his address as 355 Lonsdale Street, Melbourne, at the court hearing on Friday, November 11, 1910. The allegation is he sped at 30 miles per hour along Dandenong Road.

Police caught Jewell in the time-honoured fashion of distance covered in a given time. In 1910 in Melbourne, the speed limit was 20mph generally, and councils allowed to specify 10mph in city streets. Dandenong Road was then, and still is in 2021, a significant road connecting the city and satellite town of Dandenong.

Police staked out Dandenong Road, from the west side of Denbigh Road to Shirley Grove, a distance of 880 yards. Constables Irwin and Mooney gave evidence that on October 12, at 19 minutes past 5pm, Jewell drove a motor car along Dandenong Road between their trap in 59 seconds. This equated to 30 miles per hour. Police said it was a trade car, meaning a vehicle used as a demonstrator for potential buyers. At the time there were eight vehicles on the same stretch of road and two omnibuses.

Jewell told the court he believed he was only doing between 20 and 22 miles per hour with five people in the car. The average weight of those aboard was a hefty 18 stone. The car was probably a Regal touring sedan. Jewell said he took the car out for a 'trial run' to show its smooth running. In this era of high-speed vehicles, it may seem hard to believe, but back then 30 miles per hour (50km/h) was high speed. It was similar to a driver doing 120km/h in a 60km/h zone in today's terms.

But, like drink-driving back then, speeding was a relatively new occurrence. After all, in 1910 there were only 3204 licensed drivers in Victoria and 2735 registered cars. Jewell forked out three pounds for the misdemeanour. It was not his last brush with an enthusiastic traffic cop, Constable Irwin.

March 1911 saw the keen motorist heading overseas: to Tasmania. He boarded the SS Wauchope, from Melbourne and landed at King Island on Friday, March 10, complete with a 35hp motor car, the first car to visit the Bass Strait island.

In no time Jewell had the car off the general cargo vessel and drove along the beach. The local *Argus* correspondent commented it was surprising to see the way it ploughed through the sand.

An old islander said he heard the car coming and thought it was a buggy with the horses running away. He ran out of the bush to stop it, but when he saw the car coming, he "got an awful start and first thought of climbing a tree", but before he could find one the car had gone past him. Jewell continued to Launceston by ship and then drove to the island capital, Hobart, and started a car yard. This dealership - probably for Regal cars - seems to have been short-lived, and before long, he was back in Melbourne.

Jewell's enthusiasm for motoring was a continuation of his love of cycling. He threw everything into it. His first competitive event came in September 1911 in the Automobile Club of Victoria's Hill Climb at Mt Macedon. This time he could speed without fear of police traps.

He entered a work car, a 20hp Regal Runabout. The two-seat roadster had an underslung frame and cost 275 pounds. It was, most likely, his demonstration vehicle used with permission of Acme. Hill climbs were one of the first forms of Australian motorsport. Victoria generally has wet winters. In the early motoring era after winter rains, roads became quagmires. Queensland is the opposite with a more defined two seasons, the dry in winter and the wet in summer. The seasonal rains made a massive difference to motorsport in both states.

Once roads dried, they were rutted and threw even slow automobiles around like rag dolls. It was no place to hold any race. Rutted roads are one reason early vehicles had high clearance and large-diameter wheels. Twenty-six-inch wheels were not uncommon.

The Automobile Club of Victoria came under criticism from within for proposing to hold the hill climb at Mt Macedon, outside Melbourne. It argued that only a dozen cars would take part and as such, it was a waste of time and effort.

Those critics within the Automobile Club of Victoria sports committee misjudged the motorists' mood. Drivers wanted a place away from public roads - and police - to see how their cars would go and improve their driving skills. As always, there was a competition between the drivers and their choice of vehicle.

Plenty of makes and models rolled up within the 46 starters at 'Derreweit' the Mt Macedon property of host Gerald Buckley. A crowd of almost 300 people also arrived to witness the spectacle of cars racing up the twisting dirt track.

The weather was good, and only a couple of showers fell in the afternoon, not an unusual occurrence at Macedon.

The cars came in all makes and horsepower ratings. It was a gathering with WOW factor. There were 28hp Lanchesters, BSA, 25/30 Mercedes, 24hp Lancia, Clement Bayard, De Dion, Talbot, Star, Imperia, Minerva, Austin, Renault, Dennis, Nagant, Hudson, Fiat, Humber, Hotchkiss, SCAT Chalmers, Ford, Berleit, Swift and the single Regal with Alec Jewell.

The cars used a 300-yard flying-start, and as each car crossed the line the starter pressed a signal lever, giving a distinct buzz at the top of the hill. The timekeepers stationed at the top pressed their stopwatches.

There were no fewer than three chronographs at the finish line, besides a host of amateur checkers, 'who very kindly informed the official time-keepers that their timing was correct according to their own turnips,' reported the *Australian Motorist*.

Handicapping was calculated according to horsepower and weight, and the handicap winner was H V McKay in his Lanchester, representing Sunshine Motor Cars Ltd. His 28hp car crossed the finish line in 95 2/5 seconds.

Coming second was another Lanchester driven by W Hinson. Alex Jewell came 26th with a time of 91 2/5 seconds in the 20hp Regal. The fastest time was set by a 38hp Minerva driven by Jim Moffatt, who covered the track in just 56 2/5 seconds. Another Moffatt, called Allan, would be a regular guest on the winner's podium in a much later era. But that's another story.

Jewell crossed the finish line 8th fastest out of the 46 entrants. He loved the competition, the buzz that comes with high anticipation and the throbbing purr of a willing engine. It was as if this event was the sole purpose he had been aiming for since he first stepped into a car. It took him back to his teenage days as a competitive racing cyclist around Melbourne and Perth. As one of Australia's first motorists, he felt as he had done his motoring apprenticeship in Perth. At last, he had found a passion for replacing the thrill of competitive cycling.

Unfortunately, Alec Jewell failed to distinguish between the track and Melbourne's public roads. He was not the only motorist pushing beyond the speed limits. Jim Moffat, who took line honours earlier in the day, also got the fastest time back to Melbourne - according to the *Australian Motorist* he went 'fast enough for anyone outside of the Brooklands track.'

On July 6, 1911, Jewell faced court again - this time the Prahran Court - still giving his employers' address in Lonsdale Street, charged on June 13, with having driven a motor car on Toorak Road at speed dangerous to the public.

Constable Rose led evidence that at 3pm Alec Jewell drove between Cunningham Street and Cromwell Street, a distance of 300 yards, in 22 seconds, or at a rate of 27 1/2 miles per hour. Constable Irwin told the court he and Constable Rose were at the Cunningham Street end of the speed trap. Jewell denied the car was going at 27 1/2 miles per hour, but 'without a speedometer it was difficult to rebut the evidence of the police'. In the end, Jewell was found not guilty on a technicality - the police should have stationed themselves at either end of the trap.

The majority of the bench of three JPs said with the two constables at one end of the trap, and it was not a 'proper' one. There was doubt in the case, and the defendant receiving the benefit of the doubt. There was a lot of 'benefit-of-the-doubt' surrounding Alec Jewell in his frequent court appearances.

Police caught Jewell twice for speeding over a brief time, and it would be naive to think these were the only times he put the pedal to the metal. When caught and hauled before the courts, he had a special knack of being able to sow a seed of doubt in the magistrates or JPs' minds. Charges before an Australian court must be proven 'beyond a reasonable doubt'. This talent - to muddy the waters - is an art Alec Jewell perfected. His skill as a car salesman - the gift of the gab - came in handy in a court of law.

5

Sydney to Melbourne

With Alec Jewell needing to think-over his driving habits on public roads, his future adversary in the quest for an Australian land speed record - Fred Z Eager - made his first motoring trip to Melbourne from Sydney. He too was starting his motorsport career, stepping out from behind the substantial shadow of his adventurous father, Edward.

The time had come for Fred to create his own identity. It was an inauspicious start, a drive between Australia's two main capitals. It was not an officially timed race, but Fred was keen to experience speed on well-made roads. For his purposes, he timed the jaunt.

After leaving Sydney's outskirts and entering Melbourne's outskirts, Fred Eager saw two other cars, putting the excursion in context of the size and remoteness of even relatively populated parts of the country. His report to the *Australian Motorist* gives an insight into interstate travel in 1912. Eager drove a 30hp Overland and threw 'our grips, letter files, and other paraphernalia' into the car.

To Camden, the roads were in good shape with some fine stretches. The route took Eager from Camden over Razor Back Hill which he thought was a little disappointing, as he was looking forward to the challenge and had heard it was 'some hill'. After a rough descent, he struck good surface into Picton. They had a clear run through Mittagong and Berrima to Marulan, where they stopped for lunch.

Along here they struck 'sluits' - drainage ditches - dug across the road designed to take away rainwater, which gave some 'good jolts' forcing them to keep a keen lookout. Shortly after leaving Marulan, heavy showers fell, and after passing through Goulburn, ran into a decent cloudburst. Within

15 minutes the road was mostly underwater. The 'sluits' were torrents, pushing the car sideways. Eager thought in several places that he would drown the engine but was lucky enough to pull through.

At the same time, he had to dodge large logs which were washing down the road. At Breadalbane, he lifted the bonnet and found dead leaves, grass and twigs around the engine base, and one leaf wrapped around the carburettor air intake. The foliage washed through the radiator, giving some idea of the water's depth. Eager passed it off as having some 'close calls'. From Breadalbane on to Yass, they found the same good surface, though a little heavy after the downpour. The rain continued intermittently all afternoon.

"I picked this time to have most of my tyre trouble - it's fun to change them on a muddy road, with the rain dripping down the back of your neck, isn't it?" he told *The Steering Wheel*. After supper, they decided to keep going a bit further, to push on through the night rather than sit around.

They took it easy and enjoyed watching the rabbits and foxes attracted by the car's headlights. Reaching Jugong at about 10.30pm, they pulled up for the night. The demanding night driving caught up with them, so they started late on Saturday morning. It was a hot day, and finding a 'pub' in Gundagai, where they put 'real ice' in their drinks, they didn't leave until about noon. The road deteriorated after Gundagai, and they found alternate good stretches and light sand through to Lower Tarcutta, where they stopped for lunch.

The 'pub' was a great surprise to the travellers, who had their best meal between Sydney and Melbourne. Rain set in as they left Tarcutta, and they had a slippery road most of the afternoon, varied by stretches of fairly heavy sand. Fred Eager learned a valuable lesson from this drive, one that he would put in the back of his mind for future long-distance road trips. It was to prove a critical lesson.

The next leg of the trip, apart from occasional short surfaced-stretches, the road from Lower Tarcutta to Germanton, about 50 miles, was the worst Fred Eager had ever encountered. The gullied hillsides meant any attempt at speed was impossible and were especially bad in the rain as it flowed deep across the road. From Germanton to Albury, the next leg proved to be much better, and they arrived at 7pm. After fighting the road most of the afternoon, Eager was ready for a good night's sleep.

The pair made an early start from Albury and needed it, as two blow-outs set them back in the first 50 miles. They found the roads through this country a little rough, and with some sand, but not nearly as bad as they expected. After lunch at Euroa, they kept on over a gradually improving road. Outside Seymour, the road had a fine stone surface which lasted to Melbourne.

"My actual driving time for the trip was a little under 27 hours. I think that the road, as a whole, is really good and I am sure that we both enjoyed the trip very much. I am only surprised that the road is so little used - after leaving Sydney we saw only two motor cars until inside the Melbourne suburbs," he said.

The last statement is significant as it gives an insight into Fred Eager's upbringing. His family's relative wealth he took for granted. In 1912 few people could afford a car, let alone driving the vehicle between capital cities and risking damage to the automobile, as well as the expense of accommodation, fuel and food along the way.

Yet, Eager seems mystified as to why there were only two cars between the cities. The preferred transport between the capitals was by ship, or train - albeit with a stop in Albury to swap to another train, as NSW and Victoria used different rail gauges. He continued his report to the *Australian Motorist*. "I have been asked several times to compare this road with our roads in the United States. "This is a hard task. However, I think that bar the stretch between Gundagai and Germanton, the going is about as good as one finds in the average 600-mile trip at home (US).

"In some of our states, one may travel for days on roads like boulevards, but the Central, Western and Southern States' average roads are none too good at present.

This trip gave Fred Eager a good overview of road conditions and the eastern states of Australia, a knowledge that would become valuable as his interests expanded in future years. Road surfacing and condition would become a significant issue for the motor industry.

6

Trials and Tribulations

In May 1912 Alec Jewell lived in Tasmania and advertised a car for sale, a '16hp model in good order. Owner Leaving State'. He gave his address as the Highfield Hotel, Hobart, Tasmania. By July he was back In Melbourne and set up Alec Jewell Motors. In addition to importing vehicles, he sold used cars: Daimler, De Dion, Itala, Star, Dixie, BSA, Clement Bayard, Maxwell, Standard, Siddeley and De Dietrich.

The *Australian Motorist* reported the start of the new business. "Mr Alex Jewell, who was formerly associated with the Kellow Motor Co, and later with Acme Motor Co, is now controlling the agency for Victoria for Standard cars. His business establishment is in Elizabeth Street, north."

Jewell established a cosy relationship with Melbourne's *Punch* newspaper. It featured many editorials favourable to Alec and his new business, more like what is now called 'advertorials'. *Punch* had a motoring column and a motoring reporter with the by-line 'Magneto Sparks'.

Jewell was innovative and adventurous in his first outing at the Melbourne Motor Show in September 1912. He featured a polished Standard chassis and drivetrain at his display, exposing visitors to the 'nuts and bolts' in their full glory under the car's body. That was just the entree.

Then came the Galah, Magpie and Canary. Described in the column as "Three delightful touring cars … revealed in the highest art in body-building, the colour schemes of grey and rose pink, black and white, and pure yellow." This was 1912 when most cars were black (as they were Model Ts) or dark coloured. *Punch* gushed over Alec Jewell and his new showroom in Melbourne.

"His very handsome spick-and-span garage at the top end of Elizabeth Street is a sight to see these days. I paid a visit recently, soon after the garage was opened and received an eye-opener when I beheld the packed state of things. Standard cars of all descriptions lined the walls, and a constant stream of trial runs kept up to prove to would-be purchasers the true value of the goods.

"Mr Alec Jewell has long been associated with the motor industry, and from what I know of him personally, no man could be more popular," he said.

"Alec Jewell possesses a happy knack of making friends at every turn. He is always smiling and always in a jovial frame of mind. If there's business to be done, he's the man to do it. I think he could sell a car to any man when he is in the humour to do so, and as he is always in that humour, and good humour at that, men place faith in him and become enamoured with his broad smile and buy."

The correspondent stated Alex Jewell had untiring energy and wonderful perseverance that brought him up to the first rank, "He is one of those men who cannot sit still." Alec was not in the business alone but had a partner, Charles Keil, also from Ballarat, who controlled Keil and Loveland's firm in perhaps Victoria's coldest city. Keil was not a silent partner and worked in the Elizabeth Street premises.

Business was booming for Alex Jewell. *Punch* reported a wave of prosperous times and big business passing through the Alex Jewell Motor Co. "The Itala cars have caught on, the demand has steadily set in, and now it's a case of keeping up with it. If you wanted an Itala right at the minute, I doubt if you could get it as the last arrivals are gone."

On October 2, 1913, the *Punch* motoring column reported that it had seen a 'motor hearse' on the streets of Melbourne for the first time. Around this time undertakers used motor coffin carts and motor cars in the role of a hearse. The hearse had been built by Alec Jewell's company on an Itala platform. It became popular with mourners, more dignified than the older transporting methods for the recently departed to the Necropolis, and to Springvale Cemetery.

This innovation led to another creation, built by Alec Jewell's firm; the mourning coach, also made on the Itala platform. These coaches transported grieving families, who did not own a car, to burial places in a far more private and dignified way than the train or taxi. Magneto Sparks commented Alec Jewell led the way on funerals' dignity and solemnity, particularly the procession with the bespoke motor vehicles' innovation.

In January 1914 Alec added another win to his CV by competing in the Melbourne-to-Sydney Reliability Trial, taking out the petrol consumption test over the 628-mile journey. He averaged 21mpg from a single-seat Dixi. In April he was presented with his winning prize by the British Imperial Oil Co - a stunning gold watch pendant in the shape of a motor wheel, the hub being a large diamond. Engraved on the back are appropriate words outlining the win.

If ever there was a story to give credence to 'Win on Sunday, Buy on Monday', this was it: A New South Wales motorist, Mr McFarlane, after reading of Alec's win, took a train to Melbourne and bought the winning Dixi.

Jewell had chosen the perfect vehicle for the economy run. The Dixi was a tiny car, a single seater with a small economical engine. *Punch* reported, "Business is good these days with the Jewell Motor Co … and cars are going out rapidly. Amongst these might be mentioned a two-ton Itala lorry to the Glenferrie Ice Works."

Alec had increased the size of the premises, including a new workshop. By June 1914 he had added the Commonwealth Government to his list of clients with an order for the supply of Itala cars to the Postmaster-General's Department. Alec Jewell Motor Co Pty Ltd was sole Melbourne agent for Itala, Panhard, Dixi and Turner cars.

As ever, the motoring exploits of Alec F Jewell were never far from the headlines. On Thursday, October 30, 1913, Jewell was driving along Queen's Parade, Clifton Hill, at 8.20pm when the unthinkable took place. He was going on the inside of a slowly moving tram when he heard a thud.

In no time the police were on the spot, they did not have far to go as the crash took place outside the Clifton Hill Police Station. The victim had not just been hit but was run over by Jewell's car. The man was picked up and taken into Sergeant Stillard's office, and within minutes two doctors attended the badly injured worker. He was pronounced dead at the police station. Sgt Stillard witnessed the accident.

On Saturday, November 1, police ordered Alec Jewell to attend a coronial inquest before Coroner, Dr Cole, and a jury of 12. The Coroner was investigating the circumstances of the death of a married man, Peter Portway, a bill poster and wood salesman.

Police evidence was simple: Portway died after being run down by a car driven by Alex Jewell, motor importer, of High Street, St Kilda. Jewell found himself at the City Morgue and represented by his lawyer, Mr Brayshaw. Mr S E Secomb appeared for the family of the deceased. The case did not bode well for Jewell.

Due to previous well-publicised court appearances, Jewell had a reputation as a speedster. Portway resided in Walker Street, Northcote, and was pushing a hand-truck along Queen's Parade's tram-track. Tram gripman Patrick Deneiro said while in charge of the tram he saw Portway with his hand-truck a short distance ahead of his tram. As the tram passed Portway, a motor car came around the side, knocked Portway down and ran him over.

The motor car was travelling a little faster than a tram, and it was dark at the point of impact. Deneiro said the car's driver did not appear to have been careless. Jewell then gave evidence saying a friend, Mr R B Lawrence accompanied him, and he left the city in his car, bound for Clifton Hill "When I was near the Clifton Hill Police Station, I was running up alongside a tram. I don't think I was travelling faster than the tram, and I was dumbfounded when I felt a bump.

Dr Cole: -- What is your opinion about fast driving? Jewell: -- Fast driving is all right in open country. In the city, a mile an hour is sometimes dangerous. The Coroner said that the evidence was perfectly clear. The driver of the car did not appear to have been travelling very fast.

The question was, was there any criminal negligence, or was the driver reasonably careful? He thought the driver had been.

The (jury) foreman announced the jury was perfectly satisfied that it was an accident and added a rider that they did not wish Jewell's licence to be endorsed. Alec Jewell was free to go and still held his driver's licence.

When it came to court cases, Alec Jewell was cat-like. He seemed to have nine lives.

7

Professor Starlight

Few Australians have heard of Professor Starlight. In the 1880 and 90s and even as late as 1912, he was a legend in Melbourne and London. Edward William Rollins was born in British Guiana in 1852, was not just a boxer but a pugilist who started in the ring as a bare-knuckle fighter in Brisbane, as a 35-year-old.

A tall man, just under six feet, he had long arms giving him an advantage over shorter opponents. A sharp left jab kept them at bay while their punches fell short of the target. Professor Starlight was a black man with high cheekbones and a wide grin, and a personality known to light up a dark day. He was famous in and out of the boxing ring. A sailor, he had traveled the world. He fell in love with Melbourne on his first visit and it with him. His life story reads like fiction - a story out of a *Boy's Own Annual*.

Rollins was born on April 1, 1852, on the banks of the Demerara River in British Guiana, in the South American tropics. There were schools, but after the sudden death of his mother, the traumatised young boy refused to attend. He was sent to boarding school but ran away.

"I must have been a wild 'un," he later admitted

His next move was again to run away to sea as a cabin boy. He landed a job on an American coastal ship called the *Polly Greenwich* and ended up in New York. From the Big Apple he worked the West Indian gulf ports and then started on the England run as a crewman, with ports including London, Liverpool and Glasgow.

In the early 1880s he signed on as a crewman aboard a fully rigged sailing ship bound for Sydney. In the harbour city he took up with a bunch of coloured men from the West Indies and then met with another man of colour, Peter Jackson. Jackson arranged to smuggle Rollins off the sailing ship and found him a job.

At the time Jackson was working as a wharfie and neither man had any intention or idea of taking up boxing. The pair became firm friends and they took up boxing lessons - Rollins as a middleweight and Jackson, a heavyweight.

"He (Jackson) was a strapping boy, as strong as a lion and very active," said Rollins.

"He had all the makings of being the greatest fighting man in the world, which he turned out to be a few years afterwards.

"Everyone knows that Peter Jackson never won the heavyweight championship of the world because John L Sullivan (world heavyweight champion) drew the colour line."

Sullivan would box only white opponents.

Jackson arranged a job for Rollins on Thursday Island in Torres Strait, off the tip of Cape York, to work with the pearl fishermen. He was smuggled aboard a Howard Smith vessel bound for Thursday Island and signed in at Captain Riddell's pearling station for two years at one pound a month.

After six months on deck Rollins had saved enough money to buy a boat and hire a crew. He decided to take up pearl diving. Captain Riddell promised him 15 pounds for every 100 shells he brought to the surface. The business was going well until one day his air line fouled on rocks. He was lucky to survive after the crew pulled him into the boat, 'just about out of it'. He was too young, he reckoned, to keep on diving as he had a lot of living to do. His high income dried up.

Rollins arrived in Brisbane, broke and hungry, and ready to fight anyone in the world for a feed. He found himself at Jack Dowridge's Black Diamonds boxing saloon. The saloon was a meeting place for 'forlorn coloured adventurers' - a suitable description of Rollins at that time. Dowridge matched Rollins with a fighter called Moonlight and told Rollins he could not go into the ring with a name like Edward.

In Brisbane bookstalls Rolfe Boldrewood's novel *Robbery Under Arms* was a sensation and a bystander suggested Starlight as a ring name for the newcomer. So, Starlight it was, and remained, for the next 50 years.

He became one of Australia's best middleweight boxers and one of the most popular. He was charismatic, and even though his record was not great, he was highly regarded, in and out of the ring. A good man, a gentleman. His boxing CV stands at 91 bouts, 27 wins, 17 KOs, 36 losses, and 11 draws.

Starlight could not read or write. He could recall when events in his life took place by linking them to the year when a horse won the Melbourne Cup. He could recall every Cup winner from 1861 until the year he died.

In the mid-1930s Melbourne's *Sporting Globe* newspaper ran a five-part feature on Professor Starlight, allowing him to tell the story of his remarkable life. The introduction to the series paints a beautiful picture of the Professor.

"Well preserved even though he fought more ring battles than any other boxer in Australia, Professor Starlight does not look his age. Just 6ft. tall, he has an erect figure and dignified bearing. His voice is soft and deep, and his words are carefully chosen. His fists are frail-looking, but there is still power in his grip ... yet if you look more closely, you will notice that several knuckles have been smashed.

"However, there is no mistaking the close-cropped bullet head, thick neck, high cheekbones, scarred lips and eyebrows, and thickened ears of the fighting man."

Alongside his boxing career, Professor Starlight was an entertainer, actor and conducted boxing classes at fire stations, the YMCA, and police gymnasiums. In 1891 he entered the Melbourne Athletic Club ring to fight for Australia's middleweight championship against a formidable foe in Dan Creedon. He was then known widely as Starlight, or the 'Star' as his many friends called him. Starlight was 40 years of age, and Dan Creedon was just 23.

Despite the Star flooring Creedon twice, the New Zealand-born fighter took the middleweight belt. Starlight later revealed in the third round he had broken his hand, but he believed he could have won for that. "I got very tired in the legs, and then he beat me to the floor several times ... I was in a bad way at the finish," he told the *Sporting Globe*.

Starlight and Dan Creedon remained firm friends for the rest of their lives. After the 1891 fight, the pair met for a quiet drink in a Melbourne pub run by Creedon, his mother, and sister on Queen and Bourke streets' corner.

"Well, Star," said Dan, "Now I'm champion of Australia, and I've got the belt, I reckon I'm going to the (United) States to take the championship of the world from Bob Fitzsimmons!" The advice given by the Star was simple: "Dan, don't fight Bob; he'll beat you and end your fighting days. He's a cruel puncher."

Starlight knew his stuff. He fought Fitzsimmons twice in Sydney, "and the cruel kidney punches that beat me down are still a nightmare to me." Creedon ignored the advice and went to the US and matched up with the World Champion. "Bob Fitzsimmons punched the fight out of Dan," said Starlight.

On April 23, 1896, after completing a boxing tour, Starlight boarded a ship from Wellington, New Zealand, bound for England. He had the money for a ship's passage to London but instead opted to get a job aboard a passenger liner. As a young man, he had been a seaman and visited England many times. This time he wanted to go as a "someone ... as Starlight, colored boxing champion." He wanted to test himself against the best British boxers.

He strolled down to Wellington's docks where a stevedore put him in contact with the captain of a White Star boat, and he signed on as a third cook, "which is a nice name for potato peeler and pot-washer."

On arrival in London the first thing he did was purchase a tailor-made suit - of the type worn by posh Englishmen.

Starlight was beaten in a boxing match at the National Sporting Club of London by Frank Craig, the 'Harlem Coffee Cooler'. As usual, Star put up a good fight. He was a stylish, elegant boxer which caught the eye of the audience. Edward VII, Prince of Wales, approached Starlight after the bout and commented as he met the pugilist, "Professor Starlight – a real professor of the Noble Art."

The name stuck like super glue. The Prince invited 'Professor Starlight' to visit the Royal Palace with the Star's good friend, the great colored boxer, Peter Jackson.

"They said he (Prince Edward) would bet on anything from a man fight to a dog fight," said Professor Starlight, explaining the royal presence at a mere boxing match.

"We were invited along to see the magnificent grounds and were shown around by the Prince himself one Friday afternoon," he said. The visit capped off with Prince Edward presenting the Professor with a gold-headed Malacca walking cane as a memento of the occasion. "I am proud to say that Peter Jackson and I were, as far as I know, the only coloured men ever to visit the Royal Palace," he told the *Sporting Globe*.

No thumb sketch of Professor Starlight would be complete without the story of him meeting another royal ... boxing royalty in the form of the legendary Jack Johnson, World Heavyweight Champion 1908 to 1915. Johnson was an Afro-American; they were about the same height: Johnson just over six feet, Starlight just under. That's where the similarity ended. The Professor had a build like a flimsy old iron backyard dunny. Johnson, on the other hand, was built like the proverbial brick outhouse.

The pair met at Bill Lang's hotel on the corner of Swanston and Little Bourke streets in Melbourne CBD. The year was 1907 and Jack Johnson was in Australia chasing the Canadian boxer, Tommy Burns, for a world title fight.

Johnson had been stalking Burns around the world for several months, taunting him - looking for a match up, a shot at the world title. Jack was preparing for a fixture against Bill Lang in Melbourne - hence he was at his pub - and they wanted someone to spar with him. Professor Starlight, then aged about 54, takes up the story in the *Sporting Globe*:

"I was in Bill Lang's hotel ... when they introduced me to Jack. He had just come down from Sydney where he had beaten the colored man, Peter Felix," he said.

"They said to me: 'Star, we want you to spar an exhibition with Jack.' "I remember looking up and down that enormous frame. "ME box HIM!", I said. (He looked twice as big as I was) "No, sir, not me - too old, too small!"

"But they told me that Jack would not try to knock me about. They kept filling up my glass, and soon I began to think that I was as big as Jack and twice as good.

"I told Jack that I'd have a smack at him and that he'd better step lively!

Starlight said when he climbed into the ring at the Cyclorama, he felt like a little boy sparring with his father.

"I just couldn't hit big Jack anywhere but on the forearms. He was the most wonderful boxer! I tried hard enough, but I don't think I could have landed on him if I'd been throwing dozens of boxing gloves at him at once. Sammy Green was in my corner, and about the second round, he called, 'Go on in Star; go for his body!'"

Starlight dropped his gloves, turned to Sammy, and said, 'It's all very well for you out there to talk - you ought to come in and try yourself.

"Big Jack Johnson was always one big grin, and he joined in the laugh with everyone else."

The most interested onlooker at the sparring match was Bill Lang, who had taken a night off from training ahead of their bout to size up big Jack.

"Well, I think Bill saw enough of the big chap's style that night to know that he didn't have the ghost of a chance with him."

At the end of the third round, Starlight told the referee he'd had enough.

"Go in and have another round, Star," the referee replied, "The crowd are enjoying it."

"Wish I was one of the crowd," retorted Starlight

"Big Jack helped me through another round. I couldn't do anything with him. He let me have one or two solid ones too."

Johnson went on to defeat Bill Lang in the ninth round at the old Richmond Racecourse on March 6, 1906. Previously he took down Bob Fitzsimmons in just two rounds.

Alec Jewell liked the fight game - he was a regular in pubs and boxing nights after he returned to Melbourne in 1907. He enjoyed the company of those who undertook the noble art. Sometime between 1907 and 1913 he met Bill Lang and Starlight. It may well have been when Starlight and Dan Creedon had their second fight in Melbourne in 1912. Creedon won on points and this was Starlight's last fight in the big time.

Fast forward to January 1913 and Alec Jewell offered to drive Professor Starlight and Bill Lang to Wonthaggi in South Gippsland, to spar at a charity show. What could possibly go wrong?

A letter to the editor of *The Herald*, gives some insight as to Alec Jewell's driving:

"Sir, An article in one of the Melbourne dailies referring to a motor incident, which happened on Sunday, is worthy of notice. It refers to the road hog and his smelliful machine. That the speed rate limit is exceeded by the hog when passing through Pakenham is a matter of ordinary comment.

"On Sunday a motor passed through at a speed of about 27 miles an hour. Between the shire hall and the railway crossing there is a positive danger on the narrow road. The local progress association might get a move on by discussing the hog at the next meeting. That he will have to be stopped is a certainty. Some of us feel so indignant that a project is on foot to wreck the hog by prosecuting him. Locally owned cars are driven fairly, and the offenders are in the main flash maniacs from the metropolis."

Starlight drew the short straw and sat on a petrol can in the tray back of Jewell's utility, while Bill Lang and Mr W M (Billy) Williams scored a front seat with Jewell. Williams was a sporting personality, a boxing and wrestling referee, as well as Lang's and Jack Johnson's manager. His job was to referee the sparring match between Starlight and Bill Lang. From the CBD, they drove out through Dandenong, about 35km from the city.

Professor Starlight amused himself by singing a few of his favourite songs as Alec sped along the rough road.

"We were going along and happened to miss the melodious voice of the rear seat passenger," explained Williams.

"We looked behind and were surprised to find no trace of Starlight. The car was turned and about a mile back Starlight was found covered with dust and dissatisfaction on the roadway. He had been jolted from his seat clean out of the car."

Professor Starlight gave his version of events to the *Sporting Globe*.

"We went past Dandenong when Alex took a corner too sharply. I went spinning down the embankment, and they (Lang, Williams and Jewell, sitting in the cabin) didn't know I was missing till they'd gone a couple of miles.

"When they came back looking for me, I told them what I thought of them, believe me. We went onto Wonthaggi, but I was too sick to box. "I had to be back in the city at 9 o'clock that night to do my turn with the J

C Williamson Company at the Theatre Royal, but I couldn't go on with that engagement either.

The following day Professor Starlight took himself to Melbourne Hospital. "Doctors found I had a broken knee and a broken bone in the arm. "The knee has been crippled ever since. They put me in hospital," he said. Professor Starlight told the *Sporting Globe* he lost a lot of money through being unable to give lessons.

"I had dozens of pupils at the time, so Wonthaggi was a disaster for me. "I really think that if I hadn't got bucked out of a motor car … I'd be a handful for some of them yet."

Starlight used a walking stick for the rest of his life, the gold-handled one given to him by the future King of England 17 years earlier.

Professor Starlight and son.

8

From boom to bust

Alec Jewell Motor Co. had done a booming business in car sales in 1914, and the future looked bright as he secured sale after sale and landed a Federal Government contract for the supply of vehicles to the Postmaster General's Department.

In May 1915, the Alec Jewell Motor Co. went into liquidation. Everything left in the showroom was up for auction on May 6, at 11 am., including the lease on the premises at 675 Elizabeth Street, Melbourne, that still had eight years to run at an annual rent of 234 pounds.

Motor cars auctioned included a BSA touring car, a Wagentals three-wheel delivery vehicle, and a Dixi, similar to the automobile Alec Jewell had won the Melbourne-to-Sydney economy section Reliability Trial. There was also an Itala Touring car, many parts for Itala cars, and all the office furniture.

In 1925 while visiting Perth, Jewell described the business's failure to Perth newspaper, the *Sunday Times*. He said he was doing a high-grade business as Alec Jewell Motors but, when the war broke out, it caught him with several continental cars, the 'financial condition of which gave no hope'. Meaning the sale of all the assets would not have covered his debts.

The positive publicity Jewell generated in *Punch* was just smoke and mirrors, or as they call it today, Fake News. Gullible journalists sucked in by Alec Jewell's ebullient and charismatic personality.

Another chapter closed in the roller-coaster life of Alec Fraser Jewell.

9

Four cylinders versus six.
Motoring soap opera

The year 1914 started like most others. It was an exciting time to be alive with modern inventions changing the face of Australia: aircraft, cars, cameras, electricity. In a brief time, the world had changed dramatically. You could buy a tailored suit, with extra pair of trousers, from T T Barry in Queen Street, Brisbane, for 65 shillings, ($6. 50). You could hop on your motorcycle for 67 pounds 10 shillings ($135), or if that were out of reach, a quality 'Coventry Flyer' bicycle would set you back between four pounds and nine pounds.

Under the heading 'The Year of the Six ... The Six of the Year', CCM heavily promoted the new Studebaker Six. "Someday you'll buy a Six! Why not Now?"

CCM newspaper ads claimed Studebaker was building as many sixes as all other makers combined. Mass production allowed them to bring the Studey Six to market at 470 pounds, or 130 pounds less than other sixes. Naturally, it was only a matter of time before the inevitable counterclaim entertained *Brisbane Courier* readers and infuriated those at CCM.

"NAPIER SIX. Noiseless and smokeless NAPIER" taunted the ad taken out by Town and Country Amalgamated Motors Ltd.

"The first six-cylinder car 11 years ago, and still without a rival.

"Way back in 1903 the first Six-Cylinder Car (the NAPIER) was put on the road -- Competitors laughed - Critics? Criticised - The world wondered and exclaimed, What next! The Napier triumph is seen in every 6 Cylinder Motor ad of the day. The lead 'Napier' set has been followed by the principal motor car manufacturers of the world. The 'Napier' Six

Cylinder has had 11 years of testing - 11 years of success - Many others you hear about haven't had one -

"THEREFORE! When extravagant claims are made about 'this' and 'that' 6 Cylinder Car, it'll prove interesting to bear in mind the simple story of 'Napier' 6 Cylinder construction."

These advertisements set the tone within the new car dealerships in Brisbane. One false or arguable claim and you would be publicly exposed. It was a divisive culture and confusing to prospective buyers.

CCM seemed to swallow the bitter pill without too many hiccups and its next ad, two days later, on January 12, 1914, was for the four-cylinder Studebaker roadster at 295 pounds. No matter what the agencies did, they could not compete with Ford.

On January 14, Ford announced Francis Birtles had crossed Australia from the Gulf of Carpentaria to Melbourne, 3500 miles in 21 days in a 20hp Model T Ford.

'COMMENT NEEDLESS!' stated the simplest of ads. 'PRICE 210 pounds.'

Car companies were not the only ones vying for the reader's attention. There was fierce competition from tyre makers. One of the more innovative was French makers, Michelin.

The Michelin Brothers used a cartoon figure as their logo from 1898 after one of the brothers saw a stack of tyres at an exhibition. This stack resembled a man without arms, and tyres at the top, smaller diameter than those of the rotund body.

They commissioned French artist Marius Rossillon, who used the pseudonym O'Galup, to develop the cartoon-like figure, who we now know as the 'Bib the Michelin Man or simply as the 'Michelin Man.'

From about 1908 the Michelin Man was called Bibendum. And in January 1914 Bibendum gave his Australian friends his best wishes for the New Year and offered them a few New Year motoring hints.

If the life of your tyres you wish to prolong,
And repair bills encounter but seldom,
Read over the rules that are written below, And
take heed to the words of Bibendum. Avoid all
those faults, much too common by far,

That for tyre destruction soon make,
Such as turning abruptly, a sharp standing start,
Or too harshly applying the brake.
Take care not to run on non-parallel wheels,
Close small cuts in covers with Mastic---
Small items, 'tis true, but they save in the end,
Repairs both expensive and drastic.
Be sure that your tyres you carefully dry,
At the close of a run through the rain,
Also, after washing, or else I'm afraid,
Your labour's expended in vain.
If you pay strict attention to matters like these,
You'll find that you quickly will be,
Exempted from wasting both temper and time,
And last, but not least, LSD. (Pounds, shillings and pence)

Michelin, Continental and Barnett Glass were among the most media-active tyre manufacturers, advertising regularly. Tyre makers emulated car companies when vehicles, shod with their tyres, won motorsport events, highlighting when and what car.

"In the two Greatest tests for Reliability yet held in Australia, CONTINENTAL TYRES gain an easy first."

The contest was the Melbourne-to-Sydney reliability contest for cars and motorcycles, with eight of the 28 starters in the automobile section using Continental tyres, with the top four placings using their products. The winners were A V Turner in a 25hp Benz, 1; G F Hill in a 15hp Talbot 2; A Hoette in a 12hp Benz 3; and P Meyer, also in a 12 hp Benz.

There were also hill climb events at Bulli Pass and Melbourne's Pretty Sally hill. Turner, Meyer and Hoette came first, third and fourth at Bulli Pass on the Illawarra escarpment south of Sydney.

With the McGhie Motor Co's demise, in Brisbane, Dalgety and Co, picked up the Hudson agency and two models, the 44hp Hudson Six at 610 pounds and a Hudson four-cylinder at 550 pounds.

Edward Eager continued to run aggressive advertising, and why not, when he had a story to tell. Willys Overland company was given the 'position of honour' at the 1914 National Automobile Show in the Grand Palace, New York City.

"Even in Detroit, the automobile hub of the world, more Overlands are being sold than any other car of its type," said Edward Eager.

"The Overland has made, established, and won for Toledo with its individual plants alone, the title of the second greatest automobile city in the world."

More than 50,000 Overlands came off the production lines in 1914, more cars than all of France, three times as many as Germany's factories, and more than Italy, Holland, Russia and Sweden combined.

Town and Country Amalgamated Motors announced the 1914 Oakland at 398 pounds, including Delco electric lighting and self-starting ignition.

CCM, meanwhile, realised there was a significant opening for after-market accessories. It stocked Michelin, Dunlop, Continental, Barnett Glass, Goodrich and Pedriau tyres, foot pumps and pumps driven by the car's engine, tyre levers, puncture kits, jacks, fire extinguishers, dashboard clocks, and Jones speedometers, at four pounds 15 shillings for speedo alone and 6 pounds 10 shillings for one that also recorded trip and mileage.

Bosch magnetos, headlamps, oil, horns and spark plugs from three shillings and sixpence (35 cents). Most impressive were bonnet emblems:

"A smart and handsome little gathering including Billikens, Owls, Bulldogs, St George and the Dragon and Laughing Cat' priced from nine shillings and sixpence (95 cents) to two pounds 10 shillings ($5).

As had become his habit, Edward Eager was waving a red rag at the other agencies, when on January 28, 1914, he wrote an ad for the 1914 Overland:

The Car that made Toledo famous and Detroit jealous.

Eager's rhetoric was wearing thin on other agencies. Rival brands were wearing many badges, winning reliability trials, hill climbs and fuel consumption tests. Overland was rarely among them. Again, the angst between CCM and Eagers entertained the *Brisbane Courier's* bemused readers.

DEEDS, NOT WORDS
screamed the headline, under a drawing of a Talbot.

The ad highlighted the Sydney-Melbourne reliability trial where only one Talbot entered, a three-year-old model at that, and came second, beaten by 2.5 points in 690.

"Yet the honours of the contest did not altogether escape England's Greatest Car. It secured full points for reliability and showed 31 miles to the gallon. The victor was a new model of double the horsepower. Last year the same Talbot had to be content with second place solely because a higher-powered Talbot took first.

While Eager had grazier A J Cotton purchasing more Overlands, CCM had Mr Peter Tait of Aramac buying four Talbots for his properties.

"This is strengthened by the fact that the Blackall Show Committee for two successive years in open competition have declared the Talbot to be the most suitable car for Western Queensland conditions."

While Eager could equal the sales and reputation of others in the bush, there was one area in which the Overland was lacking. It had few bragging rights for motorsport events in Australia, or Queensland. No bragging rights meant the newspaper ads had to concentrate on the dry subjects of car specifications, price and positions at car shows. For Eager there was no 'Win on Sunday, Sell on Monday' as Overlands rarely competed. There was no 'sizzle' for the sales department.

Having a go at other manufacturers on plusses for the Overland was fine, but those plusses did not include the cherished chequered flags. Buyers love a winner. The lack of any sporting success on which to hang the Overland's name was a significant chink in the Overland advertising armoury.

The CCM ad, with its 'DEEDS, NOT WORDS' heading, must have stung 299 Adelaide Street. Edward and Frederick sat down to consider what they could do to fill this yawning gap in their strategy.

In the meantime, Cadillac won its second Dewar Trophy, awarded annually by the Royal Automobile Club of Great Britain. The trophy recognised the motor car demonstrating the most outstanding achievement towards the advancement of the Motor Industry. Caddy was the only car to win it twice – once in 1908 and again in 1914 – and the only American car to win the coveted award.

Significant advancements in automobiles started in luxury models and gradually filtered down to the cheaper brands. Self-starting, instead of cranking, was technology comparable to Electronic Stability Control of that era. (ESC Started with Mercedes in the early 1990s before being adopted by other luxury brands and then other makers)

Evers Motor Co based opposite the magnificent Customs House near the Brisbane River, announced the 1914 model Hupmobiles with the entry-level car at 345 pounds, while the self-starting electric model, including lights, cost 395 pounds. Even Buick was starting to win awards, and Howard Motor and Cycle noted two Buicks tied for a first place without losing a point in the New York reliability trial.

Ford too was crowing after a Model T beat all cars for economy in the Melbourne- Sydney reliability trial, averaging 38 miles to the gallon.

It took CCM almost six weeks to respond to the Town and Country Amalgamated ad for Napier, in which they took a pot shot at the new Studebaker Six and the fact it was new on the market, while Napier had a six-cylinder engine since 1903.

For readers of the *Brisbane Courier*, the weekly motoring ads arguably provided the best read of the week. It was a motoring soap opera, entertaining, witty at times, and reflected the dynamic, competitive and at times spiteful state of play in Brisbane's retail motor industry. *Days of our Lives* had nothing on Days of our Drives.

The CCM ad was a magnificently tongue-in-cheek, with an artist's impression of a courtroom, judge, jury, prosecutor and defence lawyer, and a media table with two journalists busy taking notes. In a large dock in the foreground was a Studebaker car and the heading was

"THE STUDEBAKER SIX ON TRIAL"

"The arraignment ... of the Studebaker Six whose price is 470 pounds.

"Represented by the Very Learned (in matters motoring) the Canada Cycle and Motor Agency (Q) Ltd.

"This is an action calling upon the 'Studebaker Six' to show cause why it should not be priced 200 pounds higher than it is.

"His Honour Justice Probonopublico in summing up the evidence said:-

"There is a minor charge which appears on the sheet that accuses you here looking wistfully at the inviting cushions of the Studebaker Six of not being the first six-cylinder car to be built. Wait! don't plead. I shall not refer this to the twelve learned citizens of Motordom on my right. The time of the court must not be wasted frivolously.

Umph! - Er - er! If I remember rightly, the first railway train was built by Stephenson, but the public doesn't want to travel on Stephenson's train because it happened to be the first to be built.

"It has been left to other men to perfect it. The same applies to Motor Cars, I suppose. "That charge is ruled off the sheet.

"Now, with regard to the second count, which alleges your price to be misleading as to your value, the evidence against you is very weighty. "In the first place, there is the authoritative statement of the 'Autocar' the leading technical motor journal of – of – of -"

"Counsel: England, your Honour. "

"Umph! Thank you --- of the World. This eminent authority criticises your low price in conjunction with your high value in the following language---

"As a marvel of value the Six-cylinder Studebaker is unexcelled by any car that reaches us across the Atlantic, it will be admitted by all who view it.

"The jury will take especial note of that. In addition by your own specific --- confession --- you are shown to be furnished with electric lights, a self-starter and a piece of modern and expensive equipment. You have a full floating rear axle, Bosch magneto, long-stroke motor, 121-inch wheelbase and six-passenger body. "There is also the evidence of a number of gentlemen whose words must count for much."

The ad then featured a number of letters from satisfied owners, plus a review by the 'motor expert' with the Australian Pastoral Review.

"THE VERDICT"

"Your reply has been heard and considered by twelve good men and true, who have expressed their opinion that it is reasonable. You are therefore acquitted without a grease spot upon your character. Your only sentence shall be an indeterminate one to years of hard work on Queensland roads.

"The court is adjourned to have a demonstration in the Studebaker Six.

"Enthusiastic cheers from the spectators.

"Sheriff (angrily): Order! Order!

And they did ----- Studebaker Sixes."

Eagers were getting the message they needed to tell more of what the car could do, than how and where it was made, and in what numbers.

On February 12, 1914, Eagers noted for 365 pounds people could buy an Overland with the same mechanical features as the Overlands which 'led the way to Burketown and Betoota --- the same car which carried Under Secretary Shannon and Assessing Commissioner Robson-Scott on their 4000-mile tour of the far West.'

Ford started 1914 in a flurry with 95 Model Ts being sold by March 24, more than once a day for every working day of the week. Worldwide there were 1000 Model Ts sold every day. At 190 pounds, it was a bargain in Australia, even compared to the cheapest Willys Overland at 375 pounds.

Queensland Motor Agency advertisements were not creative like CCM, verbose like Eagers, but simple and to the point:

'MEN SWEAR BY THE FORD, NOT AT IT'

By 1914 the automobile had reached a stage of relative reliability. Makers started refining the cars to add creature comforts, not the least the good ol' self-starter. Of course, many vehicles still retained the crank capability, just in case. You may notice a small round hole through the front bumper with two smaller indents on either side in many old cars you see at veteran car rallies. That's where the crank handle fits.

The 1914 Sunbeam prided itself on being a car designed for Australia's rough-and-ready conditions and extreme heat. Its 1914 model included improvements such as 'special sliding front seats' increasing driver comfort, anti-rattle doors, and a hood that could be raised or lowered by one man.

The foot brake pedal was much more extensive and lined with Ray-bestos, 'giving greater life and efficiency', and increased the hand brake to nearly double its size. A bigger steering wheel added, and the column strengthened with a stay to 'prevent undue vibration on rough roads.'

"The Colonial models this year have a much larger radiator with an increased wind area. Cars' overheating was a common problem in the early days of motordom. The equipment this year includes electric lights, oversize tyres, interchangeable steel wheels, improved pressure feeding of the petrol, and shock absorbers." Many early cars rode on various forms of leaf springs, giving a ride over rough terrain as you might expect from a billy cart.

On reading this book, you have found many makes that are not familiar. As mentioned earlier, the car industry is, and always was, dynamic. It was not only car agencies, or dealerships as we now call them, going out of business, car makers came and went like the tides. While there were numerous reasons for this, history tells us there was one constant: FORD.

In these formative days of the automobile industry, the single most significant cause of makers going broke was Henry's Model T. No one could compete on price. On April 25, 1914, Ford brought this fact to the attention of *Brisbane Courier* readers. As usual, it was a simple ad.

"The Ford 20. THE SURVIVAL OF THE FITTEST"
"Never, since the beginning of the automobile industry, has there been such a determined insistence for genuine motor car value as there is at present.

"THE FORD is the development of this foresight and honest policy, and now stands the greatest of all Cars." (Little did Queensland Motor Agency know how true this was: the Model T was named Car of the Century in the year 2000).

The ad. continued: "Henry Ford was the pioneer of low-priced cars, and the past decade has witnessed the passing of many newcomers. Now, that the time has arrived when motor car purchases are made on merit alone, it has been fittingly and deservedly acclaimed the greatest motor car ever produced for the money."

The Model T was never going to be beaten on price when it set back buyers 190 pounds. You got what you paid for, and in that, nothing has since altered. There was no better example than the Model T. Until 1915 this iconic vehicle carried kerosine head, side and tail-lights. The first Model T with electric headlights did not come until 1915, and even then, it was powered off the fly wheel's magneto. The faster the engine went, the brighter the lights - the slower, the duller.

As John Duncan's book *Any Colour, So Long As It's Black* explains, you did not want to be in a Model T at night if the engine stalled. "This has proved to be particularly `interesting' driving a black Ford after dark, broken down on the side of the road with no lights. Hence, they all carried kerosene sidelights and tail-light." While none of the early model cars was easy to drive, the Ford was incredibly complicated.

There were three pedals, low speed, reverse and foot brake. There was a hand accelerator and a spark advance on the steering column, while the handbrake also activated neutral and the high-speed gear. Duncan gives a description on how to start off in a Model T . . . after, of course, you cranked the engine.

"To drive the car off, one had the handbrake lever half-way back to be in neutral, pressed the low-speed pedal to move forward in low gear, while giving the engine a bit of gas with the steering column lever.

"An engine speed of 1000 revolutions per minute gave a speed of about 9 miles per hour when in low speed. "Now putting the handbrake lever fully forward and taking one's foot off the low speed pedal engaged top gear, and for 1000rpm the speed was about 25 miles per hour.

"The difference between the gears was so great that the driver learned to adjust the gas lever while changing. "If the engine 'chugged' a bit while trying to pick up speed, the spark lever would be moved with the other hand to retard the spark until the engine ran faster (all the time remembering to use both hands to steer the car).

"There was quite clearly a great deal for your hands and feet to do, and you might even need an additional hand to press the horn button to warn those ahead to keep out of the way."

Eagers took to emphasising 'value' rather than cost, and stated on April 27, "We claim for the OVERLAND that it is BETTER VALUE than any other Car in the World."

CCM was still finding reluctance from businesses to embrace the new technology of Albion motor trucks and lorries. On May 15 it ran an ad defining even further the benefits of a single lorry over horsepower.

"The Albion will increase your profits and expand your business because: One Albion covers greater radius than half a dozen horses.

"One Albion's working life (say 130,000 miles) is equal to the life of six horses.

"The punctuality resulting from a motor service is a big factor in business building.

"Your name on an Albion marks your firm as one of progress, and nothing succeeds like success.

"The Albion banishes almost totally stabling and agistment charges and wages to five drivers.

"But the initial cost?" cries one businessman ---- "Is only slightly more than for six horses and vans.

"Then, the upkeep?" ---- "Is less than the cost of six drivers, six sets of harnesses, six fodder bills, six cart sheds and stables, six rents for cart sheds and stables and so on.

"Of course, the Albion pays! If it didn't, would so many successful firms continue to make mistakes by placing repeat orders?"

The ad then noted the London firm of Harrods ran a fleet of 77 Albions, while in Australia, where wool haulage was an issue, an Albion motor lorry could do up to 180 miles in a day, compared to 12 miles a day by horse and wagon.

AV Dodwell's CCM was a worthy adversary for the aggressive Americans down the road at 299 Adelaide Street. The company was always on the ball, looking for new and innovative ways to get their message across, no matter which of its agencies it was looking to promote. In the embryonic days of motoring, many cars were roadsters or what we call convertibles. They were simply a hang-over from the days of horse and buggies where the driver needed to be exposed to the elements to control the horse or horse team.

In 1914 CCM started to promote the Studebaker 'cabriolet' as 'the professional man's car.' In particular, the car appealed to doctors who, in this era, conducted much of their business by 'house calls', which meant travelling in all weather, often at night. The single-seat, two-door cabriolet in Australia became known as a 'doctors' special,' no matter who the maker.

CCM was one of the first agencies to hit on the concept of the cabriolet, as a two-door, single-seater, was not only a car for professionals, but with electric lights and self-starter, was an ideal conveyance, 'which is also singularly suited to the lady driver.' "The terrors of tugging at a refractory starting handle or striking matches (to light the kerosine headlamps) in a storm are banished," stated CCM.

"In fair weather, passengers can fold the windows into the doors, and the hood let down, giving a luxurious roadster. When the rain or the westerly comes along, it is a moment's work to convert the open runabout into a snug closed car. No draught can penetrate anywhere; not one drop of rain can beat in and withal there is ample glass at each side to allow you a clear vision of the traffic on both sides."

CCM, like Eager, found it difficult not to have a dig at the opposition whenever possible. After all, how would *Brisbane Courier* readers get their weekly entertainment fix if the latest in the long-running serial 'Days of our Drives' did not appear?

If Eagers wanted to talk about value, CCM would come to the party with their Studebaker Four retailing at 340 pounds. Compared to Overland, which now had an entry-level price of 375 pounds, including electric lights, but no electric self-starter, which elevated the cost of the Overland 395 pounds.

"Disputes end where figures begin. Every agent claims his car gives a bigger value than any other. We do, among the rest, but there the comparison ends. For we have the cold figures - not mere persuasiveness, mind you. But cold, undeniable figures to prove the Studebaker '4' gives at least 50 pounds bigger value in Queensland than any other American medium-priced car, selling in America in the vicinity of the Studebaker price.

"If you're interested, let's cut out argument and get right down to bedrock pounds shillings and pence facts with you. Can you come round to our Show Rooms this week?"

More and more agencies were using sporting events to promote their cars. On June 2, Howards used the fact Buick was the only team to finish the 'Tour de France.' "This trial of 3600 miles, one of the most severe ever held on European roads, again proves the reliability of the BUICK CAR." Three days later, CCM announced it was importing the 'Silent Knight Minerva', popularly known as the 'most beautiful car in the world.'

"The Minerva's latest international success was the 1914 Swedish Winter Cup, which attracted competitors from all parts of Europe and America. 717 miles was the distance, and for the third year in succession the 'Minerva' conquered."

In the same edition of the *Brisbane Courier* the Barnes Auto Coy., noted the many successes of Sunbeam in 1913, under a heading, 'A review of the past season's events points to the fact that no car has done more to ADVANCE British prestige than the supreme SUNBEAM."

Four days later CCM highlighted the 'Invincible' Talbot.

"Around the Earth 6½ times equals the distance traversed by Messrs Edkins, Marsh and Co's 15 Talbot in the Longreach district, between March 1909 and January 1914."

A few days later CCM took out a large ad to highlight the changing engine landscape, again aimed at promoting the Studebaker Six which it offered was more luxurious, with less vibration and wear. It revealed in 1910 four-cylinder cars accounted for 81 per cent of the market, while six-cylinder cars made up just 11 per cent.

In 1911 the per cent breakdown was 79/17; 1912: 76/21; 1913: 62/38 and 1914: 54/45.

The response came from an unlikely quarter. CCM would have been expecting Edward Eager to come out punching. So would have the *Brisbane Courier* readers awaiting their weekly instalment of Days of our Drives.

The retort came from the Howard Motor & Cycle Co, agents for Cadillac, under the heading 'Four-Cylinder Cars Broke All Records for Attention and Sales at the Recent New York and Chicago Shows.'

"In its Price Class, the CADILLAC Drew Three Times as Much Interest from the Visitors as any other Car.

Then came the sting:

"This year's motor shows have proven conclusively that the six-cylinder troublemakers are rapidly losing ground. "While the Cadillac dislikes to see its competitors' money go down in extravagance and waste, it was indeed gratifying this year to see that the thousands of dollars spent to popularise the six-cylinder car and the exhibition of two or three 'second thought' little sixes did not succeed in diverting the public's support from the Cadillac.

"Instead, it seemed to stimulate interest in the Cadillac for the public to realise that they must pay for all this advertising and promotion expense, and their 'six' experience has been costly, they have found as Cadillac found, that the 'six' is impractical, costly, and wasteful. Yes, gentlemen, it costs money to run a six.

"Remember, if sixes were practical, Cadillac would build them. Cadillac built the best 'four', and Cadillac could build the best 'six'. But the best 'six' did not, and could not, compare with the Cadillac 'four.'

The Caddy 'four' cost 625 pounds while the Studebaker Six cost 470 pounds.

No doubt Edward and Fred Eager joined the rest of the *Brisbane Courier* readership in seeing what would happen in the next episode of Days of our Drives.

It didn't take long. Three days to be exact.

Under the heading 'Choose' CCM featured a businessman's bust with one hand pointing to a 'HEAVY FOUR' and the other to a 'LIGHT SIX.'

The heavy four was of the Caddy and the light six the Studebaker. The advertisement was remarkable in that it claimed the gap between spark plug ignition in each of the four's cylinders caused a vibration that resulted in excessive wear to the rear tyres.

"Have you ever paid a Petrol Bill on a heavy car, and then gone around to the Tyre Company and asked wearily when the price of rubber is coming down? If you have, you will know why owners feel so keen about the Studebaker Light 'Six'.

"It is not solely the weight of a car that hurts the tyres. There is a certain vibration about a heavy 'Four' that runs right through the machine to the back tyres.

"This vibration is the natural result of slight breaks between the four explosions.

"If the 4-cylinder engine were replaced by a 6-cylinder there would be greater smoothness because six explosions would overlap - no break, you understand - therefore no vibration.

"A smooth, vibrationless 6-cylinder motor wears out fewer tyres than a heavy 4-cylinder which cannot dismiss all vibration. And a light 'Six' wears much less than a heavy 'Four'. "As for Petrol --- A 'Four' uses the same amount as a similarly powered 'Six' because both do the same work - only does it better. "Yes, gentlemen, it costs money to run a 'Six' - the same, or less, than to run a 'Four.'

This ad must have caused some confusion to buyers and rival dealers. After all, CCM were still selling four-cylinder models. They seemed prepared to trash their own four-cylinder car to promote the new six. There was a good reason for this, which was yet to be revealed.

On June 19, 1914, Barnes Auto Co highlighted yet more successes for their two agencies, Delage and Sunbeam.

Delages took first and third places at the Indianapolis 500, also known as the American Grand Prix, while Sunbeam took out the first spot in the Isle of Man Tourist Trophy.

While over at CCM the Minerva added to the trophy cabinet of 1913 by taking out the 1914 Swedish Winter Cup. While most Brisbane car dealers were multi-agency, such as Howards, with their cheaper Buick and more expensive Cadillac. Ford was caught with only the Model T.

According to the heading 'UNIVERSAL CAR', Queensland Motor Agency Ltd recognised the limitations and tailored its ads.

"It's a lady's car because it is reliable and easy to control. It's a gentleman's car because it is sturdy and fast and quiet and serviceable. It's a rich man's car because it is comfortable and ever ready and trouble-free. It is the car of a man of moderate means because it is all these and vastly more economical."

At last, some good news came for Overland in the record department. Legendary Adelaide driver, and Overland dealer, Murray Aunger, teamed with Frank Beasley in late June to set a record for the Adelaide-to-Broken Hill road.

The pair left Adelaide in the most potent Overland, a 45 hp model single-seater at 6.30am on June 27 and arrived in the mining town at 4.38pm.

This broke the previous record by S A Cheney by 4 hours 22 minutes, covering the 325 miles in 9 hours 38 minutes.

Eagers recorded the win in a significant advertisement under the heading 'Here's proof of Overland's capacity for a good time on any road.'

"You may never want to make trips like this record ... but when you're buying a car, you should buy one that can do such work."

The home-grown record was significant. Aunger, as an Overland dealer, was showing the way. Ready to put the car's reputation on the line, along with his investment in the vehicle, to get bragging rights. The most crucial element was the record was home-grown, not some European race, on roads with which Australians could identify. Rough roads. Outback roads.

In racing parlance, Overland was starting from the back of the grid. Other makes were regularly in the news for various exploits from economy runs, reliability trials, road racing and hill climbs. Overland had a lot of catching up to do. The day after Murray Aunger set his record, a relatively minor event on the other side of the world set other wheels in motion.

On June 28, 1914, heir to the throne of Austria, Archduke Franz Ferdinand, and his wife Sophia were assassinated in Sarajevo by a Serbian Nationalist. The Austro-Hungarian empire wanted to extradite the killer, but Serbia refused.

This murder led to a fall of dominoes due to an alliance system major powers had in place. On July 28 Austria declared war on Serbia. On August 1, Germany declared war on Russia. On August 3, Germany declared war on France. On August 4, Britain declared war on Germany. WW I started, America declared war on no-one.

On American Independence Day, July 4, Ford announced an Australian record of 40 miles on one gallon of petrol. Records were getting close to home, with the event run by the Automobile Club of Queensland. "Mr A H Sagar, in his 20hp Ford Model T, did 40 miles on one gallon of petrol, thus creating an AUSTRALIAN RECORD," states the Queensland Motor Agency Ltd ad on page seven of the *Brisbane Courier*.

A few days later the Queensland Motor Agency Ltd, took advertising to a new level when it proclaimed the Model T as a 'CAR WITH A CONSCIENCE'.

"Whatever the road, whatever the weather, the Ford is the Car to be aboard. It wouldn't think of 'letting you up' at the critical moment - it simply couldn't because the firm behind it makes certain such a happening is practically impossible."

Despite the war, life went on pretty much as usual in August 1914. Brisbane hosted an Australian Football Carnival between August 8 and 15 with clubs representing Victoria, South Australia, Collingwood, South Adelaide, Tasmania, West Australia, Perth and Tasmanian club Cananore.

"Come and see the game that attracts thousands in the Southern States," beckoned the ad. Held at the Gabba, with admission one shilling, and a seat in the stand costing a further shilling, it was an effort to promote Aussie rules football in a rugby league stronghold.

Despite CCM's earlier diatribe against four-cylinder cars it started promoting the Studebaker '4' at 340 pounds, including a full floating-rear axle, electric starter and electric lights. This was 55 pounds cheaper that the equivalent Overland with an electric self-starter. Eagers responded with dropping the price of their entry-level car back to 365 pounds, with the electric self-start model staying at 395 pounds.

W F Turk Motors entered the motoring fray in August as agents for Maxwell cars, starting at 265 pounds, and Mitchell, Argyll and Opel cars, and Thorneycroft commercial vehicles.

By late August 1914, Australians recognised the seriousness of the war. The *Brisbane Courier* started a war fund, and the Howard Motor Company donated a Buick car to be sold by art union.

To promote the art union, the car was driven to the top of Mt Gravatt, just south of the city, and was believed to be the first car to achieve the feat. As the story ran on August 25, it probably took place on August 24. Naturally, the story was given prominence by the newspaper.

Howards also took out a large advertisement on August 27, under the heading 'Another triumph for Buick, First car to climb Mt Gravatt.

"The reputation of the 'Buick' car has been further enhanced by the recent performance of climbing Mt Gravatt. The Buick was the first car to negotiate this steep and uneven climb, even though several other cars of higher hp had tried and failed."

Once again, *Courier* readers were in for an exciting episode of Days of our Drives.

Not to be outdone, Town and Country Amalgamated Motors took an Oakland 19.2hp car to Mt Gravatt on August 25, after seeing the *Courier* article that morning.

"The five-seater 'OAKLAND' ... has again established a record of hill-climbing powers by ascending the almost impossible gradients of Mount Gravatt on 25/8/14. The track was severely cut up by others trying to reach the summit and the Oakland, with perfect ease and without any sign of boiling, made the top.

"It has worthily upheld the American boast as being the Acme of Perfection."

The Oakland cost 398 pounds. Not content to leave it there, Town and Country returned the following day, August 26, this time armed with its other agency contender, the 750 pounds Napier.

"NAPIER CARS still uphold BRITISH SUPREMACY against all-comers in the COMMONWEALTH OF AUSTRALIA".

"The reliability of the 20hp Colonial Model has again been established by its recent performance of climbing Mount Gravatt, on the 26/8/14, with a complement of five passengers on board. A 15hp NAPIER CAR, belonging to the same owner, also accomplished this remarkable feat on the following day."

Interestingly, one ad contained Napier and Oakland's ads in the one space with the agency seeing no conflict in the makes both upholding American and British supremacy. For the Buick, Oakland and Napier, all ads included photographs atop Mt Gravatt in front of a picnic shelter.

The scaling of Mt Gravatt by three rivals to Overland left the Eagers in a dilemma. If they decided to conquer Mt Gravatt in the Willys, it would be a hollow event. The Buick did it first, and even the Oakland and Napier's feats carried little weight. Edward and Fred Eager had to decide: Either they got into the game, or continued to sit on the sidelines, mere spectators at the game of Win on Sunday, Sell on Monday.

On September 1, 1914, they took out a small ad. in *The Courier-Mail* with an illustration of an Overland above the heading,

"We don't go much on records, but --

"It has never been the Overland policy to make hair-raising records, but occasionally owners put them up on their account, just to show their pride in their car.

"For instance:

"The old record from Adelaide to Broken Hill was 13 hrs 55 minutes. Recently Murray Aunger lowered it to 9 hrs 48 minutes in his Overland.

"The record from Pialba to Maryborough, 23¼ miles, was set at 24 minutes by Jenkins in his Overland on August 25.

"The old record from Sandhills to Bundaberg, a matter of 8 miles, was 11 minutes. Jenkins lowered it on August 27 to 6 minutes."

The ad was almost disinterested, as if Edward Eager had something else on his mind. He did. And it would change the face of the Queensland motor industry forever. The war on the other side of the world would be the first major conflict where cars would take part in various forms, particularly ambulances.

The Australian Expeditionary Forces readied, and CCM plays its part to help young Aussies go eagerly off to war. CCM built a 'motor quick-firer gun carrier' on what appears to be a Studebaker utility. The body was designed by Mr A Wynyard-Joss, of CCM, and built at their Adelaide Street workshops. Wynyard-Joss served in the Boer War and would enlist and serve with the AFD in France. After the war, he became a partner in CCM.

Along the running boards were long ammunition boxes as well as under the seat. On the tray was mounted a water-cooled machine gun on a tripod. Tracksons donated a large searchlight while Barnett Glass provided tyres. There was no protective armour, with the driver, navigator and machine gun operator sitting up like Jacky in the open.

During WWI around half of CCM's entire staff of 120 enlisted. Fred Eager tried to enlist in the Australian Flying Corps and was rejected because of poor eyesight.

The war sowed seeds of doubt in buyers' minds and created a nightmare for sales staff. While the purchase of a lorry or truck was a business decision, a car purchase was different. Cars were luxury items. Even including the 'Universal' car, Ford's Model T. Brisbane residents managed for years using trains, trams, bicycles and horses to get around. A delay in purchasing that first automobile until the war ended would not cause any significant hardship to anyone: Apart from car agencies.

CCM recognised the potential for sales to slump.

"Talbots continue to sell freely -- we'll tell you the reason.

"These are stirring times. Times when Deliberation is the keynote of all our critical decisions.

It governs our army's advance in France; it curbs our navy's fighting eagerness as it plays a waiting game off Heligoland and in all our buying and selling transactions here in Queensland. Deliberation guides and guards our actions -- Very Well."

Besides, the Brisbane motor industry, through the Automobile Club of Queensland, was doing its bit for the war effort. In association with the motorcycle club and the cycling club they decided to raise money by holding a 'Patriotic Motor Gymkhana'. The motor agencies kicked in 80 pounds in prize-money for the Saturday, October 10, event at the Exhibition Grounds. Events to include an automobile obstacle course and zig-zag courses for gentlemen and ladies in different classes of vehicles. Admission was a shilling.

While Brisbane was gearing up to assist the war effort, Edward Eager had another project he had been working on for months. Queensland had an automobile club, but it didn't have a voice. It had no club magazine. On the other side, the *Brisbane Courier* was happy to take advertisements from Brisbane's many car dealers, but it did not have a motoring column.

The nearest thing the *Courier* had was the weekly argy-bargy contained in the entertaining automobile advertisements that lined the coffers of the *Courier* ... one of the newspaper's largest single-industry clients. The *Brisbane Courier* did very well out of Eagers, CCM, Barnes, Howard, Town and Country and Queensland Motor Agency.

Edward Eager recognised the need for a specialist motoring magazine. He also realised it was vital to get the support of the majority of agencies to make it work. These were the same agencies involved in the public bickering in the *Brisbane Courier* ads. Eager had done his homework. In its early days, the magazine could not pay for itself through subscriptions, so agencies would need to support it through advertisements.

For that to work, the magazine would have to be seen as neutral and not favour, EG Eager & Son. This was a big call, given the simmering jealousies and sniping agencies had engaged in for the past two years. What was the point in operating a magazine if Willys Overland could not get the inside running?

There was another implication. In the cut-throat car business, there were only so many advertising dollars to go around. Would the agencies be prepared to back the magazine and withdraw or reduce their advertising from the *Brisbane Courier* and the *Brisbane Mail* to at least give the magazine some hope of succeeding?

What if some agencies stayed with the *Brisbane Courier*, would they gain an advantage over those in the magazine? Would they lose sales?

It was a magnificent gamble for Eager. If it failed, not only would he lose money, but more importantly respect, among the Brisbane business community, not just those involved in the motor industry.

To help launch the magazine, Edward Eager called in a good friend, the journalist, R S Maynard, editor of the *Farm Bulletin*, who assisted Eager in penning his controversial ads in 1913-14.

"He was a keen advertiser," said Maynard years later in an interview published in the proposed magazine.

"Hardly a day passed by, and he had some new scheme that he wanted to put into practice. "Just before the war broke out, he wanted to publish a monthly magazine,"

Eager told Maynard, "Get a good name for it, and you can go ahead." "Next day I suggested *The Steering Wheel*. That settled it."

"Within a week we had formed a company, taken our oaths before the Chief Justice, and made a contract with the printer."

Speaking in July 1917, Maynard said: 'The magazine today, under its present editorship, is proof that Mr Eager's vision was true. He knew that such a journal was needed and he put up the money to start it on its way. The instructions he gave at the commencement showed the spirit of the man: "Now, forget that I have put up most of the money. Treat all the other motor firms as you treat Overland. I want no privileges for Overland that other firms cannot have.

"Spare nothing to make it a magazine worthy of the automobile, and I'll be satisfied. If you do that the financial end will not worry anybody."

Eager was true to his word, but he also knew the power of the written word and ensured the Overland was always represented in *The Steering Wheel*. Editorial space was, after all, open to all-comers.

In the *Brisbane Courier* of October 19, 1914, EG Eager and Son took out an ad under the heading, "A Story about an Overland."

"In the October edition of *The Steering Wheel* is a fine story descriptive of the advantages of the OVERLAND. It's good reading. We'll send you a copy if you just let us know your address. Free? Of course. Just your name and address on a postcard."

Edward Eager's use of the *Brisbane Courier* to promote a business succeeding in taking advertising dollars away from the *Courier* was bold in the extreme. The move speaks volumes for the determination of Edward Eager for *The Steering Wheel* to succeed. A brilliant move.

Between October and December 1914 there was a marked change in the make-up of *The Courier-Mail*. There were fewer car ads, and what there were, significantly smaller than the previous two years. There was one exception.

Canada Cycle and Motor boycotted *The Steering Wheel* and kept its ads exclusively in the *Brisbane Courier*. There was little love lost between CCM and Eagers. Why should CCM support *The Steering Wheel* when it was openly owned by Eagers, even down to giving the head office address as 299 Adelaide Street. Why should Eagers profit in any way from the sale of Studebaker cars?

Others, including Eagers, continued to run lesser ads in the *Courier* as they most likely thought it necessary not to put all their eggs into *The Steering Wheel* basket. Besides, dealers did not want to get offside with the city's largest newspaper. Edward Eager was still writing all Eagers ads.

In an October edition of the *Courier*, he wrote: 'The OVERLAND this writer drives is a 1911 model. "It saw service in the United States -- then quite a lot of work in New Zealand -- now it's doing all that asked of it in Queensland."

The war was having an impact on car sales. In August 1914 Eagers sold 42 Overlands, but in September this dropped to 24, and in October, 25. It took until late 1914 for anyone to source a car that could be brought to market at the same price at the Model T.

The Howard Motor and Cycle Co had found the British GRANT car priced at 195 pounds stating, 'No other car on the market to similar specification at under 235 pounds.' The single-seater Grant featured a four-cylinder single block engine rated at 11.9hp and a two-speed transmission.

On November 21, 1914, Fred Eager left Brisbane bound for America on business. While the *Brisbane Courier* automobile ads may have diminished in size and numbers, readers still got their weekly fix of Days of our Drives.

On December 23, 1914, CCM announced its new Studebaker models for 1915. It was in response to a Ford Model T ad by Queensland Motor Agency, that pointed out 'No new models for seven years', and the engine was 'the same as seven years ago.'

CCM did not mince words.

"They say in effect: Our cars are hopelessly out of date and even the man in the street acknowledges this, for who does not know and recognise the significant advance in Motor Car construction and design during the past five years.

"Studebakers three years ago decided to drop the old and, comparatively speaking, inefficient American type of Engine, and put in one of the very best European design and also the best designed Rear Axle of the European type."

The war of words in Brisbane gave some entertainment when a real war was costing Australian lives at an alarming rate.

Frederick Z. Eager

B.E. PRICE

10

The Steering Wheel,
Patriotism and V8s

The company name 'The Steering Wheel Publishing Co, Limited' was registered at 299 Adelaide Street; subscription rates were 3 shillings and sixpence a year. Advertising rates were five pounds a full page, with discounts for yearly, half-yearly and quarterly contracts.

Like its no-nonsense founder, Edward Eager, *The Steering Wheel* would not mess about when it came to advertising. Reading between the lines, *The Steering Wheel* did not want the same style of motoring display ads that appeared in the *Brisbane Courier*.

"Unwholesome, immoral and quack advertising will be excluded from *The Steering Wheel* it proclaimed. The Editor spelled out the magazine's editorial policy.

"The management wishes it understood that *The Steering Wheel* is an entirely independent paper, published with the idea of proclaiming the joys of motoring on land and water. The paper's policy is entirely in the hands of the Editor, and no trade concern, club, nor other body is in a position to influence that policy."

In effect, this meant Eagers, although they owned the magazine, had no more influence than any other dealer. They wanted this on the record – as did the Editor – to reassure dealerships all would be fair and above board. The statement was vital if dealers were going to put hard cash into the venture.

One of the first issues to be dealt with by *The Steering Wheel* was Brisbane's day and weekend trips. In 1915 there were no road or street signs, other than those in the cities. To take a trip to Beenleigh, Southport, Coolangatta, or the Sunshine Coast was a hit-and-miss affair unless you already knew the route. Along all tracks, roads on both sides of the main thoroughfare led to private properties and places of interest. Few had signs to help the first-time traveller in the region.

The Steering Wheel published detailed route instructions on how to get around south-east Queensland, based on odometer readings. These would instruct drivers on which roads to take and where to turn. "The account of the Southport-Brisbane roads in your November issue is an exact one. I took the car up last Friday, and had a glorious trip," wrote AHN. In the February 1915 edition. *The Steering Wheel* encouraged people to write in with their travel stories.

"*The Steering Wheel* continues to hear of motoring folk who are following some of the trips we have sketched out in previous issues.

"Sometimes we have heard the regret expressed that they were not adept with the camera. We arranged for one of our photographic contributors to be placed free of charge for anyone who wants a cameraman to capture the beauties and the incidents of the trip."

The front cover of the 1915 edition of *The Steering Wheel* is the iconic 1911 photograph of Edward Eager, and entourage, in front of the Sphinx. There was also a full-page photo spread of Willys utility trucks involved in various businesses' day-to-day running. The Premier Ice and Butter Co truck selling ice-creams, the F Tritton furniture truck loaded to the hilt, a Webster's Cakes and Biscuits truck and a truck that undertook daily runs between the Alexander Stewart and Sons factory and warehouse.

In front of Eagers premises in Adelaide Street, two mini-'war ships', mounted on Willys truck bodies, readied for the Patriotic Carnival. A bare Willys truck chassis cost 400 pounds, and customers could have Eagers body shop tailor the body to suit their business needs.

"Horses waste time. The Willys utility truck saves it," was a simple motto. Edward Eager never stood still, unless he was seated in his office, his mind ticking over, the inevitable cigar dangling from his hand. He had a strong chin that gave him a look of determination. It well matched his forthright personality. While Edward looked after the 'big picture' for Eagers, Frederick Zina Eager moved comfortably into the position of CEO. Edward was more than happy with his son's progress and took yearly trips to the US, to Toledo to see John Willys, test new product and combine that with time to visit family at Wauseon, then on to the New York Motor Show. Back in Brisbane Fred ran the business. Despite the war, car sales were still strong, even though the numbers were not as large as pre-war.

Eagers were also developing a second string to their bow with used-car sales, using trade-ins stripped and rebuilt and often repainted by the Eagers garage. Worn parts replaced with new components, hoods renewed, body-work reinvigorated to look new. Eagers gave the cars the same new car warranty as a new Overland. The company included all makes: Model T Fords, Silent Knight Daimler, Humber, Hupmobile, Austin, Studebaker, De Dion, Cadillac and Wolseley.

Despite the war and despite being only a little more than two years in business, EG Eager and Son were thriving. They had outgrown Adelaide Street, and in early 1915 Edward purchased a large tract of land on the corner of Breakfast Creek Road and Evelyn Street, Newstead, just to the east of the CBD, and the infamous Fortitude Valley. In November 1912, they had three employees. By early 1915 there were more than 100 on the payroll.

The new premises were impressive. There was an Overland showroom on Evelyn Street, offices, garage and repair shop. Just around the corner, in Austin Street, was a substantial double building housing the paint shop, body works and warehouse.

Eagers dedicated one large section to the trimmer and his staff who, with modern machinery, looked after upholstery, seat covers and hood making. There was a smiths' shop and next door a car storage area to handle Overland shipments and second-hand cars on their way to becoming rebuilds; in all, 30,000sq ft under roof.

Adelaide Street was to be retained as the 'city showroom' in the centre of Brisbane's retail motoring hub. Of the 100 or more staff there were 40 mechanics, 20 bodybuilders and in January 1915 Eagers delivered more than 60 new and used cars. It was a remarkable growth at a time of uncertainty.

Eagers' growth was recorded, complete with high-quality photographs, in *The Steering Wheel*. While it might sound as if *The Steering Wheel* was the personal public relations machine of Eagers, it wasn't. They knew how to 'use' it, and others soon caught on.

There were profiles of those involved in the motor trade, people directly in competition with Eagers and Overland.

One example was Mr W F Turk's profile. He had the agency for Maxwell and Mitchell cars. Turk started his working life as an electrical engineer, apprenticed to the City Electric Light Co.

"After acquiring a practical knowledge of matters electrical, he travelled Queensland for a year or two in the interests of Messrs Clark & Fauset, machinery importers.

"Commercial and practical knowledge thus combined, he commenced his business in electrical and marine motor and motor car work. One huge contract secured about this time was the installation at the Blair Athol Mine, totalling 7000 pounds, a massive contract. In connection with this contract, Mr Turk travelled the New South Wales coal mines in company with Mr W J Hetherington, the well-known mine-owner, seeking modern ideas and up-to-date machinery."

In 1907 Turk became involved with the motor industry, secured the Ford agency, sold 150 cars, and was the first managing director of the Queensland Motor (Agency).

After a controlling interest in the company was purchased by Messrs Davies and Feehon of Sydney, Mr Turk struck out again by himself with the Maxwell and Mitchell agencies.

The war was impacting on car sales, but not the one that would seem most apparent. German cars were, understandably, off the Australian menu. There was also a groundswell of disapproval of American product. The reason was simple: The US was an ally of Britain, why were they not fighting side by side with the Brits, Aussies, Indians, Ceylonese and Kiwis to help liberate Europe?

It was a tightrope walk for car agencies like CCM, with Studebaker and various other brands; Eagers with the US built Overland, and, of course, the leader of the pack, Ford. They each tackled the marketing problem in their own peculiar ways. CCM ran ads under the heading 'I PREFER A BRITISH OR CONTINENTAL CAR.'

"We often hear this remark from those, who, from experience, know that 'THE BEST IS THE CHEAPEST", also from those who from Patriotic Motives wish to purchase first a B.R.I.T.I.S.H. Car, failing that a FRENCH or a B.E.L.G.I.A.N. Car.

"We have the best that money can buy: The Invincible Talbot (British); the marvellous Renault (French); the Light Standard (British) and the beautiful Minerva (Belgian).

As the daily casualty lists grew during 1915 and were reported extensively in the *Brisbane Courier*, a rising anti-German sentiment boiled over into various advertisements. Lipton's claimed to be paying the British Government eight million pounds in tea duty.

"The British Empire has a use for all of us. Every man, woman and child in Australia can help the Nation in its hour of need. While the clash of arms and the sufferings and privations of our brave troops in Europe continue, we can help the cause they are fighting for by taking part in the trade war, and resolutely refusing to spend a single penny except on British and Australian goods, and on those of our allies.

"Since the war began there has been a tremendous increase in the exports of Java tea -- foreign tea -- to Australia. "These packets in which Java tea sells should state the name or origin of the contents. "The only safe method to adopt is to refuse to buy any tea but Indian and Ceylon. Certainly, we hold a brief for Liptons Indian and Ceylon Tea, but whether you buy Liptons or not, DO INSIST ON HAVING INDIAN OR CEYLON, OR A BLEND OF BOTH, and you will be helping the Empire.

"You will help because Indian and Ceylon Tea is British -- because it is grown and cultivated by Britons with British money -- because these two teas give the British Government eight million pounds in duty every year and help to build more ships and finance the war -- because India and Ceylon have sent thousands of men and millions of rupees against the enemy."

Australian life went on with hardships, but also entertainment. Snowy Baker's Brisbane stadium presented fights on Wednesday and Saturday night cards, an international bout between Frenchman, Marcel Lepreux and Queensland's Wally Vincent, and Fernand Quendreux matched against Jimmy Coffey.

Visiting Australia, the man credited with popularising surfing, Hawaii's Duke Kanahamoku and his fellow Olympic swimming teammate, George Cunha. The 'Duke' was given a civic reception at Brisbane Town Hall on January 14, before he and Cunha, 'the world's fastest swimmers', gave exhibitions at Carnivals Dock, South Brisbane.

The car agencies were anxious to boost public confidence in the automobile. Times were uncertain. Never before had the world seen such a war, and never before had Australia's youngest and best been slaughtered in such numbers. The names of the dead were there, every week, to read in every capital city newspaper -- column after column of names, rank and Australian State. To bolster confidence in the automobile, agencies printed a monthly list of the number of cars sold.

The list was published not so much to sell an individual brand but to get out a message that it was okay to take the chance to buy a car: hundreds of people were doing it every month. If it was the judgment of your neighbour, your boss, or your brother that the time was right to buy an automobile, then it was also all right in your household. While Australia was at war with Germany, the car industry was battling with the horse. Eagers used a practical example of why a truck, Willys, of course, was superior to its four-legged counterpart.

"Edison says: The horse is the poorest motor ever built, his thermal efficiency being on 2 per cent." Every use of a Willys Utility Truck is proving Edison's words.

"Mr W Shead, Baker, Highgate Hill. The Champion of the Day Baking, whose progressive business methods are known all over Brisbane, has decided against the horse --- the poorest of motors --- and bought a Willys Utility Truck.

Judge of Mr Shead's progressiveness is that nine months ago he consumed 8 to 9 tons of flour per day, now the daily average is 25 tons.

"Now read carefully: "Mr Shead says: I use a Willys Truck for my contract work, that is for delivering to the Adelaide, Howard Smith, and AUSN Wharves, also for carrying 2000 2lb loaves of bread daily to the Enoggera Encampment.

"All this work is done by a WILLYS UTILITY TRUCK BEFORE MIDDAY. PREVIOUSLY IT TOOK 4 CARTS, 6 HORSES AND 4 MEN ONE WHOLE DAY TO DO THIS WORK. I save the expense of

6 horses, four carts, half the previous time, while three men are released to do other work I require."

To put automobile purchases in Queensland in context with competition from the horse, 1400 cars were sold in Queensland in 1914. Of those, 413 were Fords.

While the agencies were intent on selling cars, there were agents of another variety flogging land. The first stage of Pacific Ocean Estate was placed up for auction by Brisbane auctioneers, Newman & Dawber, on February 27, 1915.

The estate featured, 'beautiful beach frontage with cosy, secure river moorings for boats. There was also 'surf bathing on the Finest White Sandy Beach in Australia.' That suburb is now called Surfers Paradise, and that fine, white sandy beach on Christmas Day 1916, would host Australia's first attempt at a land speed record.

On February 27, 1915, Eagers announced it would be moving into the new Breakfast Creek premises. Eagers had quickly outgrown 299 Adelaide Street to the stage it was useful only as a showroom. The Breakfast Creek premises were large and gave the mechanics room to move. There were 40 mechanics, with enough space to build a race car, or, best known in this era, a speedster. With so many mechanics on the payroll, car body builders, painters and trimmers, all work would be in-house.

Over at Queensland Motor Agency, it decided to apply the blowtorch to car pricing. The Model T roadster reduced to 180 pounds and the touring car to 195 pounds. The reason for the price decrease was simple and stated as the heading for the advertisement. "No 'new models' emanate from the Ford factory -- the Ford never gets out of date."

This was a real-life edict from Mr Ford: If it ain't broke, don't fix it!

To launch the new premises, Eagers combined patriotism and capability. A large motor ambulance was anonymously donated to the Queensland patriotic fund. The fully equipped ambulance was built and equipped at Eagers' new facility. It was most likely a trade-in vehicle, completely refurbished for the task to specifications laid down by the military. Eagers fitted it with four stretchers arranged in bunk form and room for four people across the front, one for the driver and ambulance officer and two for 'slightly' wounded soldiers.

The anonymous donor asked Queensland motorists -- around 2000 in the state -- to donate the equivalent, about 500 pounds -- to be divided between the Red Cross and the Belgian Fund. "We ask your help so that in after years when the Kaiser's exiled to St Helena (an island prison), you'll be able to look back with pride and say, "The motorists of Queensland gave 500 pounds and a motor ambulance."

That the ad states that the ambulance was donated by 'motorists of Queensland' and suggests it was Eagers, or to be correct Edward Eager, was the anonymous donor. By early 1915 Fred Eager had returned from his business trip to the US and gave *The Steering Wheel* a 'stop press talk'. The trip home was most likely his first since moving to Australia in 1912, in which time Edward Eager had groomed his successor in all aspects of the motor trade.

Like his father, Fred was bright, quick to learn, and loved the Queensland way of life. Fred had poor eyesight and wore glasses from an early age. *The Steering Wheel* interview marked another coming of age of Fred as a businessman, out from under the vast shadow cast by his larger-than-life-father.

The sub-heading on the interview read,

'We're neutral -- Don't care a damn who licks the Germans.'

On this US trip, Fred landed in San Francisco and crossed the States to Chicago, Toledo, Detroit and New York, including the New York Motor Show. "I spent a week at the show -- the only striking development exhibited was the eight-cylinder motor. "It is expected that many manufacturers will be experimenting with this type of motor during the coming season."

As usual, the Willys Overland exhibit had 'pride of place' at the New York Show. "Several new makes of cars were displayed in New York, each one, of course, claiming to be the 'Sensation of the Show'. "Never has there been such interest shown in the Exhibition before -- the motor car industry is experiencing a terrific year.

"There has been a loss of business in America, but this has been more than covered by immense orders for cars and trucks placed by the Allies. The great war has had sweeping effects on general American business, sometimes beneficial, but with the balance on the other side. "Every State has thousands of unemployed, and the hard winter has called for much domestic relief work.

"A great deal of effort has also been put forth for the benefit of the suffering Belgians. Except for the German element, the American war sentiment voiced by a card displayed in many offices and houses: We're neutral --- don't care a damn who licks the Germans. "Yes, I am glad to be back in Queensland out of the zero weather."

Eagers continued to use the *Brisbane Courier* to promote *The Steering Wheel* and Overland.

"If you had an Overland, yes, if you had you'd be able to slip away midday Saturday to some of those far beauty spots. You'd be able to visit your good friends in other towns who are miles away now.

"You'd be independent of train whistles and tram timetables. Time would be your servant, not your master.

"You'd be able to go that wonderful 30 miles through the Samford Ranges that *THE STEERING WHEEL* has told us of this month, or the run-up to the Summit --- beyond One Tree Hill (Mt Coot-tha) --- one afternoon, again following *The STEERING WHEEL'S* lead."

Meanwhile, Cadillac introduced to Australia an engine that would revolutionise motoring. The 1914 model Caddy, brought into Australia by Howard Motor and Cycle Co in 1915, featured the world's first V8 in a mass-produced car. We think today of V8s being gutsy engines emitting a rumbling, roaring exhaust note most commonly found in Australia's V8 Supercars. So much for an engine delicately named 'Antionette' in patents taken out by Frenchman Leon Levasseur.

Levasseur named the engine after his financial backer's daughter, and from 1904 the motor powered boats and aircraft, and a few cars. De Dion-Bouton introduced a 747 cubic inch V8 at the 1912 New York Motor Show. Numbers were limited, but American manufacturers sat up and took notice.

Mr Levasseur has a lot to answer for when he invented the gas guzzling V8. Cadillac sold 13,000 V8 units in its first year. It was this car that made its Australian debut in early 1915. "Serious-minded car manufacturers have sought the ideal power principle for 15 years," stated the Howard ad.

"The Cadillac Company has never relaxed for a month, a week, or a day, its patient pursuit of that underlying principle which would prove to be ultimate and final. In the course of that long journey toward perfection, the Cadillac Company has given serious consideration to every reputable type of motor -- endeavouring to scrutinise with scientific impartiality the virtues and the limitations of each and every one.

"Building and experimenting every type from the single cylinder to the six, and from the poppet to the rotary and the sliding valve, the Cadillacs have been carried forward irresistibly by the impetus of their research to the highest form of frequent impulse motor --- the V-type Eight Cylinder.

"We believe this company produced a succession of cars in the four-cylinder field which earned a title, "Standard of the World." "Beyond that loomed for them only one hope and possibility --- the promise of a motor in which there would be no lapse, no pause, no hesitation between impulses, but an overlapping of strokes so complete as to produce a flow of power almost liquid in its continuity."

According to the ad the driving experience was extraordinary, at least compared to, for example, the Model T described earlier. "As the Cadillac softly speeds along under the almost magic influence of this new power-principle, you become oblivious to the beautiful mechanism which gives you motion. The sensation is unique as though [it] had never motored before --- the sense of floating through space comes to you, as it never came to you before.

"It is useless to try to depict in words the thrill which you have never felt --- or to portray a degree of ease which you have never experienced. "Good roads yield up a velvet quality of travel undreamed.

"In operation, you enjoy the extreme of flexibility --- from less than three miles an hour in crowded city streets and congested traffic to more than sixty miles an hour on the open highway, without change of gears."

The cost of this experience was 650 pounds, for which you could buy three Model T tourers or two Overlands, Buicks or Studebakers. As if Ford cutting the price was not enough, Town and Country Amalgamated Motors lost one of its key brands: The British Government required the entire 1915 output of Napier cars for the war effort.

"The unrivalled performances of N.A.P.I.E.R. in time of peace are the strongest argument in support of its use in a time of world war!" wrote *Town and Country*. "The Imperial War Office has requisitioned the whole output of the NAPIER WORKS for active service use.

"We have on hand and landing Electric Lighted and Electric Started SPECIAL COLONIAL MODEL NAPIERS, fitted with English Touring Bodies, which will probably be the only stocks procurable until December owing to the War Office requisition."

CCM turned to a unique way of selling Studebaker, having a cut-out chassis on display. "Don't stand on ceremony with the STUDEBAKER come right along and probe its vitals" beckoned the headline within an advertisement. Ah, reading ads has never been so much fun.

Mr. F. Z. Eager in his 45 h.p. Overland Speedster

Eager's 1912 Overland before modifications.

11

Hamilton Hillclimb

In late 1914 the Automobile Club of Queensland staged its Patriotic Gymkhana. The emphasis was on raising money by entertaining the crowd in a series of fun events, rather than serious competition. The day was a great success with organisers surprised at the interest shown by spectators in what the automobile could achieve. Throughout Queensland, cars were now given a small part in most community sports programs. The car was a novelty and in some smaller communities still a rarity.

These novelty events were becoming a drawcard in their own right. On April 4, 1915, at the Ambulance Sports at the Brisbane Cricket Ground, the Gabba, one event was included -- Motor Musical Chairs. The Automobile Club took the cue that serious motoring events were likely to be popular and on April 17 organised a hill climb at the inner-city suburb of Hamilton.

The course commenced in Cooksley Street, alongside an iron fence which bordered Albion Park Racecourse. On the flat for 200 metres, the steep climb then began with a sharp right-angle bend. The course finished at the corner of Toorak and Queens roads, where a signaller with a flag stood in full view of the officials at the starting mark.

The hill climb at Hamilton is possibly the first organised motorsport event held in Brisbane. The Club proposed two events: a Class A, open to club members only, and a Class B, open to all motorists. There were 12 starters for the first run and in the second event 18 starters.

There needed to be a recipe to place all cars on a level playing field. The club decided on a horsepower formula, multiplied by time in seconds, divided by the car's tare weight in pounds.

Horsepower was arrived at by the cylinder's diameter in inches, squared, multiplied by stroke and number of cylinders divided by 10. *The Steering Wheel* was there to record the event.

"A well-known motorist, who has had considerable experience in contests of this nature, expressed the opinion honours would go to the small-powered cars of fair weight and tipped the Minerva as the winner on formula," reported *The Steering Wheel* correspondent.

"He contended the shortness of the course would be the greatest factor in the success of the small cars."

Even before the hill climb started, there was a shock in store. In Class A entrants appeared the names of Edward and Fred Eager. Just seven months earlier, September 1, 1914, in the *Brisbane Courier* Eagers proclaimed, 'We don't go much on records, but --- it has never been Overland policy to make hair-raising records. Occasionally owners put them up, to show their pride in the car."

There had been a change of heart regarding motorsport at Breakfast Creek. Mt Gravatt's ascent by three rival brands and the popularity of motor events at various shows meant Eagers could no longer ignore reality. They, of all the Brisbane dealers, should have been ahead of the game. After all, they grew up knowing Barney Oldfield in Ohio and saw first-hand the relationship between race success and a spike in sales.

To state, 'We don't go much on records ...' flew in the face of Eagers advertising having the Overland as the 'best value for money automobile' people could purchase. No cars, in original form, were built for racing. So, for Overland not to be involved was unacceptable. There were no short-cuts – Eagers had to have the confidence in their product to put it to the test against rivals: Not privateers that owned Overland cars, but Eagers itself. Like it or not, Eagers had to get behind the wheel and compete.

While the Queensland contingent rolled up in their Napiers, Minerva, V8 Cadillac, Buick, Vulcan, Hispano-Suiza, Maxwell, Hudson, Waverley, Ford, Metz, Calcott, Overland and Studebaker cars there were a couple of interlopers from south of the border. They were a New South Wales team of CJ Munro and Boyd Edkins, both driving Vauxhalls. Not your garden-variety Vauxhalls either.

Think of the Hamilton Hillclimb in the same vein as the Sydney to Hobart yacht race. Line honours and handicap honours. Forget handicap honours, the real winner, in the minds of serious contenders - was fastest across the line. Boyd Edkins, ironically a born and bred Queenslander, took out line honours with 36.8 seconds, ahead of Munro on 40 seconds flat, in the members' event.

Boyd Edkins, aka Boyd ed, would become the world's most successful Vauxhall race driver. Munro won on formula. Next in line honours came the V8 Cadillac, driven by W Cooke, who recorded 43.4 seconds. Edward Eager came sixth in line honours and seventh in formula, while Fred came ninth in line honours and 11th out of 12 in the formula. For Fred Eager, it was an inglorious start to his motorsport career.

So, how had his father outdone him? No doubt, this arose out of Edward Eager's frequent visits to Toledo checking out Willys product, including going over the factory floor and taking the new models for test drives. He probably took a pew as a passenger in cars driven by a test driver. In this way, Edward would have seen, and experienced, cars being driven fast on a test track. He may well have been tossed keys to take the vehicles himself on a test run. Edward's credible performance at Hamilton was most likely as a result of his previous experience.

In the Class 'B' event Munro and Edkins again dominated, taking out both line honours and formula in first and second places. The New South Welshmen dominated, although it could be argued Edkins drove for Queensland! Interestingly, neither Edward nor Fred competed with their Overlands in the Class B event. Fred, in particular, wanted to have a close look at how these southerners drove.

How could they be so fast, and he so slow? There was more to Edkin's car than met the eye. One of Edkins main rivals was A V Turner. Turner had found a vehicle faster than Edkins' Vauxhall, leaving the highly competitive, loyal Vauxhall distributor, uncompetitive.

Edkins cabled England and asked for more power. Laurence Pomeroy, Vauxhall's designer at the time, was bench-testing an engine from an A-Type tourer. He had made modifications to the engine, which in modern Australian parlance means he had 'hotted' it up. This engine was the most powerful 20hp the firm had built. Pomeroy fitted the motor into a Standard 1912 model chassis and shipped it to Boyd Edkins, at no cost to the Australian Vauxhall legend. Such was the esteem held for Edkins by a company half a world away.

The vehicle landed in Sydney in 1915 and Hamilton was one of its first outings. Hamilton proved two things to Fred Eager. His new speedster required more power and he, as a driver, needed more knowledge and practice in this new sport of car racing up hills.

A CCM Studebaker Six finished 13th in line honours and 16th on formula in a field of 18 cars. That too was a poor start to a racing career. Studebaker was determined to make the Six a huge sales success wherever it was sold. Dealers like CCM Brisbane were told they had to do everything possible to create publicity for the Studebaker Six. They needed the Six to win whatever was put in front of it. Win on Sunday, Sell on Monday.

Boyd Edkins was a motorsport legend of this era. In racing vernacular, the man could 'steer.' He was also a decent bloke, committed to advancing Australian motorsport.

Edkins wrote to *The Steering Wheel*. "Dear Sir, Mr Munro and myself will have left Brisbane before we have a chance to see any of you club officials tomorrow (Monday). "I was absent when the result of the hill climb was declared, but I see that I have scored the second formula prize in each event, and the absolute fastest time, making a total of six pounds six shillings in all. "We intended to give anything we won to the Belgian Fund, so I wish you to hand this six pounds, six shillings to that fund in my name, mentioning how it has come to be donated."

Motorsport, as always, had its detractors. The Vauxhall cars were far from standard. Edkins continued: "You might please announce it in the motoring notes of the papers to let those who felt somewhat sore about 'noisy exhausts' see that we were not out for paltry personal gain, but purely for the sport of the game.

"If our entries and presence have helped to create a little interest in the sport, both Mr Munro and I feel amply repaid for the time and expense incurred coming up from Sydney. If you make the next climb a mile long or more, we shall be up again for certainty. The longer, the better -- three miles if possible -- for the greatest test of man and car.

"The result is a great surprise to us, and the only explanation why the smaller powered cars did not win is that they were not tuned up to concert pitch and were not handled to best advantage; otherwise, they must have had a walkover."

Edkins hit on two key factors. Firstly, the Queensland entrants were most likely all competing in their first hill climb, while the southern visitors were accustomed to this form of motorsport, which had taken place in Sydney and Melbourne from around 1904.

Secondly, the two Vauxhalls were tailored for hill climbs, mechanically and suspension-wise. The two Overlands and the Studebaker were in novice hands and stock-standard cars. Edward Eager's car was a four-door, 30hp tourer, while Fred had a 35hp single-seat roadster.

Munro and Edkins's results were a reality check for both CCM and Eagers: If they were to be successful in motorsport, they would have to undertake significant work to the cars, and drivers needed to drastically improve their skills to be competitive on the national stage, with aces like Edkins and Munro happy to visit Brisbane for competition.

MEN ABOUT TOWN

A. V. DODWELL,
Managing director, Canada Cycle and
Motor Agency (Queensland), Ltd.

12

Steering Wheel Independence

Significant management changes came to the 14-month old *'Steering Wheel'* as the war dragged into 1916. Owned by Edward Eager, the magazine prospered and was making money. It almost enjoyed the full support of the Brisbane motor industry and other advertisers who saw merit in being involved in a quality magazine that reached every corner of Queensland. Wherever there was a car dealership in the State, there was a copy of *The Steering Wheel*.

It had grown to become an influential publication, confronting issues of importance to the motorist: The state of Queensland's roads, road signs for bush tracks linking Brisbane to towns north, west and south; drink driving, safe driving, pedestrians, technical aspects of the automobile, police, you name it *The Steering Wheel* doled out good advice every month. Launched in October 1914, it quickly became part of Queensland motoring's fabric and took on the vital role of lobbying governments.

The Steering Wheel's success forced the *Brisbane Courier* to appoint its first motoring writer in 1916.

The first move to give the magazine true independence came in January 1916 when, EG Eager & Son, sole shareholder in *The Steering Wheel*, turned it into a 'Limited' company, 'The Steering Wheel Limited'.

"Every phase of motoring life is represented in the shareholder's list of the new company," proudly announced the magazine's editorial in January 1916.

"Practically the whole of the motor trade and many motoring medicos, pastoralists, and businessmen constitute the new influence of *The Steering Wheel.*

While the ownership changed, the editorial and management staff remained the same. The head office was removed from Eagers headquarters at 299 Adelaide Street to the 'Inns of Court', also in Adelaide Street.

Physical distancing was vital for the perception that EG Eager & Son was no longer in the wheelhouse. "It is proposed to widen the paper in its scope. Probably with our next issue there will be for the first time a motor-boating section," states the editorial.

"It is felt that the aquatic interests of the State will welcome an official organ and there is every reason to expect the wholehearted support of the fraternity that delights in the smell of petrol, combined with that of sea brine."

The move to include powerboats editorial was logical. Many of those who could afford cars were also boaties. The well-to-do motor agency businesses such as CCM also sold farm machinery and engines for boats. Fred Eager was already a keen boatie.

To the January 1916 edition of *The Steering Wheel*, CCM had not advertised in the journal. In the first edition, under the new company, CCM took out a full-page ad for 1916 model Studebakers. There was no way CCM's managing director, AV Dodwell, would place any advertising dollars in Eagers hands while they were sole shareholders. The new share-holdings overcame that hurdle. The fact that CCM refused to advertise in *The Steering Wheel* would have cost them sales throughout the State. And it shows the depth of the rift and ill-feeling between CCM and Eagers.

It was not just boating news and features in the pipeline for the new *Steering Wheel.* "Arrangements are afoot to enlarge and intensify the interest of Motor Cycling Department.

"There are in Queensland some half-dozen Motor Cycling Clubs. The interests of the motorcyclist very largely overlap those of the motorist. Petrol, tyres, roads, tours, taxation -- in all these, the two stand on common ground. We hope by the time January appears again on our title page, we shall have built up a large and vibrant Motor Cycling Department.

"Then there are our photographic competitions -- but they're worth a paragraph to themselves." There was more than photographic competitions on people's minds.

Toowoomba was preparing a Motor Gymkhana for Australia Day, January 26, 1916. There was a spectacular procession of automobiles leaving Toowoomba Town Hall at 10am with trophies on offer for the best-decorated car and motorcycle. In addition to a variety of events for motorcycles, there was an obstacle driving track for cars with vehicles to drive forwards and reverse, with the winning driver avoiding the most obstacles in the fastest time.

There was also a Motor Car Musical Chairs, with a male driver and female passenger, with the female running to the centre of a circle to secure a chair. Those who missed out retired. There was also an accelerating test for cars: with the vehicles to drive on one gear only. First half to be operated at slowest possible speed and the second half at top speed, with the best average time to win. The Automobile Club of Queensland (ACQ) and motorcycle clubs organised the event.

Besides the uncertainty in large purchases - houses and cars - due to the Great War, other issues held back car sales in Queensland. The state of the roads continued to concern everyone, choking not just car and truck sales, but the economy. It was a problem not unique to Queensland, but Australia-wide. *The Steering Wheel* tackled the subject in its January 1916 edition stating the question was also raised in other states, and a move was due in Queensland'.

"Of late there are indications in various parts of Australia, to say nothing of England, that the question of Good Roads is, at last, taken up with something approaching earnestness. May the effort be a sustained one. The belief is fast becoming unanimous that the main highways should be taken over, built and maintained, by the (Federal) Government.

"The next step in the progress of public opinion is Main Roads should be financed out of revenue raised by the imposition of a Wheel Tax, where every wheeled vehicle is called upon to pay proportionately to the wear it gives the road."

The Steering Wheel then gave a rundown of what was happening in other Australian states and mentioned the 'Victorian Good Roads Association'. "The Association contacted all Victoria's Fruit Growing Associations, pointing out to those bodies how urgent is the necessity for road reform. "Leading residents, graziers, doctors, businesses also contacted to organise country branches of the Association.

"Every country newspaper in Victoria has learned of the country branch movement, and its editor strongly urged to advocate good roads."

In Tasmania, there were different issues. The State built the roads and then handed them over to the local council to fund and maintain, with help from an annual State subsidy.

"But the allocation of that subsidy has always been a matter of considerable heartburning. Some districts got too much, and others too little, or they thought they did. In some parts of Tasmania, there is a drift in the state of roads that needs to be stopped."

In New South Wales, a Good Roads Association was formed in 1914 but foundered after just a couple of years. Their practical achievements, through no fault of their own, have been small," wrote *The Steering Wheel*.

A group that had a direct personal interest in the roads' state was The Commercial Travellers' Association which took representation on the Association, both from a pecuniary standpoint and that of comfort.

"Those who have the greatest pecuniary interest in the matter are, first, the producers of the country, and second, the merchants and these should be more appropriately be leading in the chorus of public insistence for decent transit facilities."

Therefore, there was a call for the NSW Chamber of Commerce to take the question up seriously, as it ought to do. It will have the advantage, to begin with, of a more powerful organisation, and it will be better able to arouse interest in influential quarters, both in the city and the country.

The state of Australia's main roads --- the highways linking the capital cities --- was deplorable certainly up to and including 1916, and for decades after. While that meant a hard time for producers and merchants, it also reduced motorsport to hill climbs.

The concept of out-and-out speed trials limited by unmade roads, pot-holed, and rutted from the wheels of carts pulled by horses. Beaches that at low tide and hard, flat sand were the most suitable locations for speed trials. Australia's remote and mostly unexplored inland contained salt flats, used for speed trials by Sir Donald Campbell in the 1950s. In 1916, the salt flats were not an option.

The Queensland Automobile Club (now the RACQ) was also doing its bit for the war effort. In conjunction with the Taxicab Drivers' Association, the club had 'fallen in' with the military's invitation to provide cars to meet returned soldiers. Only those cars with an Automobile Club pass were allowed on railway platforms or wharves during soldiers' arrival. *The Steering Wheel* then listed those who were already meeting the diggers, and those names comprised most of the car agencies, including arch-rivals, CCM managing director, AV Dodwell and FZ Eager.

The Club was also showing it had clout. It lobbied the Coomera Shire Council in December 1915 (one of many councils that would merge and eventually become Gold Coast City Council in the mid-1990s) to reduce ferry charges for cars crossing the Coomera River. The Coomera Shire Council reduced from three shillings and sixpence, the same amount applied to a bullock wagon and full team, to two shillings for the lighter and smaller cars.

"It is hoped the tax will be reduced at the end of those 12 months to an even more reasonable amount," commented *The Steering Wheel.*

"Meanwhile motor tourists feel a sense of gratitude for even half a loaf."

Ferry charges were a significant disincentive for car tours and tourists wanting to visit the South Coast, now known as the Gold Coast.

Australian Model T's came from Canada, but Ford Canada and Detroit's relationship continued to cause resentment in Australia. Ford dealers or agents and the Australian Government were at loggerheads about the company that supplied our Model Ts.

There was a good reason for this. The Australian Government prohibited any Commonwealth Department from purchasing Ford cars. Ford was a US-founded company, and the US was noticeably absent from the theatre of war. Anti-US sentiment was strong in Australia. The Ford Company of Australia told *The Steering Wheel* the Ford Company of Canada was distinct from Ford's American company. And Ford Canada wrote it was 'not subsidiary to the Detroit company.

"Only five Detroit Company shareholders own any stock in this Company," Ford Canada told the magazine. The Detroit Company or its shareholders do not control this company or its shareholders. Our car is manufactured in Canada by Canadians."

Ford Canada employed 2400 staff, and a further 1500 Canadians were also employed indirectly making parts for the Model T. "Let Australian Government send inquiries to Canadian Manufacturers Association at Toronto or appoint some representative here to investigate, as we can satisfy them that our resources and sympathies are absolutely with the Allies in this fight."

Queensland Motor Agency continued to run its ads under the heading 'Made in Canada under the British Flag.' On January 12, 1916, Queensland Motor Agency reported it had sold 871 Fords in Queensland in 1915. A massive increase in shipping charges caused another blow to car sales. High-profile dealers took out a *Brisbane Courier* ad on January 24, 1916, stating ocean freights lifted from 37 shillings and sixpence a ton to 127 shillings and sixpence a ton, forcing agents to increase the selling prices of cars.

"We ask the public to understand this action was taken reluctantly and has been forced on us by the phenomenal freight increases."

CCM, Dalgety and Co, Eagers, Evers, Howards, Queensland Motor Agency, Trevethan's and WF Turk Motors, commissioned the ad.

To February 1916 CCM enjoyed a two-year product advantage over Eagers. Its Studebaker came in both four and six-cylinder configurations. Overland was limited to four cylinders. That changed in February when Eagers announced the imminent arrival of the 'SENSATION OF 1916' the Knight Six engine, renowned for its silent running, that would now go on sale as the Willys Knight. On top of that, it would sell at half the price of other 'Knight' powered cars in the luxury division, including Daimler, Panhard, Mercedes and Minerva, selling between 800 pounds and 2000 pounds.

This seemingly routine announcement would have consequences way beyond its face-value importance. It would lead to bitterness, public sniping, and in late 1916 be the indirect cause of the decision to hold trials for an Australian Land Speed record on the beach at Southport.

The retail cost of the Willys Knight was directly related to production numbers.

"The Daimler, Panhard, Mercedes, Minerva and others generally make no more cars in a whole year than John Willys makes in a single week," stated an Eagers *Brisbane Courier* advertisement.

"The Silent Knight engine was designed in 1904 and was revolutionary. Instead of poppet valves, the Knight motor had sliding valves and no cams and no valve springs. It used sliding sleeves. There was nothing about the valves to wear and require grinding, all of which combined to make for silence. It eliminated the objections of even the best of other motor types.

"It had more power. It had longer life. It was so quiet that standing next to the hood one could hardly tell whether or not the engine was running. The greatest of all European manufacturers immediately equipped their cars with it. Since then, they have used none else."

While Eagers were preparing to do battle with the Willys Knight against the Studebaker Six - and vice versa, Ford dealers had a win over the Commonwealth Government after the intervention of the Prime Minister of Canada, Sir RL Borden. He advised the Australian Government all Fords coming into Australia were a product of the Ford Motor Company of Canada, and not 'in any way connected with the United States.' An ad in the *Brisbane Courier* said in conclusion: 'In Buying a Ford Car your money remains in the British Empire.'

Hard business, the car game, for people like Eagers who not only sold US-built Willys cars but were Americans to boot, a rarity in Australia in 1916.

Richard Cobden was appointed editor of *The Steering Wheel* in early 1916 and immediately put his stamp on the publication by slating the Coolangatta Shire Council over the state of roads. Visitors could get to the border of NSW and Queensland by a 70-mile train excursion. Alternatively, they could drive more than 100 miles on dirt roads, via Murwillumbah, using a road chart issued by *The Steering Wheel*. There were no Melways in 1916.

"You can imagine how we feel, and how these seekers react, when we tell them this most desirable of all resorts, within easy reach of the capital, cannot be reached except by tortuous route which adds nearly 50 per cent to the distance as the crow flies. (We never thought we would envy the crow).

"Can't you do anything to help these folk, who want to go to your district often ... can't you do anything to open your gates and let them in? If in one month only 25 cars visited the Tweed and each car party spent only five pounds in the district, it would not take long for you to recoup yourselves for the few hundreds (pounds) needed to make that last 2½ miles stretch into your town passable."

Cobden delivered the article with logic and force, providing an even stronger tone for *The Steering Wheel*. It was a publication to be feared (excuse the pun) when it got on its high horse. With support of large organisations, Brisbane's car industry, business leaders and the motoring public, a vibrant circulation throughout the State, *The Steering Wheel* had come of age. It was flexing its muscles on issues that matter and were relevant to Queensland motorists.

Mr F Z Eager.

13

A change of heart

EG Eager & Son, the company that placed little emphasis on motorsport, did a 360-degree flip on the eve of the Hamilton Hillclimb. Edward and Fred Eager knew they must join the fray. AV Dodwell of CCM Brisbane reached a similar conclusion, but for a more specific reason - he needed positive publicity for the new Studebaker Six.

The Hamilton hill climb was the Eager's first outing and left no doubt they needed to put engine, chassis and suspension development into Fred's car, and Fred's driving skills were not up to scratch.

The obvious starting point was the most potent Overland in the lightest body. In the days leading up to the Hamilton hill climb, Fred went into Eager's car storage area, which housed new cars and used vehicles awaiting refurbishment. In the used car area he spotted the perfect vehicle, a 1912 Overland 45hp roadster.

The neat soft-top was on its way to the workshop for conversion into a delivery van. It was a 61 T model, (T61276) and had the largest horsepower in the Overland range courtesy of the 270 cubic inch, four-cylinder engine. In modern terms that's a large engine, 4.4 litres.

Eager's service manager, Wally Webb, who joined the company at the start and remained in that position until his retirement in 1957, was assigned the task. Fred Eager's instructions were simple. "Turn the car into a speedster." Wally Webb had no time to work on the car before the Hamilton hill climb, and immediately after went to work with a passion. He replaced the tourer body with a light racing-type body which he painted white. The car stood out like a beacon among the dark vehicles on the road at that time, many Fords of course, that came in any colour, so long as it was black.

'Whitey' was born. Webb did not undertake the transition from roadster to a speedster in one hit. Systematically, Wally Webb worked the car over. After testing it was fine-tuned in every aspect, as Fred Eager reported performance issues back to Webb. Webb, also a competitive steerer, tested the car regularly - he was more than a mechanic and understood car dynamics.

Whitey was a genuine work in progress for around 18 months, covering some of her racing career. Webb drilled the chassis to reduce weight. However, due to instability at speed because of chassis twisting, he strengthened the frame: Steel braces welded across the ladder-type chassis' front and rear. Then, full-length steel plating was hot riveted within the parallel rails. In the end, the chassis weighed more than it did originally but was much more rigid than a standard Overland.

Rigid chassis extensions replaced ¾ elliptic rear springs and 58-inch ½ elliptic springs. Webb installed Eight Hartford friction shocks in pairs, front and rear.

He tried BE or clincher wheels, but the tyres were prone to roll off the rims under speed and heavy cornering. A set of imported 25-inch Houk SS wire wheels and hubs replaced the clincher wheels. And a unique crown and pinion was made for the transaxle. Webb probably had several differentials on hand for Whitey, with different ratios to suit the need whether it be hill climbs, long-distance touring or high-speed runs. For easy replacement, differentials were wheeled under the vehicle.

Lightweight drilled steel pistons with a crown riveted on replaced heavier standard pistons. These were about half an inch taller than the original pistons and gave a significant boost to compression. Engine bore remained at 4 3/8 inches. There were no alterations to the camshaft, but the cam followers were re-forged with feet to give earlier, and quicker, valve openings. Webb added double dippers to the big ends boosting oil circulation.

A Zenith carburettor replaced the 'unreliable' Schebler and Webb made a special muffler that reduced backpressure. A narrow brass radiator replaced a wider cooler, probably to reduce weight. Fred Eager ordered the final touch for the bonnet sides: F Z Eager driver and W Webb mechanic. Whitey was ready for action in January 1916, in time for the Toowoomba Gymkhana.

The need for Eagers to have a speedster became urgent as Webb worked on Whitey. Toowoomba CCM agent, W A Elvery, was ahead of the Bris-bane dealers and set a record time for the Brisbane-Toowoomba inter-city run. Along with pilot J Adam, Elvery steered a Studebaker to a record of 2 hours 35 minutes.

In November, a West Australian CCM dealer then set a record for the marathon distance between Perth on Australia's west coast, to Sydney on the east coast, in eight days 23 hours and 40 minutes.

AV Dodwell was over the record wins like a rash and splurged money on large display advertisements in the *Brisbane Courier*, telling the world how well the Studebakers performed.

Eagers had no motorsport ammunition to fire back.

It was not easy for Brisbane people to attend the Toowoomba motor gymkhana in 1916 as Australia Day was not an official holiday and fell on a Wednesday. Some six Automobile Club members from Brisbane attended with their cars, including Fred Eager and AV Dodwell, from CCM.

"Toowoomba people are congratulating themselves on having staged the finest motor gymkhana that Queensland has seen to the present," reported *The Steering Wheel*.

Fred Eager's Whitey and W Elvery's Studebaker, fresh from its record-breaking between Brisbane and Toowoomba, were to have staged a friendly speed race. AV Dodwell firmly supported Elvery.

Unfortunately, organisers had not read the fine print allowing them to use the facility: The Toowoomba turf club lent the course on the understanding no cars would be allowed on the track. The crowd swelled when word got around there would be a race. They left disappointed. No doubt Eager and Elvery shared this emotion.

How 'friendly' the race would have been being debatable. Fred Eager, like his father, did not like running second to anyone. He inherited his father's not inconsiderable competitive genes. W A (William) Elvery was cut from similar cloth. In addition to the CCM agency, he was the owner of Toowoomba Taxi Cab and Motor Company and a fully decked-out garage for vehicle servicing and all repairs and paintwork. He was a goer.

By March 1916 car design had moved on. Automobiles were sleeker, more streamlined and had a host more features. It was even possible to get headlamps that moved in the same direction as the front wheels, an innovation that took the luxury car world by storm in early 2004!

Back then they were called 'Swivelite Headlamp Fittings' and cost five pounds, plus brackets and took just a couple of hours to fit any car brought to Howards. The Model T was looking dated. That it would survive more than another decade is one of the miracles of world marketing. Queensland Motor Agency, buoyed by the fact Federal Government agencies had lifted the black ban on the Model T, went to town in their ads.

BUY THE FORD Because it's a better Car Because it's a British Car. Inter-city racing was in its heyday around 1916. Today it would be called street racing, and anyone found guilty of it would probably have the car confiscated and be locked away in jail for a considerable time. But these were the pioneering days of the automobile. The new-fangled aircraft were barnstorming the US and Australia, and inter-city racing events were simply an automobile variant on what Tiger Moths were doing in the air.

The inter-city timed races took place for a few reasons. First, they were not illegal, so they could. Secondly, there was prestige for the driver involved. Thirdly, intercity records were really reliability trials and that's why the buying public took notice. Lastly, there were bragging rights. Win on Sunday, Sell on Monday. Tyre manufacturers sponsored rubber for the cars competing in these events. If there was stiff competition between car makes and car retailers, the rivalry was no less between tyre manufacturers.

Buy Australian, not foreign, was a call to our allegiance to the flag in time of war. And the Aussie tyre brand had a ball when that great driver, Boyd Edkins, set a Melbourne-to-Sydney record.

In his Vauxhall, Edkins covered the distance in 16 hours 55 minutes, eclipsing the Melbourne-Sydney train time of 17 hours 11 minutes and the previous record by more than two hours. In the early days of intercity racing the car's time was always compared to that of the express trains, both the Sydney-Melbourne and the Sydney-Brisbane.

A Dunlop advertisement pointed out the train had tracks to run on while by road, it is vastly different. There are a hundred miles of rough, unmade, rutted, bush tracks; mountains to negotiate, hundreds of horrible 'V' gutters and water crossings, yet Mr Boyd Edkins ... averaged over 33 miles per hour from the capital to capital covering 565 miles. "He used Dunlop tyres." "Think about what this means for the tyres. The strain is terrific --- for the pace to be maintained irrespective of the road surface."

In an article on the record-breaking trip, *The Steering Wheel* recorded that Edkins was not unknown in Queensland having "only last winter ... journeyed to Brisbane in his Vauxhall car for the express purpose of competing in the Automobile Club's Hill Climbing Contests.

"In this competition, Mr Edkins showed Brisbane motorists that it was possible to go round corners on practically one wheel. Knowing the way he handled his car on this occasion, we are not surprised to learn of his wonderful performance from Melbourne to Sydney."

March 1916 was also an important milestone for *The Steering Wheel*. It proved itself a respected voice for the motorist and motorcyclist tackling the raft of issues facing these motor-users as Queensland, and Queenslanders underwent a metamorphosis from the horse to motorised horsepower. *The Steering Wheel* was appointed official organ of Queensland's three most influential road-motoring bodies, the Automobile Club of Queensland, the Queensland Motorcycle Club and the Toowoomba Motorcycle Club.

"We are proud of this triple distinction," wrote *The Steering Wheel*. "May the ideals for which the Clubs, and this paper, are striving become concrete and may the first to take shape be Good Roads and a Wheel Tax with proceeds earmarked for Road development, thus banishing forever the objectionable Motor Class Taxation bogie."

Edward Eagers 'baby', *The Steering Wheel*, achieved much more than being appointed the Automobile Club of Queensland's official organ. Edward Eager arrived in 1912 when the ACQ was already formed; however, it had lost its way and lacked leadership; it could not even attract anyone to fill the secretary's role. At this stage the *Brisbane Courier* was happy to take money from the car agencies but lacked any motoring section, let alone a motoring scribe. *The Steering Wheel* helped lead the Motoring Club out of the wilderness by giving it a voice, and more importantly, clout.

That club, now known as the Royal Automobile Club of Queensland or the RACQ is the equivalent Victoria's RACV or New South Wales' NRMA. The RACQ would later launch its journal, the *Queensland Motorist*, which would later be re-branded with its current title, *The Road Ahead*.

The State of Queensland's roads were a genuine impediment to car sales, commerce and tourism even though the state now boasted more than 5000 motorists. Many motorists were doctors who made house calls all over this massive state. For doctors, the car was more than a luxury; for them, it was a necessity.

Night emergencies were not uncommon with doctors often called at ungodly hours. Cars could get them quickly to outlying homes and farms to help save lives and deliver babies.

The following story from the March 1, 1916, edition of *The Steering Wheel* gives some idea of what confronted motorists.

"ROADS: An Undeveloped Country's Need Some instances of Queensland Roads Costing Hundreds of Pounds, yet Useless because not Maintained."

"DURING the month there reached us from a medico motorist a note which read; "Re Good Roads: I am sending you a news clipping......... Keep Plugging. Those last two words did quite a lot to buck us up at a time when we were feeling rather dismal over this Road business.

"We had just returned from the Toowoomba Gymkhana, having made the trip by car, and for stretches of miles had to run on an improvised black soil track on the side of the road while a couple of yards to the side of us ran the properly made route --- unused.

"Thoroughly made, but thoroughly neglected. Some local authority had poured out the money of its ratepayers to build a road that, when new, must have been above criticism. Now, for want of the merest few pounds of top dressing, the road lies useless, a monument to the short-sightedness of somebody. The improvised track is used daily by the road using ratepayers of the districts, and it must be a source of much heart burning to pass regularly by the built road which has proved to be nothing more than the grave of hundreds of pounds.

"And the Brisbane-Toowoomba road, mind you, is the most main of all main roads. Probably next comes the road which links (or rather should link) the capital to the largest coastal towns to the North --- Gympie, Maryborough, Bundaberg and others. But the memory of two and three quarter hours spent on a five mile stretch during the latter part of 1915 still remains, and we may be forgiven for not reviving the experience again in print."

CCM was doing everything they could to capitalise on Studebaker's various successes. It had become clear CCM were throwing everything at promoting the Studebaker Six. It also appeared every Studebaker dealer in Australia was doing the same thing.

CCM produced a full brochure called 'Fraser's Nine Day Six, the graphic, enthralling story of the Fremantle to Sydney world's record trans-continental trip in a Six-cylinder Studebaker Car. This artistic souvenir costs nothing and is posted free to all on request.'

Meanwhile, Whitey was becoming one of the best-known cars in south-east Queensland since the decision taken in mid-1915 to develop the speedster specifically to participate in various contests on offer.

By April 1916 it had traversed Spicers Gap, near Cunningham's Gap several times, three times been to the summit of Mt Glorious 'it being the first car to make the ascent' and four times up Mt Gravatt. "Also, it is one of only two cars to cross Tambourene (sic) Mountain from the Brisbane side," reported *The Steering Wheel.*

"In it Mr Eager recently pioneered a new and short road to Coolan-gatta from Brisbane across Currumbin Creek. The machine is enamelled white and had quite a docile appearance." After Whitey and Fred Eager's modest results at the Hamilton hill climb, possibly Whitey's first outing before Wally Webb had a chance to lay a spanner or a lick of paint on the car, both car and driver had come a long way.

Whitey was developed and improved over time by Wally Webb. Fred Eager and Webb were both prepared to experiment with the car to give it the extra speed and handling. At the same time, Fred Eager used the weekend wanderings around south-east Queensland to hone his driving skills and determine Whitey's limits.

The Hamilton hill climb was an eye-opener to the former Toledo bank clerk. He took on board how Boyd Edkins driving style, how he took corners at high speed, prepared to have the car's back wheels slide sideways in the corners, raising clouds of dust and then how Edkins and Munro corrected the front wheels and sped off out of the corner in full control. He took note of how Edkins used every possible inch of road space. He marvelled at Edkins' times.

The real lesson for Eager was how Edkins handled the car. For Fred Eager, it was compelling. How could Edkins get that performance out of a British Vauxhall? By the exhaust note alone it was apparent Edkins car was far from standard. But it was the combination of car and driver that was the key to the fast times. His trips to explore the great south-east were Fred Eager's self-taught speedster apprenticeship that combined road trips he wrote about for *The Steering Wheel*. But these were touring events, not competitive races.

By the end of March 1916, Fred Eager was ready to show his skills as a driver and Whitey's development as a speedster. The war heightened interest in automobiles, not just as transport, but an object of sport and recreation, all in the name of raising funds for the Patriotic Fund.

ACQ officials selected the iconic Brisbane Cricket Ground, best known as the Gabba, to hold The Grand Patriotic Motor Gymkhana in late March. It was a phenomenal success.

"This afternoon a crowded program was run off ... in the presence of a bigger crowd than the Brisbane Cricket Ground has held for many years," reported *The Steering Wheel*.

The day raised more than 100 pounds, mainly from the motor trade. The events were of a novelty type, and it was Fred Eager's first taste of success. The motor car sprint ran with two heats and a final. Whitey took the first sprint in 9 3/5 seconds. The second sprint went to Geo Whatmore in a Model T at 10 seconds. Whitey 'blew out a plug' in the final, leaving Whatmore to take out first prize. The sprints, held in the cricket oval's tight confines -- about 130 yards -- were not serious competition. They did, however, give Fred Eager valuable experience in a competitive environment.

One of the prime movers behind the gymkhana was Eager's business rival, AV Dodwell from CCM. Dodwell was involved in the organisation and did not compete. Dodwell planned to leave the driving side to WA Elvery, the Studebaker 'speed merchant' from Toowoomba, but he failed to make the day. Elvery's absence, for whatever reason, may have frustrated AV Dodwell and left the door open for another driver to enter the scene, one that Dodwell could ensure would turn up on race day: Alec Fraser Jewell.

While many saw the day as fun with a great cause, and no doubt Fred Eager shared that sentiment, he was also a competitor. If you played the game, you played to win. The Gabba has that effect on people. In the first cricket test held at the Gabba in 1931 against South Africa, Don Bradman made 226 in the first innings.

It is the Brisbane Lions' home, an AFL team that could barely win a game at Carrara on the Gold Coast as the Brisbane Bears, but won three consecutive premierships with the Gabba their home in 2001/02/03.

Eager's competitive nature came out in the obstacle race. "The Obstacle Race held some surprises, the climax coming with the ascent and descent of a see-saw of 20 feet overall length and height of three feet at the centre," reported *The Steering Wheel*.

"The secret of crossing it comfortably lay in going steadily up until the weight of the front wheels tilted the see-saw, when the run down could be taken without jar." Eager lined up Whitey for the run over the see-saw, having negotiated earlier obstacles, gate driving, water carrying, and hurdle jumping.

"The winner took the see-saw at speed with unfortunate results: a stub axle broke but held until the winning post was reached, when the near front wheel collapsed."

It mattered little to Eager that his car was busted. In no time Wally Webb would have Whitey back on four wheels. Eager won the Obstacle Race in 2 minutes 3.4/5 seconds; winning is addictive, and Fred Eager was hooked.

Naturally, Eager received publicity in *The Steering Wheel*. The big loser was CCM and Studebaker that did not compete. With *The Steering Wheel* under new management, other agents joined Fred Eager to explore south-east Queensland, take photographs, and submit the articles to Richard Cobden, the magazine's editor. Geo Whatmore was quick to pick up on the benefits and was an enthusiastic motorist exploring the state in his Model T.

On the April 1, 1916, edition of *The Steering Wheel*, a newcomer joined the ranks, AV Dodwell, of CCM. Interestingly, both Eager and Dodwell submitted pieces on 'touring', Eagers under the heading 'TOURING a few observations by FZ' on page 31 of the edition. On page 33 under 'TOURING TIPS', AV Dodwell' had his say. Eagers' piece took up a full page while Dodwell's took a full-length single column.

Once again, the rivalry bubbled under the surface. Eager's column started with 'Automobile touring is the King of Outdoor Sports. The man who wears his tires (sic) out on city pavements has not yet discovered the most valuable phase of his car ownership to himself, his family, and his friends.' Neither article makes mention of CCM or Eagers, Overland or Studebaker. It is likely Cobden commissioned the pieces and probably tossed a coin to see whose story would go first, adjusting the layout accordingly.

For Dodwell, the article was a test of *The Steering Wheel* and its new management. Under Eagers' ownership, he suspected he would have denied a fair go. Dodwell's piece began, 'The experience gained on some ten trips overland to Sydney and back moves me to pass along these few touring hints.' A second AV Dodwell story, recounting his visit to Mt Kosciusko at Christmas 1915 in a Studebaker Six. He was accompanied by his wife and family and Henry Kennady, like Eager, an American, and managing director of Australia's Studebaker Corporation. For AV Dodwell, *The Steering Wheel* had passed the test. He could rely on a fair go.

There was a need to lobby governments and agitate further in the newspapers and magazines for improved Queensland roads and better signage, and late 1915 or early 1916, a Roads Committee formed. No doubt Fred Eager was appointed chairman because of his intimate knowledge of south-east Queensland roads, particularly those south of Brisbane to the Gold Coast and Coolangatta region and tracking south-west to Spicers Gap and west to Toowoomba.

There was a strong push to make Coolangatta more accessible to Brisbanites who loved the laid-back seaside resort with its beautiful beaches, Tweed River and Coolangatta Beach House, perched on a high on a hill overlooking the Pacific Ocean. The fishing was great. The biggest obstacle was getting there via the MacPherson Ranges and Murwillumbah, a distance of 105 miles.

With a colleague, Jack White, Fred Eager set out in April 1916 to find a shorter route, and later, reported his findings in *The Steering Wheel*. After the usual run of 47.5 miles to Southport from Brisbane, covered in two hours 14 minutes the pair arrived in Southport just in time to miss a heavy storm and spent the night there.

"Leaving at 7 o'clock next morning we proceeded along the usual Tweed Road through Nerang, Worongary and Mudgeeraba to Reedy Creek. From Reedy Creek two tracks lead to the South. One goes direct to Tallebudgera, 3.6 miles, but is the worst bit of road on the entire trip. The other track leads from Reedy Creek to a bend about mid-way between Burleigh and Burleigh West on the Burleigh-Tallebudgera route. The distance to Tallebudgera over this route is 6.3 miles, but the road is infinitely better than the direct one." By 9 o'clock Eager and White, in Whitey reached the deep crossing of Currumbin Creek and met the Currumbin member of the Nerang Shire, Mr Cronk.

They learned the Shire could not justify putting even the most minimal of crossings over the creek. The party camped on the creek bank for three hours, waiting for the tide to drop, revealing a sandbank in the middle. As they waited, they discussed the potential crossing and concluded a few large logs and some infill would make a reliable crossing of the creek, as long as it was not in flood.

They found a patch of sand at low tide and put Whitey to the test to the southern side. No issues arose. They proceeded south and found a road that ran parallel to the railway from Currumbin. "This road is good to a point 2.5 miles from Coolangatta from which point money will require to be spent in filling before the road can be recommended to tourists.

"There are also three steep ridges on a neglected part of the road on the Brisbane side of Tallebudgera which need attention. "It is understood a prominent Tweed resident, alive to the value of the tourist trade, has said he will donate 50 pounds to the improvement of the road. A 78-mile run on roads, that after the attention indicated above, can be considered good would certainly be exceedingly popular with a host of motorists."

Fred Eager and Jack White were probably the first motorists to drive this route and pioneered Coolangatta-Tweed motoring tourism, remembering the train already connected Brisbane and the Tweed.

If today's car salesmen think they have it tough, they might like to spare a thought for Mr C E Skinner, a salesman with the Motor House in Warwick in 1916. The buyer's horse kicked Mr Skinner while trying to sell a car, forcing him to seek medical attention. An instance of horsepower's strength, perhaps the horse led by example in the fight against the automobile.

By May 1916 Fred Eager had covered tens of thousands of miles in Whitey. Since the Hamilton hill climb he had worked on getting to know the car, not just as a conveyance but as a 'speedster.' His time of 2 hours 14 minutes from Brisbane to Southport, mentioned above, was extraordinarily fast. The roads were rough, and there were crossings using ferries at Coomera and Logan Rivers. There's no doubt he used his 'excursions' to hone his driving skills and test the limits of Whitey's capability. Frederick Zina Eager would soon have the opportunity to put his skills, complete with the upgraded Whitey, to the ultimate test.

On the business front Willys Overland had consolidated, bought more car factories, and between 1912 and 18, became the second-largest manufacturer of cars in the US, only Ford building more cars, on the back of the ubiquitous Model T.

14

Whitey at One Tree Hill

The Hamilton Hill Climb had been a massive wake-up call for Fred Eager. His time was barely middle of the pack, and if hoped to 'Win on Sunday' to generate sales, he needed a minor miracle at the May 27, 1916 Automobile Club of Queensland's Hill Climb at One Tree Hill. He spent weekends driving Whitey over the rough bush tracks of south-east Queensland since the Hamilton embarrassment. The trips were not practice runs on steep climbs at breakneck speed. He had passengers to take care of on these outings and he became more aware of the rear-end sliding out on corners and slight steering correction to get Whitey back under control.

Another obstacle to overcome at One Tree Hill was driving up from Sydney. The speedster, Boyd Edkins, a good friend, announced he would bring his fast Vauxhall to compete on the 1.6-mile One Tree Hill track. In terms of race experience and success Edkins was as good as it gets in Australia, while Eager was a rank amateur. The ACQ had found a longer, more challenging hill climb at Edkins' suggestion after the Hamilton outing when he suggested the track was too short for good racing.

After driving the dirt track up One Tree Hill, Edkins was "loud in his praise of the fitness of the site." According to *The Steering Wheel* scribe, many motorists considered this event a "foregone conclusion for Edkins", since his equally fast compatriot, Munro was absent.

All drivers could conduct trial sprints up the hill climb track. The spectators became excited at what they saw from two competitors: a six-cylinder Buick driven by Albert Harrington and a white Overland steered by Fred Eager. There were 14 entrants in total including some familiar names, Ford dealer G W Whatmore in a Model T, Toowoomba's W A

Elvery in a Studebaker Four, AV Dodwell's Studebaker Six, W F Turk in a Maxwell Four, and W M Trevethan in a Chevrolet Four.

They were all competing for two trophies: Handicap honours and Line Honours. There was only one category that mattered to those who were serious about winning, the fastest time, line honours. First cab off the rank was the Buick crossing the finish line with clocks recording a great time of 3 minutes, 1 and 1/5 seconds.

This time augured for great day of racing with close times. A little 14.5 hp Fiat came next and recorded a disappointing 4 mins 16 seconds, but good enough on handicap to grab the second spot.

The big Moline Knight put up 3 min, 13 2/5 seconds, a nice curtain-raiser to the main event – Boyd Edkins' Vauxhall. Along the winding track, the crowd were on their toes with anticipation as they waited for Edkins' Vauxhall to race past. They had heard so much about this speedster. Vauxhalls were scarce around Brisbane, and now they were about to see Australia's fastest. Edkins pushed hard, and clouds of dust blew up behind the car like some massive jet stream. Onlookers had a few seconds to hear the Vauxhall coming, and then suddenly it was in front them then gone leaving dust clouds to settle over the crowd.

They gasped in amazement at the speed and control he had over the machine. Brisbane's speed limit was 12mph. Edkins crossed the line in just 2 mins 56 1/5 seconds, a full five seconds faster than the Buick and about triple the legal speed limit. Next off the line AV Dodwell's Studebaker Six with R de Mattos behind the wheel. With 45.2hp from the 5.7-litre straight six it was the most powerful car in the Hill Climb. Coupled with that it tipped the scales at 2842lb – light for its size.

It crossed the line in 3 mins 10 4/5 seconds, but its power and weight relegated the car to 12th spot on handicap. The Elvery Studebaker did not race. The *Brisbane Courier* reported the Model 35 Studebaker, "was not seen to advantage. Speed on the level is more suited to the present gearing of his machine."

After a couple more cars dusted onlookers, it was Fred Eager's turn with Whitey. Whispers relayed along the track were that Whitey in trial runs had come in nearer to 2½ minutes than 3 minutes, putting everyone on edge.

Could a Queenslander carry off the fastest time? Could Eager, the bespectacled former bank clerk in his second hill climb, lower the colours of one of Australia's best-known speedsters? It was too much to ask. Eager was dressed in a suit, wore a tie and providing eye shade was a flat cap, also known as a 'Cabbie Cap'.

On the starting line, Fred Eager was nervous, but not overawed. He knew Whitey better than the back of his hand. They'd covered thousands of miles together on rough roads … this was just another test, albeit one with the pedal flat to the floor.

The timing system were telephones at the start and finish. Those at the top rang the starter and as it tingled the flag dropped and the timing clocks on the hill punched. Eager took off like his life depended on it. It was not going to be another Hamilton!

He pushed Whitey to the limit and took the three big corners like he had seen Edkins do some months before. Whitey responded beautifully, and as he powered out of the corners, the noise of the car and the tyres on the dirt track drowned out the spectators' cheering. The onlookers erupted into applause. Whitey was faster than Edkins' Vauxhall - or so it seemed: more dust, most noise and less time to see the white car flash past.

Whitey rocketed to the finishing line in 2 mins 43 2/5 seconds, a whopping 12 4/5 seconds faster than his good friend, Boyd Edkins. The speed averaged out at 37 ½ mph from a standing start.

The Steering Wheel was generous in its praise, stating the course, which has at least three tricky corners, 'gives drivers little time to think'.

"The Eager record was probably near the maximum attainable on this course. We shall be surprised if the average is ever brought up to 40mph," it stated.

How did Fred Eager go from the first time, middle of the pack, hill-climber at Hamilton to blasting away the best driver and car from Sydney or Melbourne? Did he seek advice from his fellow Wauseon, Barney Old-field? Was he self-taught? Or did he seek tutoring from one of the hill-climb guns from Sydney or Melbourne?

Records show Fred Eager made a 'business' trip to Sydney in December 1915. Not unusual for Fred, as a CEO of a sizeable Australia/N.Z.

Mr. F. Z. Eager in his racing car, 'Whitey'

Fred Eager in 'Whitey' on One Tree Hill.

business. Could he have arranged some hands-on lessons from Edkins on one of Sydney's hill-climb tracks?

Wally Webb had done his part in turning Whitey into a genuine speed-ster, which accounts for some of Whitey's performance. At the end of the day though, the driver is the difference between winning and losing, and Fred Eager drove the hill like a seasoned racer. How Fred Z Eager, in such a short time, transitioned to that elite level remains a mystery. Having said that, later events indicate Eager and Edkins had a lot in common and helped each other out when they could when it came to motor sport. I'm 99 per cent sure Edkins took Eager under his wing and taught him everything he knew about driving on dirt roads in the summer of 1915/16. Eager, I believe, felt he owed Edkins big time. He would later repay that debt in a most unusual way which would leave Edkins forever in debt to Fred Eager.

Boyd Edkins driving his Vauxhall, set the Melbourne to Sydney record in 1916.

15

Whitey first car to conquer Mt. Glorious. Impossible, say detractors

Fred Eager had the exploration bug. Whitey, with her light body, good ground clearance, powerful engine and low first gear, made a capable car to conquer Brisbane's hills and mountains. Some might claim Fred Eager was nothing more than a headline-seeking car dealer intent on publicity alone. That would not be a fair or accurate assessment of the man. Yes, he believed in publicity, but there was more than one motivation behind his exploits.

When his father, Edward, set up *The Steering Wheel*, one of the publication's foundation stones was to show people where they could go and what they could do if they owned an automobile. It's called selling dreams or selling the sizzle. You are not buying a steak, but when a waiter passes your table delivering a T-bone to a customer, and everyone can hear the plate sizzling, that's the dish many people want. That's what gets their mouth-watering.

Fred Eager was following the advice his father wanted to give to all motorists and would-be motorists: That was the job of *The Steering Wheel*: to sell the sizzle of car ownership. Get out there and explore one of the most beautiful, uninhabited places on Earth: Australia and south-east Queensland and northern New South Wales.

While a horse and buggy might take people a dozen miles in a day, the car could take them ten times further. This freedom of travel opened up a whole new vista. It opened up a new industry, the touring motorist, the forerunner of today's grey nomads and those who love getting away from the big smoke.

When Fred Eager gave his stories, accompanied by photographs taken with a Kodak camera to *The Steering Wheel*, he pioneered what we now call lifestyle journalism and marketing. Not that it was all plain sailing.

His exploits attracted attention from the daily press in Brisbane and, in particular Whitey's climbing of Mt Glorious --- the first car to have conquered the mountain.

The *Brisbane Courier* reported, "On Saturday last, an Overland car made a trip which is unique and record-breaking but is of more than usual interest to the general public.

"The car, a rebuilt 1912 model, left Brisbane at 1.20 p.m., driven by Mr F Z Eager, with Mr Chas E Hall as a passenger.

"At 1.45 Samford post office was reached and Mr Geo Stevens added to the passenger list. Picking up Mr A J White at the Samson Vale turnoff the car reached the head of Cedar Creek at 2.30. This point is about 22 miles from the Brisbane GPO."

The men spent the next two hours climbing Mt Glorious by building a road of their own.

"There were stumps to cut, rocks to move, etc," Eager told the *Courier*.

"At 4.30pm, the car and party reached 'Gentle Breeze,' the home of Mr Thos Lindsay, on the summit of Mr Glorious (at one time called Cedar Mountain).

Gentle Breeze stands at an elevation of between 2200 and 2300 feet, or approximately 350 feet higher than Toowoomba."

Eager described the views as 'quite beyond description', with Mt Glorious rising above the entire range, except for one peak, thought to be Mt Samson.

"The panorama includes all of Moreton Bay, Brisbane, Tambourine (sic) the McPherson Range, the Liverpool Range, Cunningham's Gap, the Mistake Mountains, Lowood, Fernvale and the Brisbane Valley."

Fred Eager was excited and enthusiastic about the trip. Here was one of the best views possible within a short drive of Brisbane. All it needs was a good road to be put in, and the entire city could share what he had found.

"A good road up Mt Glorious means that a better climate than that of Toowoomba, and the finest scenery in Queensland will be accessible to all, and just under 30 miles from the GPO."

Eager said authorities should build a graded road, and EG Eager & Son would help pay for it and 'intend to do their best to have a road put through.'

"The present track is good for most of the way," he said.

"We venture to predict that within the near future, more motor cars will go over this road than to any other point near Brisbane and that Mount Glorious will take its natural place as Brisbane's summer resort."

It was an innocuous story. But not everyone believed it.

In the August 1916 edition of *The Steering Wheel*, there was a full-page story on Fred Eager's conquest of Mt Glorious, naming 11 people who witnessed the event.

"I have given you full details of my recent trip for a good reason," he said. "During the past three weeks, three gentlemen have called on me for the evident purpose of proving to me, and themselves, that a car can't reach Gentle Breeze and that, therefore, I had not made the trip.

"I am afraid that at least two of these gentlemen went away unconvinced. I have now supplied you with the names of 11 witnesses, any of whom will be willing to answer questions for doubters."

Eager believed those behind a failed attempt were trying to undermine his credibility.

"I have only heard of one other attempt to scale Mount Glorious in a motor car. I am told that a party camped at the bottom on Saturday night, July 24th, intending to do the climb on Sunday.

"The rain, which caught us at the summit, dampened their spirits and, abandoning the project, they started to return. When we were returning on Sunday evening, we saw traces of their struggles on the hills along Cedar Creek, and we were told that they finally were ingloriously pulled out by horses.

"A few of us are still working quietly for a good Mount Glorious road and think ultimate success is sure. Mr Thos Lindsay has already started work on the upper part of the road and is making a half-mile of new cutting to reduce the gradient.

"Yours for more touring and better roads," F Z Eager.

Fred Eager's high media profile led to what is now called the tall poppy syndrome. That three men would individually confront Eager, basically calling him a liar, reeks of an organised campaign against him. His exploration exploits with Whitey: Spicers Gap and now Mt.Glorious triggered responses out of proportion with what he achieved. In both instances, he had photographic evidence, and witnesses including those who were with him when Whitey graced the summits. He publicly named who witnessed the deeds. Yet, some questioned and belittled the achievements.

Eager's response was to name his witnesses and invite detractors to contact them for confirmation. He also believed so firmly in the need for a road to Mt Glorious he would put money from EG Eager & Son into a roadworks program to open up the mountain to all motorists and motorcyclists. Mt Glorious is a highlight of Brisbane: it is to the tropical capital what the Dandenongs are to Melbourne, even down to the magnificent rainforests and steep, winding roads.

While the serious business of developing Queensland's roads for improved interstate touring and local day trips high on the agenda, the business of competitive hill climbing was about to be taken to a new level in Queensland.

Goodyear tyre ad for 'Whitey'.

16

Battle lines drawn

When ex-Victorian driver Alec Jewell was nominated to steer the Stude-baker Six over the dusty One Tree Hill track in October 1916, all friend-ly-rivalry signs disappeared.

It was CCM v Eagers, Studebaker v Willys, AV Dodwell v Edward Eager and Alec Jewell v Fred Eager. The stakes soared several notches -- the highest ever with two modified Queensland cars vying for bragging rights. Much had changed since the One Tree Hill event in March 1916. Although AV Dodwell's Studebaker Six had performed well at the hill-climb, Fred Eager took the chequered flag and was streets ahead of the standard Studebaker Six.

Dodwell was as competitive as any Brisbane dealer, perhaps more than most, and the loss had stung him. He, like the Eagers, had learned a lot as a result of the Hamilton Hill Climb. But he too, was still to come to terms with developing a speedster. When Alec Fraser Jewell joined the CCM ranks as a salesman in mid-1916, that all changed.

After Jewell joined the company, the stars began to align. Dodwell now had a driver, but the Studebaker Six needed special treatment, like Edkins' Vauxhall and his nemesis, Fred Eager's Whitey. The Stude-baker was a big, heavy car compared to the nimble Overland. The CCM mechanics and body shop got to work, closely watched by Dodwell and Jewell. Most likely working on the vehicle were Mr B H Bohrdt, CCM's foreman mechanic and Mr Jack Walsh, tuner and tester, and no slouch behind the wheel.

Dodwell knew something that only Studebaker importers were aware of in Australia. From 1915 Studebaker in South Bend, Indiana, had a new president, Albert Russel Erskine. Erskine brought down a firm policy moving forward: Studebaker had a six cylinder-only policy. As far as Dodwell was concerned it meant the end of 4-cylinder cars and it was in his own best interests to do everything in his power to promote the new six-cylinder Studebaker cars. This explains why Australian Studebaker dealers were entering the 'six' into competitions and setting intercity records. The Studebaker Six was THE future for Studebaker, worldwide. It could not be seen to fail and had to win motorsport events at all cost. The company's future depended on sales success early in the life of the Six.

Boyd Edkins was unable to make the October 1916 hill climb. *The Steering Wheel* reported: "...but the interest which is usually excited by his appearance in the Queensland Club's competitions was merely transferred to Mr Alec Jewell, who is a redoubtable performer from the Automobile Club of Victoria and connected with the CCM in this State.

"When Mr Jewell's entry was announced, it was forecast at once that a great contest would ensue. Last May Mr F Z Eager was comfortably faster than the next best, so Mr Jewell's appearance created an interest in the speed contest which might otherwise have been less keen.

"As one spectator put it, Mr Jewell 'made' the contest. His welcome from the crowd and fine driving gives rise to thoughts of a Queensland team to the South when competitions are revived in the other States."

As usual, two events were contested: One for private member's cars and the other open to the trade and private owners.

In the lead-up to the Saturday, October event, One Tree Hill was open several days for practice. AV Dodwell took no chances and gave Alec Jewell all the time needed to prepare for the event. Jewell used it wisely. He took advantage of the time to familiarise himself with the car and track and sort out any bugs in the Studey.

For Jewell and Dodwell, a great deal rode on this event. It was a greater risk for CCM than Eagers. CCM was doing everything possible to promote the Studebaker Six, in light of the Willys Knight arrival at Eagers. Racing against the four-cylinder Whitey would have no consequences for the Knight but would for Studebaker Six sales if it lost. The hill climb was about six cylinders versus four, with CCM anxious to prove the Six - if it could beat the reigning One Tree Hill champion, then Win on Sunday, Sell on Monday, would look after itself.

Dodwell was adamant six-cylinder engines were the future of the motor industry. In the Brisbane market, the Studebaker Six would get a mighty edge over the Willys Knight Six - the closest rival to the Studebaker Six. He was not alone. Studebaker agencies in every State were heavily pushing advertisements for the Studey Six. The order had come down from the top, from HQ in South Bend, Indiana.

Fred Eager's record time of 2 mins 43 2/5 seconds from the May hill-climb was the time to beat. In the lead-up to the hill-climb, rumours were flying about that Alec Jewell in an early morning trial had clipped no-less than 13 seconds off Fred Eager's time. After this, talk gripped the punters that Fred Eager lowered his previous best in two runs, first by 11 seconds and then by 12 seconds. Next whisper was that Alec Jewell had reduced the time by still another five seconds, bringing his time into the vicinity of 2 mins 25 seconds. Early Friday morning Fred Eager went out and blitzed the track in 2 mins 29 3/5 seconds.

A third contender emerged, a stripped-down Buick Six, piloted by Albert Harrington, who beat Fred Eager's time in practice at the May hill-climb, It was going to be one hell of a meeting. The weather was fine, track dusty and hundreds of people lined the route on Saturday morning. On the big corners, there were new mounds in place to stop cars going over the edge.

At the finish line, the telephone rang urgently:

"Next to start, Alec Jewell, Studebaker Six; next ring will mark his start." The crowd closed in on the cliff overlooking the finish line. Mr AH Ruddle rode with Jewell.

CCM had added bucket seats. The Studey, with doors removed, was as unsafe as a speedster can be, so driver and pilot had makeshift seatbelts.

Jewell wore a racing helmet similar to the type used by Queensland's crack motorcyclists, Power and Lahey. The telephone rang at the finish line and down at the start line Jewell flattened the Studey. Two minutes from the finish line, the Studebaker's engine's deep roar was heard by all those on the hill as it echoed through the trees. A hush came over the crowd.

As the Studebaker appeared, a Hudson Super Six suddenly backed onto the roadway at right angles. It had been parked temporarily at the foot of the final uphill stretch.

It was a disaster in the making. A huge crowd roar went up, the Hudson stopped. It appeared to be blocking the way and Alec Jewell was at full tilt. He had a fence on his left with a steep hill below, the Hudson's back end on his right, barely enough room to get through if he skirted the fence. Just inches in it.

"Someone on the hill who knew his man was heard to exclaim, 'He'll never put his brakes on,' -- nor did he," reported *The Steering Wheel*.

Jewell held his nerve - and the pedal to the metal - and, in an astonishing feat of driving, shot through the tight opening and thundered across the finish line 'at a tremendous bat'. His time, a record: 2 minutes 25 1/5 seconds or 18 seconds better than Fred Eager's best in May. The 18 seconds represented 350 yards in distance.

Alec Jewell had only driven the road four or five times in practice. Any lingering doubts of his driving prowess were gone. If there were two emotions apparent, it would have been a satisfied, but relieved, look on the face of CCM's AV Dodwell, and concern from Fred Eager.

Excitement was running high. Eager's best run was 2.29 3/5 sec. And most onlookers did not think he could improve this time. But some still had faith in the bespectacled former bank clerk.

"Someone else forecasted that if the car could hold together, and to the road, its driver would do it," reported *The Steering Wheel*. Eager would have to wait a while. Walter Trevethan's Chevrolet was next and came up in 3 minutes 20 2/5 seconds, 22 seconds faster than his previous outing.

Brisbane drivers were showing with a little practice they could significantly improve their times. Mr MA Green's Swift, driven by Mr F Barnes, was next and returned a time of 3.48 1/5 seconds. As the dust settled on top of the mountain, the finishing line telephone rang.

"FZ Eager, Overland," came a voice relayed from the foot of the hill. A few seconds later, the telephone rang sharply, and Fred Eager was on his way. The timekeeper's thumb went down, and the battle was on. If the One Tree Hill record was to remain his, Eager had to better his best practice time by 4 1/2 seconds.

Mr. Alec Jewell (Studebaker), runner-up on time, 2 mins. 25 1/5 seconds.

Mr. F. Z. Eager (Overland), winner on time, 2 mins. 21 1/5 seconds.

'Whitey' wins again at One Tree Hill.

"To get the full interest of a climb on the snake line course up One Tree Hill one would want to be above in an aeroplane for at no point on the hill can you follow the course more than two or three hundred yards," stated *The Steering Wheel*. All of Whitey's balance and Fred Eager's newly found talent for driving would be put to the test.

"One official photographer declared that Mr Eager swept round one of the turns at such a bat that the back of the car fled across to the far embankment, but the mountain brought it into line again, and the race went on.

"At a few seconds after two minutes, the car came into view between the trees and opinions at the finish were evenly divided as to whether he would do it.

"At 2.21 1/5, the car flashed past the flag, and it was minutes before the crowd's excitement cooled. The speed was an average 42 miles per hour uphill, with 22 2/5 seconds cut off last year's record.

Fred Eager's mechanic, Wally Webb, was in the passenger's pew. "The wildest ride of my life," he excitedly told the crowd which surged towards the car. Eager finished four seconds ahead of Alec Jewell in CCM's Studebaker. It was a crushing blow to AV Dodwell's hopes for positive local publicity for the Studebaker Six. He had not yet opened the champagne, but it was on ice. There would be no celebrations at CCM.

For AV Dodwell the result was pure frustration: he'd recruited the best driver available. He'd poured whatever money needed into the Studebaker. And it still was not enough. "Bloody Yank!," he cursed.

Dodwell cringed when he thought of what ads might appear in the *Brisbane Courier* and *The Steering Wheel*.

To beat a stock-standard Studebaker was one thing. To defeat one prepared for a hill climb -- Brisbane's most significant to date -- was another. Dodwell's pessimism about the fall-out was not let down when *The Steering Wheel* hit the streets.

'A DECISIVE VICTORY'

Eager did not mention Studebaker or Buick.

AV Dodwell and CCM took Eager to task in a *Brisbane Courier* on October 27. Days of our Drives was about to get dirty.

"You can't drive a nail home with one blow of the hammer. You've got to hit it fair and again. "Likewise, one good performance of a car doesn't create a decisive conviction in the mind of the buyer; it only awakens his curiosity to see if it will do as well next time.

"STUDEBAKER CARS have followed up every big record established with another, proving that not a 'happy chance' but consistently increasing Efficiency and Improvement unfailingly maintained, give the only trustworthy guarantee of the permanent presence of Quality and Reliable Service. STUDEBAKER Cars have broken every standing record they've ever attempted.

1913 model broke the WELLINGTON to TAUPO, N.Z. Record.

A 1914 model broke the BRISBANE to TOOWOOMBA Record.

A 1915 model broke the Across Australia Record,

FREMANTLE to SYDNEY. A 1916 model broke the ALBANY to PERTH Record.

The problem with the impressive list of Studebaker achievements was something that was missing. Only one of the records was set locally, and even then it was established in Toowoomba by a Toowoomba dealer-driver after starting in Brisbane.

Also, these were four-cylinder cars. A key to Win on Sunday, Sell on Monday, was people relate more to local news than news from elsewhere. No one knew this better than AV Dodwell. That opportunity was stolen from him by Fred Eager and Whitey.

The *Courier* loved the car industry, especially the advertising revenue, and the on-going sniping helped circulation. It was good for business, which had slackened off since the introduction of *The Steering Wheel*. Fred Eager was furious and took out a large advertisement in the *Courier*.

'Concerning the Overland performance in the latest ACQ Hill Climb.'

'THE GOOD SPORT LOVES A CHEERFUL LOSER' it was headed.

"When you can't win, the next best thing is to lose gracefully.

"It's quite true that 'You can't drive a nail home with one blow of the hammer.'

"It's also true that you have to hit it fair.

"For five years we've been fastening the banner of Supremacy to the highest point on the motor flagpole with the nails of performance and the hammer of publicity.

" Every nail we've used has been a straight one, and every blow has been a fair one. It's now fastened so firmly that it can't be blown down by a gust of conversation, and so high that the futile attempts to reach it remind one of the fox and the grapes." (*The Aesop fable with the moral of the story being … "you often hate what you cannot have."*)

"OVERLAND leads in CONTESTING and WINNING competitions, not in losing and then contesting them."

If the relationship between Dodwell and Eager was on shaky ground before, it was now in tatters. In the past attacks between dealers had been based on sales, performance and equipment. Suddenly, it got personal.

Fred Eager felt the CCM advertisement was a below-the-belt attack, and the use of the word 'fair' implied he cheated. The ad also failed to acknowledge Eager and Whitey won the best time at the ACQ Hill climb just six months earlier. They set the standard against the best competition in the land, Boyd Edkins.

The CCM advertisement revealed just how important winning was to car sales, specifically the Studebaker Six. Any dealer who had a perceived 'edge' would get a direct spin-off. Conversely, second place was also second best. In the end, if CCM had entered a standard Studebaker, as it did in May, it left Eager as fastest time winner with hollow bragging rights. By contesting the hillclimb with a modified car, CCM left itself open to losing and copping the consequences from a rival who was adept at using the 'hammer of publicity' to get his point across to the buying public.

CCM was not only outdriven but out-foxed, by a master of marketing. To rub salt into the CCM wounds, Fred Eager ran the 'Decisive Victory' advertisement a second time in the *Brisbane Mail.*

CCM's decision to invest in a six-cylinder speedster was to counter the latest addition to motorists' shopping wish-list: the Willys Knight Six, a direct threat to Studebaker Six sales. To win the hill climb would have brought credibility to the Studey Six even before Willys Knight sales could get off the ground.

While the Willys Knight was 495 pounds, the Studebaker Six was 470 pounds for the equivalent touring model. An extra 25 pounds was not a lot more for a car with the famed 'Silent' Knight engine. Eagers were not backward in coming forward about who drove a 'Knight' powered car, including His Majesty King George of England, Her Majesty Queen Mary, Her Majesty Queen Alexandra, Czar of Russia, King of Sweden, Emperor of Japan, King of Spain, King Albert of the Belgians, King of Greece, King of Norway, Prince of Wales, Duke of Connaught, and Prince Henry of Battenburg.

For a fraction of the price paid by European Kings and Queens, Australian drivers could become highway royalty. In today's market, the Studebaker Six and Willys Knight would be considered prestige vehicles. In this era, well above Ford's Model T, the car for the masses, and below the European luxury marques Rolls-Royce, Minerva and Mercedes, and the US, Cadillac and Packard.

As such, the Willys Knight was a car for the well-heeled and the extra few quid more than the Studebaker Six, was unlikely to deter buyers. Having the 'Knight' engine also added snob value. Most of the Knight powered Willys cars had six-cylinder engines, although there was a V8 in the 8-88 model sold between 1917-19.

There was a lot more riding on the One Tree Hill hill climb than met the eye. Dodwell was acutely aware of this, and the failure to beat Fred Eager was a dent in his marketing plan for the Studebaker Six and, indeed, all Studebaker sixes into the future. Dodwell and Alec Jewell returned to Adelaide Street to lick their wounds and develop another strategy to put the cocky American in his place.

The pair sat down and discussed how the Studebaker Six handled the hill climb. Jewell told Dodwell the car had the speed, but not the handling of the sprightly Overland. Jewell knew Overlands well - he sold them and drove them in Melbourne. Fred Eager had indeed gone wide on one corner on One Tree Hill, and luckily the oversteer - the tail skidding out - was corrected by an embankment, plus Eager's ability to control a skidding car.

The Studey heavily oversteered on most corners, losing precious seconds. The fact remained this was the Studebaker's first outing while Whitey was in its second year of development by the talented Wally Webb.

In mid-November 1916, AV Dodwell went into damage control. Unable to wait for the next edition of *The Steering Wheel*, called senior management of the *Brisbane Courier*.

He wanted an 'independent' *Courier* journalist to take a ride in the Studebaker Six. Not an off-the-shelf model, but the losing car from the One Tree Hill hill climb. Again, he had a passing shot at Fred Eager and showed how desperate CCM could get in the quest for favourable publicity for the Studebaker Six.

"We have heard that some people are questioning the abilities of the Studebaker Six," he complained. "This is an ordinary stock car of 50hp, 1916 model. It has been lightened for demonstration purposes by removing the touring body, which has been replaced by two low seats for the driver and observer.

"The gears, pistons, and everything is exactly the same as in any stock car made by the Studebaker Corporation and sold by us to customers every day.

"We challenge anyone who questions this to put up 1000 pounds, (more than twice the value of the car) which we will cover with a like amount.

"If all we say in regard to the car is not true we will forfeit the whole amount to the hospitals; they to do the same when we can demonstrate the accuracy of our claim."

This was a direct taunt at Fred Eager.

The *Courier* journalist met Alec Jewell at CCM's headquarters for the road test. AV Dodwell was able to pull this stunt as he had something over the *Courier*: He was a big advertiser. He remained loyal to the *Courier* when most others had not. Other agencies allocated large chunks of advertising money to *The Steering Wheel* and reduced to the *Courier*, accordingly. Dodwell was also a close friend of the *Courier's* chairman.

"Everybody agrees that this is an age of speed and power, remarked Mr Alec Jewell to a *Courier* representative this week as he took the wheel of a Studebaker six-cylinder car, and the Pressman climbed in beside him.

"I want to show you, or any independent observer, that the stock model Studey Six is the greatest proposition in speed and power in Australia today.

"The trip had been arranged at the special request of Mr AV Dodwell, managing director of the Canada Cycle and Motor Agency (Q'land)."

(The above paragraph suggests the journalist was not happy to be given a job where he had to write a favourable report.)

"As our car swung out of the CCM garage, the driver started in second (gear) and changed at once to top gear. Within 100 yards of the exit the short ride in Creek Street, to the railway overbridge, was encountered. And up this, the car travelled at 30 miles per hour, the remarkable response to the slightest touch of the accelerator being at once noticed.

"Travelling via Wickham Street, Gregory Terrace, and Petrie Terrace to the Toowong tram route the car raced over the hills with ease. "From the Toowong Cemetery gates to the road to Mt Coot-tha was taken.

"The observer had frequently driven over the route, and in common with other metropolitan motorists knew all about the problematic jump just beyond the cemetery boundary. This jump where the grinding of gears usually racks the ears of passengers, and where they drop first into second and then into low gears tests the driver's ability on almost any car.

"Mr Jewell sat tight without so much as a move in the direction of the gear lever. His right foot pressed almost imperceptibly on the accelerator and the jump-up successful with the speed index wavering from 28 to 30 miles per hour.

"On the sharp turn into the gate of Mt Coot-tha reserve the driver eased up the car. Up to the summit the car raced at speeds at no stage dropping below 25mph and ran up to 48, the observer was hanging on, with eyes glued to the speedometer.

"The last steep pinch to the top was done at 48 miles per hour, and it was with a breath of relief the Pressman let go the strap beneath the shade of a tree above the kiosk."

The Pressman was not used to being in a car driven at speed and was somewhat in awe of Alec Jewell's driving prowess. He was also aware they drove up to four times over the speed limit - for Alec, old habits died hard.

"The grades, the sharp corners, and the road camber are all against the motorist ascending this hill, and it required some confidence in the driver to avoid a 'nerve storm' as the engine raced up the incline, cleaving the air with a shrill whistle of defiance," he wrote.

This article is interesting, not just for the favourable content, but how it came about. When *The Steering Wheel* launched in late 1914 only one large agency -- Canada Cycle and Motor -- remained entirely loyal to the *Courier*, or put another way, CCM did not want to finance Edward Eager's new motoring magazine.

"Coming down the route to Paddington was taken, and so round to Gregory Terrace and down to Water Street. Then, bringing the car to a standstill at the foot of Hill Street, Mr Jewell raced it to the top of that incline, starting on top gear and keeping at that. The speedometer seemed to jump in a second to 15, then to 25, then to 30 miles per hour is something that every motorist will understand."

(In this era the bane of all drivers was changing gear, so if an engine had enough torque to take on hills without gear changes, it was a significant selling point. Gearboxes in this era were very often crash boxes and challenging to use).

"At no stage on the trip did the driver change gear, though at times the speed on the level was brought down to 5 miles per hour to illustrate the flexibility of the engine."

It was a glowing report that rates at 10/10 for damage control. But, the best was yet to come.

Hidden away at the foot of the story was an announcement by AV Dodwell, interviewed by the pressman after he returned to CCM, and where Dodwell grilled him about the tour he had just completed in the Studey Six.

"In the course of a subsequent chat with Mr Dodwell, he said he was planning another novel test for the 'Stude Six'. The proposal is to establish a motorists' camp on the Main Beach at Southport during the Christmas holidays. The tides during this week will leave a wide stretch of beach about 10 miles in length, very suitable for speed tests. Over this, Mr Jewell will run the 'Stude Six' in an effort to establish new speed records for Australia, and it is anticipated that with some little attention to gearing 100 miles per hour will be reached.

"Mr Dodwell invites others to join the camp and partake in speed contests each afternoon. "Several competitions will also be promoted amongst the motorcyclists. This will be the first camp of its type in Queensland, and probably Australia."

It is not difficult to read between the lines: If the Studebaker could not beat Whitey and Eager in a hill-climb, CCM would try on the flat. Perhaps this idea came from the item on Mr Elvery who pulled out of the hill climb at One Tree Hill, advising his Studebaker Four was geared "more for flat land than hill climbs".

And it laid down the gauntlet to one other vehicle in Queensland that was capable of such high speeds: Fred Eager's Whitey. The prize was Australia's first land speed record, followed immediately by the much sought-after newspaper and magazine coverage.

Mr. F. Z. Eager in the white Overland Speedster shod with the **PERDRIAU 3-RIB TYRES** on which he made his fastest time on Southport Beach at Christmas—81·8 miles p.h
NOTE HOW STRONGLY THE 3 RIBS STAND OUT.
It is noteworthy that these Perdriaus submitted to the severe strains of Racing were standard touring Perdriaus as supplied to every user·

17

Speedsters Paradise

The Southport racetrack: low tide, hard sand, high speed. Plans were under way for the erection of a large marquee, CCM organised food supplies and drew up the invitation list. The camp would last for four days with clients coming and going as they liked, at what is now known as one of the world's finest surfing beaches.

The Steering Wheel reported the event on December 1 . "Hats off, motorists of Queensland, to the Canada Cycle and Motor Agency (Q) Ltd, whose novel and original suggestion for a CCM Camp at Southport during the Christmas holidays marks the establishment of a real institution, the like of which are all too rare in our motor sphere.

"To our knowledge this is the first occasion on which such a function has been attempted in Australia." *The Steering Wheel* then alluded to the strained relationship between CCM and Eagers.

"Although primarily intended to the matter of establishing new speed records for the company's cars and motorcycles, it is hoped the meeting will improve the of purely social relations with the CCM Coy's many friends, patrons and also associates in the motor industry."

Guests had to travel via Meyers Ferry to access Southport beach. Meyers Ferry crossed the Nerang River, close to what we now know as Cavill Avenue, in the heart of the Surfers Paradise CBD.

CCM spared no expense in the camp. Company executives would have their living quarters in large tents, and a chef was in charge of the commissariat.

"The establishment will comprise a self-contained colony where good fellowship and conviviality are promised as a standing dish," reported *The Steering Wheel.*

The camp would be set up by December 23, the Saturday before Christmas, and preliminary racing and testing expected to start on Sunday, December 24, racing against the clock on Christmas Day and Boxing Day.

"It is intended that Mr Jewell's much-discussed Six Cylinder Studebaker, which provided a stock car sensation in the recent ACQ Hill Climb, will be put against the watch, and it is anticipated some 'breath-catching' figures will result. The Indian Motor Cycle 'Chiefs' are expected to contribute their quota to the 'thrill' programme, and they are all riders who are to be depended upon to provide tests worth watching."

In November 1916, the *Courier* finally acknowledged such an industry as the motor trade and appointed their first motoring writer, AJ Leaver. This appointment had everything to do with leakage of the lucrative motoring advertising income from the *Courier* to *The Steering Wheel* since its inception in October 1914.

Mr Leaver also wrote a regular column in *The Steering Wheel* and was highly regarded for his technical knowledge of the automobile -- he owned an independent garage -- and his independence when it came to makes, models and car agencies.

On December 6, Mr Leaver heaped praise on the instigator's foresight of the Southport Speed Trials. "Mr AV Dodwell is to be congratulated upon having hit on the idea of running some speed trials on the beach at Southport during the Christmas holiday," he wrote.

"The afternoon tides will be very favourable, and a good hard beach should be available, particularly if the customary north-easterly breeze prevails during the time. Much trouble has been taken to perfect the arrangements, and something quite spectacular should be provided for those fortunate enough to be present."

"The primary undertaking, I understand, is to establish official records for 1 to 5 miles. Arrangements have been made to ensure the absolute safety of the public, and a horse will be available to get the cars across the stretch of very soft sand to the splendid surface that is provided by that part of the beach, subject to the tides."

A problem facing any contestant was a lack of facilities to test their car leading up to the contest. Not only were the roads abysmal but required a police sanction to push a car above 12mph. Mr Leaver lamented; "At present any testing of a car at a speed of over 12 miles per hour renders one liable to heavy fine, and yet a speed test of a car can hardly be so called if the car is only tested up to a speed of 12 miles."

At the CCM garage mechanics were busy turning the ugly duckling that tackled One Tree Hill into a high-speed racer. "The chassis has been shorn of all outward embellishments, and attachments, such as headlights, mud-guards, footboards and windscreen," reported the *Courier*.

"Speed possibilities increased due to the decrease in weight and the removal of anything that offered resistance to the air.

"The broad, deep Studebaker radiator had been enveloped in a projecting sheet-steel shield reduced to a few inches in width in front, forming a slot through which the air will cool the radiating water. Immediately behind the bonnet, a typical racing body of the lightest sheet metal has been attached."

The transformation was astounding. The bare-bones, squared-off raw street-racer was now an elegant, streamlined torpedo on wheels. It was a no-expense-spared conversion.

"The scuttle-shaped dash cowl extending backwards, protected the various gauges, speedometer, and electrical instruments, which, during every second of the bursts of speed, will telegraph their record of the performance of the engine, lubricating system, charging dynamo, batteries, etc, to the watchful eye of the driver."

"The steering wheel was dropped to a low rake to match the low position of the bucket seats, set low on the floorboards. These seats are two narrow niches for driver and observer. Flush from the radiator to taper tail, the side and top lines sweep out and converge, forming an outline mould, dolphin-like in shape."

"The gradual taper characteristic of racing bodies, from the radiator to a foot or more beyond the back axle line, has its justification in the fact that unless the air split by the racing shell is allowed to come together in smooth streamlines, a following vacuum is formed, which causes wind eddies materially affecting the speed and steering control."

"The wheels on the outside were covered with metallic discs, to offer low resistance, and the whole car has been painted a dull silver."

With the Studebaker Six attracting plenty of press attention, there was little news from the Eager's bunker. No doubt Fred Eager and Wally Webb read the *Courier* reports and prepared Whitey accordingly. The most significant change would have been to the differential with a higher gearing installed, replacing the lower gearing suited to hill-climb work. They would have also discussed wheel and tyre choices at length and prepared several sets to transport to the beach.

Both camps packed up mobile workshops. On December 13, AJ Leaver, writing in the *Courier*, said considerable interest 'is already displayed in regard to the forthcoming CCM speed trials, to take place at the Southport beach at Christmas.'

'The timing is to be done by officials of the (Queensland) Automobile Club, so that results may be properly established.' Mr Leaver then wrote about formulas, in much the same way as hill climbs were run, with a formula winner and the fastest time winner.

In this, he missed the point. Competitors who were out to win were only interested in the fastest time or line honours, no matter who won with what engine. Irrespective of engine size, or modifications made to the cars, the intent was to set new Australian land speed records. And to the winner would go the all-important glory.

"Although not strictly competitive, the times made by the different makes of cars will no doubt be closely followed and criticised by the motoring public, and this criticism should be based upon displacement (ie: cylinder capacity) in relation to the speed attained," wrote Mr Leaver.

"For instance, to compare the actual speed made by a car with a cylinder capacity of, say 400 cubic inches to that attained by another car with only 300 cubic inches or less, without taking into consideration the big difference in power, would be absurd.

"Another factor of course is the actual weight of the cars, and this should be officially checked and vouched for. With these factors at hand, a true value of each individual performance is easily arrived at without difficult calculation."

In mid-December, the first contender came forward against the Studebaker Six. Singer and actor Allen Doone, was in Brisbane playing in 'Geisha' and announced he would enter his 90hp racer, based in Sydney.

He challenged Alec Jewell to an 'actual race on the beach.' Adding spice to the contest was the fact Fred Eager was yet to declare his intentions. No doubt, he was weighing up his options and looking at likely outcomes. If he were to enter and beat the Studebaker, then everything would look after itself. Just like it had after the One Tree Hill hill climb result. But what if he lost? How could he mitigate the impact to control any possible damage to Knight and Overland sales?

The Overland cause got a leg-up with another record across the other side of the vast island that is Australia. A model 83 Overland 'speedster' established a record in Western Australia between Albany and Armadale covering 238 miles in 5 hours 25 minutes, averaging 44 miles per hour.

"This establishes a New Record for Road Racing in Australia -- the best previous average being forty-one and a half miles per hour put up by a car nearly twice as big as the Overland" stated Eagers advertisement on December 21, 1916. "Comment is unnecessary. This new performance establishes the Overland as the Champion Road Racer of Australia."

On the fine, white sands of Southport in a few days, a sleek Studebaker Six would put the Overland name to the test. As news of the Southport speed trials spread there came the inevitable conjecture: what speeds would be obtained? The Brisbane *Daily Mail* explored the theme in their weekly motoring column 'Midweek in Motordom,' under the heading 'How many MPH?

"On Monday and Tuesday next (Christmas Day and Boxing Day) Queensland will be given her first experience of a new sport. As these lines are written, the public interest is hinged a good deal with wonderment. As Australia is concerned, we have not the advantage of precedent to guide us in our attempts to gauge the likely speeds that will be achieved.

"First estimates spoke of a hundred miles an hour, but slightly more moderate figures have been mentioned. One wonders will an estimate of 85 miles per hour be far out when the numbers go up on Monday and Tuesday next."

During the week the *Daily Mail* received a 'wire' from the actor Allen Doone, confirming his competing interest. On top of that, he challenged Alec Jewell to an open contest - his 90 National racer to go head-to-head against the Studebaker Six. Jewell too was wired by Doone and accepted the challenge, saying he "welcomed his appearance and feel confident I can beat him."

Doone's National racer was no stranger to Brisbane. The green '90' National came with the actor two years earlier and was frequently seen around the city. It had a reasonable racing heritage too: Six years earlier, at an average speed of 78mph, it won the Indianapolis 500!

The actor failed to tell everyone in Brisbane the car was 'piled up around a tree some weeks earlier.'

Reading between the lines, Motordom says Doone's car is a wreck and there's no way it would be racing. Doone's wires were simple self-promotion for his show at Her Majesty's Theatre. The *Daily Mail* Motordom editor was also on the ball as to the intentions of Fred Eager.

Newspapers had heard nothing from Eager since AV Dodwell announced the speed trials. It was as if he'd gone to ground. There was good reason for his low profile.

In a letter to Motordom, Eager broke his silence and stating if Whitey could have a mechanical overhaul and a light racing body was ready, he'd be at Southport for the speed trials. Whitey's engine was a 270 square-inch four-cylinder. That's 4.42 litres. For Southport, the engine gained new pushrods, wire wheels fitted along with a new radiator.

"I am told Mr B Bohrdt is co-operating with Mr Jewell in regard to the Studebaker, while Messrs W Webb and and H Rabson are acting similarly in the tuning up of Mr Eager's car," explained Motordom.

There were only two legitimate contenders with just days to go before Christmas. Despite this, there was a high degree of enthusiasm for the event.

Motordom stated Southport beach at low tide was particularly suited to high-speed work and if it established records, 'it is probable that some of the southern cracks may be tempted to come north and try our natural speedway.'

(It is ironic the Surfers Paradise beach where the speed trials took place are just metres away, and parallel to the back straight of what was the Gold Coast Indycar circuit.)

"I understand the distance for Christmas has yet been not decided, though two miles and five miles are mentioned. It would be interesting to have a record of the one-mile time."

Motordom then raised some reality for readers.

"The world's best speeds for this distance have been accomplished by a 300hp Fiat and Blitzer Benz, each of which did slightly better than 140 miles per hour. Some idea of the monster size of the Fiat may be gathered from the fact that the highest point of the bonnet is over 5ft from the ground. 1916 has been a very revel of speed. In the United States, new speedway after new speedway has sprung into existence.

"In the US a car averaged 104mph in a 250-mile circuit. Soon after in a 100-mile test, another car averaged 105mph, in the first 50 miles the pace was 109mph.

Bespoke racers set these speeds, vehicles far in advance of modified standard cars. Interestingly, in 1915 the American Automobile Association capped engine size for speed records attempts at 300 cubic inches (4.9 litres).

"The Indianapolis race of last year was the first race with the reduced engine dimensions and the speeds of the past year are therefore all the more remarkable," stated Motordom.

At a date unknown Fred Eager ordered an experimental V8 Willys Overland sleeve-valve engine. According to David Crisp, from the Willys-Overland Club of Victoria, that engine was an S4R-8 racing version, adapted from the Knight sleeve-valve engine. This motor was publicly available between 1917 and 1919, in the Willys Knight 8-88.

Whitey was possibly fitted with the engine in 1918 as Willys engineers had been developing the powerplant from around 1915. When the V8 arrived Fred Eager called in Wally Webb asking him to strip Whitey down and fit the monster engine. Webb completed the work at the Breakfast Creek workshops, and Fred Eager told Whitey was ready to roll. Legend has it Eager hopped behind the wheel and waited for Wally Webb to take his usual position in the passenger seat. Webb

'Whitey' fitted with the V8 engine in 1918, developed by Willys for
the Indianapolis race.

refused the offer. In testing V8Whitey, Webb found the car now possessed straight-line speed to burn; but cornering was another story.

It did not take Eager long to find out why Webb declined to take a ride. "Wally Webb stated that this made the car go very fast in a straight line but wouldn't go around corners, and since Fred only drove with the accelerator in one position, he scared the ... 'T' out of himself a few times and then ordered the engine removed and the original Overland 4 re-installed," wrote David Crisp.

The story has it Fred Eager took Whitey out for just 20 minutes before making his decision. Luckily, the V8 engine survives (see below) and is owned by Mr Crisp in Melbourne, along with a Willys Knight type radiator fitted by Webb. Both the *Courier* and the *Mail* were giving regular space to the Southport Speed Trials, and along with *The Steering Wheel*, it was the largest concentration of motorsport news ever in Queensland. This publicity set the stage, players primed, their cars overhauled ... all were in anticipation of the first straight-line speed contest in Australian history. Fred Eager must have felt like a moth lured into a spider's web, with CCM the organisers, and the opposition.

18

The Southport Speed Trials

There were no speed records set for those getting to Southport beach to take in Australia's first attempt at land speed records. It was a mini-marathon for many Brisbanites. Most took the train to Southport Railway Station, a block or so north of the Del Plaza Hotel (now Railway Hotel), on Scarborough and Nind Streets, just a few hundred metres north of the Southport CBD. From there it was a four-mile drive by hire car or bus to Meyers Ferry, where they could park vehicles unless they were of the racing variety and needed to cross the Nerang River.

Visitors were not happy that there was so little infrastructure in the sleepy hollow that was Southport in 1916. "I travelled to Southport to see the motor racing on the main beach and was most disagreeably surprised to find the difficulties which were encountered in the reaching of the scene of the events," one spectator told the *Courier*.

"After a four-mile drive from the station in a hired car, of which there seemed to be rather a shortage, it became necessary to cross on 'Meyers Ferry'. Occasionally, I understand two boats were running, but when I crossed there was only the one, and caused a considerable delay on the bank awaiting this boat's arrival.

"Having crossed, there remained possibly a quarter of a mile walk to the beach, the last 200 yards over exceptionally heavy sand. Altogether, the trip from the station to the beach occupied considerable time, and hardly served to put pleasure-seekers into a cheerful temper."

On the beach, the visitor found a local crowd who were not savvy to motorsport's needs; indeed, some were irate 'their' beach was a racetrack.

"Then, again on the beach, where time for the running of events was naturally limited due to the fact tide waits for no man, there appeared to be a considerable delay with spectators wandering on to different points of the beach throughout the course.

"I also noticed a very unsportsmanlike action by a party in a sulky travelling towards Burleigh Heads, who insisted upon driving on the part of the beach used for the racers, cutting it up with hoof marks and wheel tracks. The driver assured the traffic policeman that he was quite within his rights. So he was, but it is an extremely objectionable type of man who declines to waive his rights occasionally for the convenience of others."

This spectator told Southportians if it were to host more speed trials the beach must be temporarily closed for motorsport events: "Thus encouraging a fair run to those who are enthusiastic and public-spirited enough to spend as much money as was spent at the CCM camp.

"There is no doubt the holding of these motor races attracted many people to Southport who would have not been there otherwise. The town is a pleasure resort, and not an industrial centre. But it is not unreasonable to expect the local council to do something for the convenience of patrons, such as those who made the beach a rendezvous at Christmas time."

He recommended council put 100 yards of corduroy (logs laid sideways) across the sandhills near the beach and a large water tank for campers. In 1916, apart from Meyers Ferry, there was little infrastructure in Elston, the original name of Surfers Paradise. Even Meyers Hotel had closed its doors and only the ferry -- the first business enterprise in Surfers Paradise -- remained.

Of Cavill Avenue fame, Jim Cavill was yet to build his first hotel, and the road network consisted of nothing more a few sand tracks connecting back to the ferry and north to MacIntosh Island.

"It is decidedly up to the people of Southport to consider the revision of the transport arrangements between the station and the main beach, and to attend to the two above little matters referred to," he stated.

Although there were shortcomings, around 1000 people flocked to the beach between December 22 and 26. The tides would be best between around 2pm and 4.30pm on Christmas Day and Boxing Day. There would be time for test runs on Sunday afternoon, Christmas Eve. With

Christmas Day falling on Monday the beach was busiest with most businesses closing down on Friday.

Holidaymakers were heading for various Queensland beach resorts to the south on Friday afternoon and Saturday morning. Southport Beach was a well-worn highway for locals commuting between Southport and Burleigh Heads and beaches beyond.

In 1958 this string of magnificent beaches would be named the Gold Coast. In the early part of the 19th century, the beach was the fastest, most comfortable route, to southern shores using a horse and sulky.

While CCM had revealed most of the changes it had made to Alec Jewell's Studebaker speedster, it held back some information. In mid-October, CCM cabled Studebaker Corporation in South Bend asking for a set of six racing pistons and other lightweight parts.

It was public knowledge that Whitey was fitted with similar pistons. Lightweight components allow the engine to rev higher and quicker than a standard motor. There was also a risk. Racing pistons lacked the reliability of standard pistons, designed for speed, not longevity.

By late November the lightweight racing gear failed to arrive from the US. CCM found a local manufacturer and ordered six aluminium pistons to suit the Studebaker Six. These were fitted, ready for the first practice run on Christmas Eve. Alec Jewell fired up the Studebaker and cruised south along the beach, warming the engine and getting the feel of the sand through the steering wheel. As he drove south, he waved to traffic police indicating he was about to make a high-speed run, asking them to clear the beach of spectators, and the troublesome horses and sulkies. There was irony in this: The new clearing away the old.

At his starting point, he turned the car around, to face north. It was a magnificent sight. Most spectators had only seen cars like this in newspaper columns ... they were from the US. It was big and dolphin-like, all curves and smoothness, designed for speed, slipping through the air with little resistance.

Alec Jewell was a happy man. Even the bonnet's front curled back allowing the wind to ride over - not trapped before it, slowing the car. The beach cleared, Jewell started slowly then gunned the car. There were no starting or stopping points, just a clear beach. He raced through

40 miles an hour, then 50 then 60. To Alec Jewell, it felt like the car would keep on accelerating; it was as if it had unlimited power.

Suddenly a deafening explosion came from under the bonnet, loud enough to drown the sound of the car's exhaust and the pounding surf. He glanced down at the speedometer. He was tearing along at 70 miles per hour and took his foot off the accelerator as fast as he put it down a few seconds earlier. He nursed the car past CCM's tent and could see the crowd's cheers had turned to dismay. The engine's roar replaced by a noise not unlike that of an amplified kids' rattle. The car limped back to the service tent where mechanics were already rummaging through the spares box for standard pistons.

Jewell's assault on the Australian land speed record and his chances bettering whatever time Fred Eager could set took a nose dive. He thought of what AV Dodwell would be thinking. Not nice thoughts. His mechanics, BH Bohrdt, the foreman mechanic at CCM, and Jack Walsh, his tuner and tester, discovered one of the six aluminium pistons had given out under strain. No surprise there. The mechanics had no option but to re-fit the original pistons.

Jewell took another risk. To reduce weight the shock absorbers were removed. With flat sand and driving in a straight line, he saw no need to have more than leaf springs tie the body down. Saturday saw the arrival of Fred Eager and Whitey with an entourage of mechanics and Eager's staff. Notably absent was his father, Edward.

Fred Eager had a terrible secret. His father was dying as a result of the Toledo accident. His internal injuries were massive, and it was only due to his stubbornness to keep on living that saw Edward Eager emerge from hospital months after the crash. In late 1916 Edward decided to take an extended working holiday in New Zealand and missed the Southport Speed Trials.

He toured New Zealand with his wife and called in to see Overland agents as they travelled. It was the last hurrah for a man who lived and breathed cars, revered Willys, loved New Zealand and lived for travel and meeting people. It was with heavy heart Fred Eager drove from Brisbane to Southport two days before Christmas. He did not know long his father would last but knew the time clock was ticking ... just like it was on Southport Beach.

Standard three-rib Perdriau tyres dressed Whitey's new wire wheels, bespoke for the speed attempt. Fred had his father's blessing. Business came first. They set up camp away from the CCM marquee. The ACQ were using the same timing method as the One Tree Hill track. A telephone cable was laid above the high-tide mark, the finish line almost opposite Meyers Crossing. As the Sun rose warmly over the Pacific Ocean, it fought to penetrate Christmas Day storm clouds.

Not ideal conditions for racing. Light rain fell on and off during the morning, while breezes from the south-east fanned sea mist across the beach. Ideal conditions would have been a light westerly, with dry sand packed solid below the high-water line. As it was, the light rain kept the sand damp and uncompacted which would create tyre drag. The rubber needs to rid itself of water to reduce drag that slows the car. Any hopes of hitting 100mph were gone, lost in barely visible water.

CCM mechanics worked through the night to replace the Studebaker's lightweight pistons with the originals. The mechanics fired up the engine as the sun rose. Alec Jewell was a big man, heavily framed. Since his days as a champion cyclist, he gained five stone and now tipped the scales at 17 stone 6 pounds.

While there were no roll cages, not even a roll bar behind the driver's seat of either car and was unlikely either driver was strapped in. Jewell started the Studey, which roared back to life with the familiar sound of the big six. He felt reassured and steered south towards Burleigh Heads, as traffic police started to clear the beach.

It was just after 2pm Christmas Day. The ideal racing window was between 2.30 and 4.30, an hour either side of the tide's lowest ebb. Day trippers joined the core of CCM and Eagers guests and the crowd swelled to more than 1000 as Alec Jewell, now just a blur in the distance, turned the Studebaker around about two miles south of the start line. Jewell gave the Studebaker more than enough room to reach top speed as they crossed the start.

Officials from the Automobile Club of Queensland, Messrs W Johns and T Langford Ely, tested the telephone connection by ringing the finish line from the start line. It checked out. All systems go. The first timed attempt was over a half-mile. Jewell accelerated slowly and then changed from second into top gear gunning the Studebaker and raced past the start line at around 80 miles per hour. The starters simultaneously clicked their watches, and the first attempt to set an Australian land speed record was on.

Even the roar of the breakers and waves rolling in was drowned out by the scream of the Studebaker's Six as it revved to its peak in top gear. There was a second, underlying hum ... that of tyres reacting with sand, working hard to push out any water. The crowd gaped in amazement as the sleek machine raced past the CCM marquee at full pelt, Alec Jewell hunched over the steering wheel, his hands making minor steering correc-tions to keep the car on track. In 22 seconds, it was all over. Using time expired from the start and finish lines, his speed was 81¾ miles per hour, the fastest time recorded in Australia.

Jewell slowed, executed a U-turn, and drove back past the audience, as they erupted into applause. It was rare to see a car on the street doing more than 20 miles per hour, even that well above the 12mph speed limit. For some, the sight of a vehicle doing four times that speed was awe-inspiring, if not frightening. For others, it was pure joy. Jewell made history, and they were there to witness it.

The actor Allen Doone, 'Australia's most popular actor', failed to show up with his car and some were disappointed he used the event to promote his current theatre show, 'Happy Go Lucky O'Shea'. Doone, however, was in attendance, taking the trip down with AV Dodwell and Alec Jewell. The only other competitor was Fred Eager. It seemed the small Brisbane motor racing community, based mainly around car dealers, knew the speed trials were little more than a grudge match between CCM and Eagers. They kept away to let them fight it out alone. Even Geo Whatmore with his new white Model T speedster did not bother to enter, not even for the sport, or fun.

Fred Eager's turn arrived. Compared to the Studebaker, Whitey looked more like a streetcar than a race car. There was little attempt at streamlin-ing. On looks alone, the Studebaker won best in show. Fred Eager took Whitey briskly south towards Burleigh Heads and turned the car near the U-turn tracks Jewell created with the Studebaker. He waited as the timekeepers went through their routine, and after a final check, the traffic police waved him away.

Like the Studebaker, Whitey started slowly and built speed, passing the start line at about 80 miles per hour. Without the Studebaker's streamlined styling, the Overland created more wind resistance and made more noise, as it forced its way through the air. The engine roar was also deafening as Fred Eager gave the car everything. Around 300 yards before the finish he crossed a water film that took the edge off his speed. Jewell suffered the same fate. Fred Eager passed the finish line in 23 seconds, a second slower than Jewell.

As he sat in the driver's pew back at the finish line, he was given his time and offered a second run. A quick nod and again Whitey headed south along the beach, past the start, keeping well away from the racing line. His second run was faster, and he passed the finish line in 22 seconds. There was nothing between the two cars.

The committee then asked Alex Jewell if he would like a second run. He accepted and eclipsed his first run by 3/5 of a second at 21 2/5 seconds which was about 84½ miles per hour. Jewell broke the deadlock. To say the large crowd were enthralled would be a vast understatement. They had seen nothing like this. It was a shootout of dramatic proportions. Again, the committee asked Fred Eager if he'd like to try one more time. Once more Whitey cruised south towards Burleigh. His third attempt was gallant but peaked again at 22 seconds.

Alec Jewell set Australia's first land speed record. Jewell was the winner by 3/5ths of a second over the half-mile. At this moment Fred Eager must have realised the Studebaker would also win the one-mile trial unless something untoward happened. He had given Whitey everything in his three attempts. There was nowhere else Eager could go for more speed.

He probably mused that the difference between the two cars was not in the drivers or even the engines. The Studebaker's sleek bodywork was the crucial element between the two vehicles … the 3/5 of a second had come from streamlining. Fred Eager and Wally Webb should have put more work into Whitey's bodywork to give her every chance. They hadn't, and it cost them.

"And at this, the attempts to establish half mile records for Australia rested," reported Richard Cobden, editor of *The Steering Wheel*, a member of the organising committee.

"On the first day's running the beach had proved to be a good deal softer than had been expected, and it was noted the cars at two or three soft patches appeared to lose their speed momentarily. The softest spot was about 300 yards from the finishing line, where there was a slight dip in the beach. This patch was quite wet long after the rest of the beach was firm and dry.

"The roar of the racing cars' exhausts compared with the roar of the breakers was much commented on, and it was rumoured that the squally weather of the second day was Father Neptune's revenge for the way in which he had been outdone."

"In his first two attempts Fred Eager used the Perdriau three-rib tyres, changing to Goodyear cords for his last run. Alec Jewell used Goodyear on the front and Barnett Glass on the rear in his first run, switching to Goodyear all round in his second run," wrote Cobden.

Time and tide wait for no man, so racing was abandoned for the day. That night the CCM guests were treated to a feast of music and food. A Beale piano player tickled the ivories, and when he wasn't playing the Beale, a Brisbane music store supplied a gramophone 'adding greatly to the enjoyment.'

A large dining room in the marquee was in full swing and between 40 and 50 guests at a time sat for meals. At night 30 to 40 people slept in the same space. The next day the weather was again disappointing.

"Boxing Day morning gave evidence of threatening rain, and at about noon the weather began to grow squally," reported *The Steering Wheel*.

"Storm after storm came up from the south-east, rendering driving difficult, and onlooking unpleasant. It was evident that what tests were conducted would have to be done between squalls. The first event listed was an attempt to establish an Australian one-mile record. Mr Jewell traversed the course first in his Studebaker, rolling the distance off in 44 seconds, equivalent to 81¾ miles an hour. Mr Eager followed, taking one second longer, his speed being equivalent to 80 miles an hour."

In a second attempt, Fred Eager clipped 2/5th of a second off his previous time, bringing his average up to 80¾ miles per hour. Alec Jewell then headed off towards Burleigh for his second attempt, 'but the rain set in so heavily that the idea was abandoned.' Jewell took the Studebaker to 60 miles an hour, but with the rain bucketing down, he could not see anything in front of him. Alec Jewell was probably the most adventurous motorist in Australia - given his driving record off the race track - so his decision gives an idea of how dangerous it was.

"The successful attempts, therefore, to establish Australian records for the half mile and one mile stand to the credit of the Studebaker Six," reported Richard Cobden. As Alec Jewell returned to the finish line, Fred Eager hopped from Whitey and was among the first to congratulate him. The win sent AV Dodwell into a spin.

"The wonderful power and running of the Studebaker engine ... convinced CCM that it would be able to show the public that in the present Studebaker (Six) car it had something exceptional, and events proved that its conviction was well founded," he told the *Courier*.

"The only parts used in the trials at Southport not supplied by Studebaker were the crown wheel and pinions, introduced to secure a higher gear ratio, these made in CCM's own workshop. It is doubtful whether any car has previously attained a speed of 85 miles an hour without shock absorbers -- a wonderful tribute to Studebaker springing -- but it was demonstrated in the recent One Tree Hill hill-climb the Studebaker had a wonderful 'roadability', hanging to the road at high speeds and rounding corners in a way which astonished experts.

"Many motorists were emphatic that 80 miles an hour could not be reached, but the fact that just on 85 miles was attained, and this with no chance of trying the car except the day before the contest, showed the wonderful faithful workmanship throughout the car, not in the engine alone, but in every part."

Dodwell said the two days of trials led to intense excitement and could not resist having a parting shot at Eager's Whitey.

"Mr Dodwell points out that a six-cylinder engine is not usually looked upon as a racing engine at all, every test throughout the world, and every record, having been held by a four-cylinder engine, therefore

Mr. F. Z. Eager in action.

Alec Jewell in his Studebaker Six at Southport Beach in 1916.
Fred Eager in his Overland - 'Whitey'.

Mr. A. Jewell on the Southport Beach.

Fred Eager congratulates Alec Jewell on winning the
Southport Speed trials in 1916.

the performance of this Studebaker Six was one which stands out in a remarkable way."

The Southport Speed Trials were a massive success for AV Dodwell and Alec Jewell … the decision to have the trials was a stroke of genius by the pair. They recognised the Studebaker Six, which they had fully committed to as their speedster, was not going to win hill-climbs. It was too big and too heavy to compete with nimble cars like Boyd Edkin's Prince Henry Vauxhall and Fred Eager's Whitey. Jewell would have told Dodwell precisely this when they met to discuss the Studebaker's showing at One Tree Hill.

As part of that discussion, both men canvassed every alternative that would put the Studebaker's attributes to best advantage and get some sort of local credibility. They desperately needed publicity for the Studebaker Six. They would have discussed road racing between Brisbane and Toowoomba and, of course, the Sydney to Brisbane. The time was not right, nor the season, for the Sydney-Brisbane. The wet, and storm season, was already under way.

That led Dodwell and Jewell to think outside the square. Land speed contests had become popular in the US where they used Ormond Beach, Daytona, at low tide. The Europeans too were into speed contests. The Florida beach has hosted the Daytona races annually since 1903. It was a magnificent stretch of sand, 27 miles long and wide as a football field.

More importantly, it was probably the world's flattest racetrack. Daytona-Ormond beach racing often made the columns of Australian newspapers, most likely that information, and the proximity of Southport, gave impetus for the AV Dodwell decision to host a Studebaker-friendly competition. Not that Mr Dodwell said that in as many words.

The choice of a Southport Speed Trials was inspired, out of the left-field, that left most dealers little time to prepare. It was a competition designed to take honours over one other car, Whitey, that had blitzed two ACQ hill-climbs in succession and appeared unbeatable in that form of racing.

CCM urgently needed a peg to hang its hat on. On Wednesday, December 27, the *Courier* reported, 'It is stated that Mr Jewell's time is the fastest officially time speed attained in Australia or any part of the world, with the exception of the Florida Beach, United States.'

While the record captured the headlines across Australian newspapers, *The Steering Wheel*, the Automobile Club of Queensland's official organ, which organised the timing equipment, cast doubts over whether the times established were able to be ratified. It described how the event's timing system worked in a similar way to the One Tree Hill event.

"Had it been practicable, it would have been better to have timed the events by an electrical apparatus, which would start a watch going as the cars crossed the starting line, and stop the watch as the finishing line was passed," commented the magazine's editor Richard Cobden.

"As one of the starters remarked, while the human element enters into it, there is always the possibility of some variation, however slight, from the accurate.

"In all cases the runs were made with the wind behind the machines and the method of timekeeping the same conditions held for all cars and motorcycles, and there was perfect fairness for all. A question has already been raised as to whether the times established, though authentic and official, will be recognised by the established bodies of motoring. It is customary when setting a record to run both with and against the wind and strike an average."

Authentic, officially ratified or not, so far as the contestants were concerned the records were just that: records. Australian speed records. Cause to celebrate, complete with bragging rights; the *Courier* was again about to benefit from Win on Sunday, Sell on Monday. CCM could not wait for Monday and launched its campaign on Wednesday, December 27, to capitalise on the Studebaker's two wins.

A display ad featured a full-length profile image of the Studebaker Six with Alec Jewell at the helm … an image at worst striking, and best magnificent.

The heading was simple:
STUDEBAKER MAKES FASTEST TIME -- AND AN AUSTRALIAN RECORD.

Fred Eager drove Whitey south to Tweed Heads on Tuesday after the rain stopped racing. The speedster went from attempting records to Fred Eager's preferred mode of holiday transport. A keen fisherman, Eager could not wait to head to the open sea in the clear waters off Tweed Heads.

The Steering Wheel, January 1 1917

But first, he had to make a telephone call. The master marketer had a plan. If he had won the speed trial, that would be easy.

However, if he came second, as had happened, he needed to mitigate the damage, to take the edge of any publicity that CCM might capitalise on for Studebaker. So it was that he called his advertising agent late on Boxing Day.

A few days later an advertisement appeared in the *Brisbane Courier*. The below wording took up more than the top half of the display ad, underneath a photograph of a speedster which had an uncanny resemblance to Whitey.

OVERLAND FIRST AGAIN

The devil was in the fine print, and it was an advertisement for a Model 83 Speedster that had set a record between Albany and Armadale in Western Australia. Goodyear Tyres also did Eagers a favour with its ads, splitting the winners into the Studebaker' 6' and Overland' 4' with their respective records, under the heading 'Goodyear Shod Cars Break All Records.

EG Eager & Son also ran a series of ads outlining their take on the Southport Trials.

"The Same Overland that holds the Hill Climbing Championship - a car which is five years old and has covered over 125,000 miles - holds the AUSTRALASIAN SPEED RECORD in its horsepower class - 81.8 miles per hour. The only other greater speed developed by a motor car in Australia - 84.1 per hour - was made by a new six-cylinder car of 20 per cent greater horsepower."

The Eager advertisement did not turn defeat into victory, but it did, in marketing terms, balance the ledger with CCM. Despite AV Dodwell's claiming four-cylinder cars held most speed records, the public still thought of six cylinders as better and faster than four cylinders. Economy, though, was seen as a negative.

CCM advertisements expounded the merits of six cylinders being better than four when marketing the new Studebaker Six. They claimed fewer gaps in the cylinder explosions in a six-cylinder engine; therefore, it ran more smoothly. CCM had also been busy and under the heading: REMARKABLE RECORDS detailed the Studebaker records for the one mile and half-mile at 'almost 82 miles an hour and 85 miles an hour', respectively.

"These new Australian records for a stock chassis were made by the above car -- a 6 cylinder Studebaker at Southport Beach (Q) December 25th and 26th, 1916."

CCM would run advertisements along the same theme in the following weeks under headings such as STUDEBAKER MAKES FASTEST TIME --- AND AN AUSTRALIAN RECORD and STUDEBAKER WINS AGAIN This time in the Australian speed records. The old saying of winners are grinners was evident at CCM. And why not?

Compared to the Studebaker's off-the-shelf chassis, the reference to a 'stock' chassis was a further dig at Whitey's modified platform. However, the real game for CCM – and rightly so – was to give the Studebaker Six as much exposure as possible before the Willys Knight Six's arrival.

The engineer, A J Leaver, writing in the *Courier* on January 3, was in disbelief that only two cars arrived for the contest. He apparently had not followed the latest edition of 'Days of our Drives' and missed the on-going antagonism between Eagers and CCM. Another factor could also have been that it was, after all, Christmas.

"We are all very familiar with the motorist whose car 'has done over 70, old man,' wrote Leaver. "It is surprising what a great number of cars appear to be able to touch racing speeds, yet only two cars availed themselves of the facilities for timing provided by the Automobile Club at Southport," he lamented.

"There are very few touring cars in Queensland fitted with touring bodies and equipment that can exceed 55 miles per hour," he said.

Leaver could not resist having a go at the state of Queensland roads.

"After all, is there any good reason why they should be capable of attaining even so high a speed as 55mph when we have no roads. Every car owner likes to think that his car could hit 60 if only he dared 'let it out,' just as every motor boat owner will tell you that his little ship can do '15 knots'; yet the number of Brisbane motor boats that are capable of making their 12 knots ... can be counted on two hands."

In the same article, he again broached the subject of the two cars. "It is a great pity that only two cars availed themselves of that splendid stretch of beach and the timing and other facilities provided at Southport. There are at least eight well known makes of cars that could have taken part there with a corresponding increase in the interest and the instructive nature of the enterprise."

"As it was, only the Studebaker and the Overland cars ran speed trials. Outwardly, the two cars looked almost like pure racing machines, but this effect was due to the very light racing bodies that had been fitted to them. The chief point of interest to the motor buying public is as to the alterations that had been made from purely stock models in the cars that ran on the beach. I am glad to be able to say that these alterations were very slight. Take the Studebaker. The power unit was standard; it was as to bore and stroke, valves cam shaft, crank shaft and reciprocating parts. It had been fitted with a higher gear ratio than stock, but this was the only radical departure."

"Of course, it had been lightened by cutting step irons and lessening the number of leaves in the front springs. Discs had been fitted to the outside of each road wheel. With these minor alterations, it did the full mile, flying start, in 44 sec. Dead equal to 81.52 miles per hour. I witnessed this official trial, which was run with wind almost abeam, but slightly on the quarter, therefore somewhat in the car's favour."

Leaver then turned to Whitey. "The Overland car was standard stock pattern of its year as to bore and stroke, and it had not been rebored, it had stock pistons, cam shaft, crank shaft, valves and timing gear. It had a stock Overland gear of three to one and had been fitted with a special exhaust manifold and exhaust pipe. A splendid set of shock absorbers had been fitted, and the great utility of these was apparent in the remarkable way that all four wheels held the track; an object lesson to all motorists who desire the ultimate best in tyre economy and power transmission. Thus equipped, the car did the full lime (shortly after the Studebaker trial) in 44 3/5 seconds, equal to 80.68 miles per hour."

Leaver said the Studebaker could have reached higher speeds had it been fitted with shock absorbers, 'which are a quite legitimate device, and really essential at racing speeds.'

The Steering Wheel's front page, January 1, 1917, featured photographs of both cars racing along the beach at top speed. Significantly, the Studebaker appears to have its left rear wheel spinning well above the sand, no doubt giving Alec Jewell the odd heart flutter and the Studebaker losing vital traction.

Leaver's observation that Whitey had stock Overland pistons is also at odds with other reports. Probably the fact remains that both cars had some mechanical variations from stock standard, showroom-variety models. As Leaver points out, most motorists were interested in how standard these cars were to the models they could buy. The closer to stock, the better for publicity for both vehicles. And the more sales 'come Monday'.

AJ Leaver was impressed by what he saw that Christmas and Boxing Day on Southport Beach. "It is fervently hoped that a big official motor carnival will take place at Southport next year," he wrote. "Private enterprise has shown the way and proved that a crowd of spectators would assemble, but such a large meeting as is possible is too big for private effort alone.

"To make such a large carnival a success, strong and effective efforts are necessary for the provision of proper means of motor car access to the truly magnificent beach, a faster working ferry and actual co-operation of every interested person in improving the roads hither."

Leaver also addressed the issue of the method of timing. "The timing system, as provided by the Automobile Club, was good, but not sufficiently free from the possibility of human error for the speeds attained. No one doubts the skill and disinterestedness of those who officiated: but it is probable that a purely electrical device will time the events at the next meeting, wherein the car itself makes and breaks its own contacts at start and finish, thus eliminating the human element entirely."

By rights, the story should end here. CCM and Eagers would return to Brisbane and live happily ever after. Thankfully, that did not happen. The Southport Speed Trials, as impressive as they were, were the entree in a menu that got bigger and better.

19

Sydney-to-Brisbane Record Attempt

WITH New Year out of the way, AV Dodwell and Alec Jewell again sat down to look at opportunities. Both were elated, yet relieved: the gamble to take on Whitey, on terms they set, had come off. There was little time for celebration. Both agreed a follow-up race was a priority – the need to strike while the iron was still sizzling. Dodwell now had a lot more confidence in Alec Jewell. The ex-Victorian contributed not only his driving skill but was forthcoming with ideas for improving the Studebaker's performance and the big-picture decisions for the speedster in 1917.

All of Jewell's knowledge had come to the fore. He was one of the first motorists in Western Australia in 1902, if not earlier. Few people had been around cars that long, let alone driving for most of the intervening period. The Studebaker Six joined in the celebration and was now daubed with the words, "Australian Record Holder 85 miles an hour", on both sides of the bonnet.

At the meeting, both men took a fancy for a crack at the Sydney-Brisbane record, a time trial that would become a pinnacle event of all the Australian inter-city challenges in the next decade. They both knew it would not be easy: the wet season was already under way across Queensland and dipping well into New South Wales, between Sydney and the Queensland border.

The first attempt at the Sydney-Brisbane record was in 1912, and the time still stood. Ironically, it was set by CCM's then tuner and tester, Andrew Lang, in a 12hp Talbot. At the time, CCM was under the control of A Wynyard-Joss. AV Dodwell did not take the reins at CCM until 1913 and would have been aware of the Talbot record. The decision made by

Sydneysiders turned out in force to take a look at Australia's fastest car.

AV Dodwell to mount a challenge to the Sydney-Brisbane record meant a lot of work had to be done in a short time. They set an attempt date of January 20 – less than three weeks away.

The Studebaker had to shed its sleek skin and return to a practical touring car body. Preparation for speed trial was one thing – getting everything in order with the vehicle and then adding in spares for every possible contingency was another. Plus, they needed detailed route directions, as there were still few signs to bring them back to Brisbane – a distance of 677 miles. They would attempt to drive in one stint - stopping only for bathroom breaks and quick feeds. J Walsh, who helped prepare the Studebaker for the Southport trials, became Alec Jewell's co-driver/navigator.

They made a formidable team for what was nothing less than a long-distance sprint on public roads. If that sounds familiar, it should. The Sydney-to-Brisbane time trial, in particular, was a forerunner to Australia's greatest race on our most amazing circuit, Bathurst. Even the distance 600-odd miles was similar. And, when races started at Bathurst in 1938 the circuit was also an unmade road, called the Mount Panorama Scenic Drive.

Jewell and Walsh had to get to Sydney in the first place, ideally, along the reverse route they would follow, to gain as much route knowledge as possible. The record set by the 12hp Talbot was 36 hours and 50 minutes. Jewell decided not to take the Cunningham's Gap route that he already knew well, instead opting to go via Lismore, south-west of the Gold Coast.

As CCM's salesman responsible for New South Wales's Northern Rivers area, Jewell knew this region well. The trip to Sydney was uneventful, but for picking up a passenger in Lismore. It was an emergency, and Alec Jewell immediately came to the man's aid. The distraught gent received a wire that day to urgently go to Sydney, as his sister was on her death bed. The fastest way was to get there was via Tenterfield, on the Brisbane Express train. There was no time to spare.

The Studebaker arrived in Lismore, and Alec Jewell was more than happy to assist. It must have been a tight squeeze with three of them in the tiny, open cabin. One wonders if the Lismore resident had known of Alec's driving record, whether he would accept the lift! All he knew though was scrawled across the bonnet, which told him this was the fastest car in Australia.

Departing Lismore at 1.55pm in a cloud of dust they headed for Casino, 20 miles away and arrived in 30 minutes, meaning an average 40mph. Alec was not wasting time and roaring past Drake to Tabulam, up the range to Tenterfield at 5.40pm, just in time to catch the train. Alec's driving did not go unnoticed.

The *Daily Mail* Casino correspondent filed a report that several people along the route complained to police about the car's speed, but "as officers were aware of the mission, the misguided ones received little satisfaction." For once, the cops were on Alec's side. He would have grinned at the irony … no one in this part of the world knew of his Melbourne motoring misadventures, including the boys in uniform.

Sydneysiders turned out in force to take a look at Australia's fastest car and farewell it on another record-breaking attempt. News photographers swarmed around the Studebaker surrounded by a sea of people, hundreds of them, all keen to see the car in all its glory.

The transformation from the sleek, dolphin-like speed machine on Southport beach to inter-city racer could not have been more stark. The nose cone was gone revealing the radiator and a curved steel bar, attached to the chassis, rose up and then across the front of the radiator and down the other side. It was stabilised with three struts, stopping it from being pushed back onto the radiator. On the steel bar were mounted three massive headlamps - each about a foot across. There would be a lot of night driving after leaving Sydney.

Departing Sydney - where the harbour bridge was still just a dream - at around 3pm, the night ahead would be long and dark. There were no street lamps on this route. Behind the two seats was a flat, open deck now covered in gear, including several sets of wheel chains if the so-called roads turned to mud. Jewell was thrilled with the Sydney send-off, and the first 170 miles greeted the car and crew with beautiful weather. They reached Singleton in five hours, after river crossings requiring two punts. The roads to Muswellbrook were firm and flat, and they maintained 35mph for most of the way. It was then the rot set in: Rain.

Roads turned to mud, and the rain seemed to follow them for the rest of the trip. As a roadster, there was no passenger protection, apart from their clothes and wide-brim felt hats. They wanted to reach Armidale by 3am, but 10 miles short, at 2am they found a traction engine had broken through the bridge and was jammed in the timber. Traction engines are heavy pieces of machinery often steam-powered. There was no room for the car to squeeze past and the heavy machine would not be going anywhere for some time.

"We wasted one-and-a-half hours there trying to find a track through the paddocks or any way to get on the road again ... but it was impossible," Jewell later told *The Steering Wheel*. "This creek must have been anything up to six feet deep and forty or fifty feet wide. Talk about looping the loop, why it was nothing to Walsh's drive through the creek. We carried an electric torch with us, which I held in advance to show him where to make for."

Walsh drove the Studebaker back to get a decent run-up. They wasted far too much time, and the only option to continue the attempt was a high-speed running leap at the creek. It was an almighty risk.

"He took a run of fully a quarter of a mile and landed on the other side," said Jewell in *The Steering Wheel*. "How he got it over we don't know, but he did it, and we don't want to do it again."

They reached Armidale at 4.25am and took a one hour break. They filled the main fuel tank and portable tanks. From Armidale, the road was sloshy to Glen Innes, Tenterfield and Wilson's Downfall. Now 10.45am, and they had worn out three sets of chains on the rear wheels. By 12.30 they were coming into Warwick, a 40-mile trip, and the Queensland town gave them a great reception.

Jewell gave high praise to Dave Ezzy, a good mate of Fred Eager's, and the local Willys dealer.

"I cannot speak too highly of Mr D Ezzy and the manner in which he treated us," said Jewell in *The Steering Wheel*. "He certainly had everything that would warm or cheer a man up for the rest of the journey."

Someone, probably Dave Ezzy, strongly advised the pair against continuing the trip – the road ahead over Cunningham's Gap and down into the black soil country was pure hell.

"As we were on the road, and while the wheels would turn … we meant to keep going," said Jewell. The comment says everything about Jewell's determination. He had his faults, many of them, but quitting was not one of them. As a champion cyclist, he had a never-say-die attitude. He was the scratch marker that had, against all odds, won a classic road race in Western Australia. That effort was etched into West Australia's cycling folklore. Jewell had the guts to keep going, no matter what lay ahead. It was just 100 miles to the finish line, Brisbane's General Post Office. In the dry, they could do in three to four hours.

It took 11 hours of torturous driving. "When we tell you that the engine had not stopped and that we went side-on and any old way to get here, you will know what we went through from the bottom of the Gap to Ipswich. We drove the whole distance in first gear, and many times our wheels were wider (than the tyres) with the mud and the clay they dragged off the road."

They arrived in Brisbane at 11.15pm. The car was barely recognisable. Several inches of mud covered the bonnet, and both men, dressed in over-coats, were inch-deep in mud-spatter. Signage proclaiming the South-port records was under clods of dirt, and the rear wheels still wearing the chains that got them home. Even at this time of night, the people of Brisbane came out to welcome the heroes. They knew what it had taken to get this far. They also knew Alec Jewell and co-driver J Walsh had just broken the Sydney-Brisbane record by 4 hours and 32 minutes. Their demanding mud-caked journey of hard-labour took 32 hours and 18 minutes. Similar weather and road conditions also hampered Lang's Talbot record.

Once again, AV Dodwell could smile. The record received massive publicity across Australia for the Studebaker Six and Jewell and Walsh. Coming as it did on the eve of the new Willys Knight Six's release, the timing could not have been better.

The record was short-lived as in June 1917 the legendary driver, Francis Birtles, steering a Maxwell, reduced the time to 29 hours, and 25 minutes. This did not matter as CCM had more advertising hooks to hang the Studebaker Six's hat on for months to come.

Records are made to be broken, and there were plenty of speedsters waiting in the wings to challenge Birtles time.

Fred Eager read Jewell's account in *The Steering Wheel*, taking on board the poor conditions, the time and month of departure, the gear needed to get out of trouble and other snippets that might come in useful.

Sometime after this and before June 1918, the relationship between AV Dodwell and Alec Jewell appears to have fractured. He would never again step into the driver's pew of a CCM Studebaker Six speedster for racing.

SYDNEY-BRISBANE RECORD
Studebaker covers 677 Miles in 32¼ Hours.
LATTER HALF OF ROUTE A MUD-FIELD.

Mr. A. Jewell and his recently acquired interest in the soil.

20

The end of an era

The long journey started on June 18, 1917. Edward G Eager was 53 when he passed. A young man. He fell ill in Sydney after returning to Australia from his six-month tour of New Zealand. It was supposed to be a holiday, but he visited Willys dealerships in between sight-seeing. It was ironic that the industry he loved, nurtured and developed was responsible for his early death.

Two years earlier he was seriously injured in a car crash in Toledo while testing a Willys car. He spent months in hospital, but never fully recovered from internal injuries. The New Zealand trip - a country he loved dearly - was his swansong. He was the super salesman, even on his holiday he took his order book, and Willys 1917 New Zealand sales doubled that of 1916.

Returning to Brisbane from Sydney he did not last long. Enough time to say his farewells to Fred, along with any advice on how to run the company he founded just six years earlier. He lived a good life, an honest life and was known as a 'white man'. That's not a racist term but refers to purity. He was a damn good bloke. At work, behind his back, the young male staff called him 'Dad'. He knew it and liked it. He was a father figure - someone to look up to. He earned respect, never demanded it.

In his old office in Adelaide Street, above his desk, hung a card. It was his mantra for life: "And when the Great Scorer comes to write against your name, he'll write, not that you won or lost, but how you played the game." In football parlance, Edward Eager was a hard man, but a fair one.

The Steering Wheel carried a two-page obituary to Mr Eager, individually written by Richard Cobden and RS Maynard.

"Queensland, and particularly motoring, is poorer for the loss of Mr Eager. Many in this city - and some beyond - have had to stand by to see a best friend go. Charities will miss him. His generosity to these, and to patriotic appeals never failed, and was always anonymous," wrote Cobden.

"Scarcely a dozen people know that one of the biggest patriotic gifts that has gone from Brisbane was one for which the Commandant thanked Mr Eager privately in his little office in Adelaide Street. He never paraded his generosity, and he was a difficult man to thank for kindness shown."

RS Maynard knew Edward Eager better than most.

"He was a lovable fellow - one of those who live in the hearts of their business associates, and such men are rare these days. With him there was always room for laughter and good fellowship in business. His sense of humour was as large as his sense of honour," wrote Maynard.

"Sometimes he tried hard to be the stern businessman with the darkened brow, but he was never successful at that role; he preferred to play the part of the fellow worker when he was in touch with the men in his big business."

The company he founded, EG Eager & Son Limited is still a registered company under the parent firm, Eagers Automotive. In 2020 the company had sales revenue of $5.8 billion and employed more than 8000 staff.

21

To race or Not to race

Motorsport has always been divisive. It is dangerous, sometimes fatal for contestants, pit crews and onlookers. It is also responsible for the development and improvement of many of the safety innovations in automobiles. Racing provides one of the great buzzes in life for those involved. In today's purified, politically correct world, it is a sport not all that far removed from Roman days' chariot contests.

The risks are high. In pursuit of fame and fortune, drivers lose their lives. They race chariots of dreams. For winners, the benefits are many. The sport gives comfort to many people in times of high stress: wars, pandemics, bushfires and floods, to name a few. The holding of sporting events while 'our boys' were dying on the other side of the world, to some people, understandably, seemed improper.

The Automobile Club of Western Australia did not believe contests such as 'sporting events' or 'trade hill climbs' or 'reliability trials' were needed in a time of war. Some clubs felt otherwise, and even within the ACWA in mid-1917, there were voices with the opinion the club should not 'drive sport altogether from the land.'

The ultimate test was to stage an event and see if the people wanted it. Were they prepared to enjoy themselves while across the seas our lads were bleeding to death in the trenches of France? War news dominated Australian newspapers -- with long lists of dead and injured from every state -- Australians needed some respite from the horror of losing loved ones. Sport - not just motorsport - provided that escape. It gave hope to the future - some sense of normality - even for only a few hours.

There was no more exciting contest than the relatively new sport of hill-climbs.

"Whether these hill climbs should be held during the war is a question that has been very fully thought out by the officers of the club (ACQ) ," wrote Richard Cobden in *The Steering Wheel*.

"One great value lies in the undoubted influence they have in drawing the attention of motorists to the club and thus assisting in the effort to secure a tremendous numerical membership.

"That this influence is genuine, is shown after each of the more important club fixtures, there is an acceleration in the number of applicants for membership received.

"The main objection to which expression has been given is that, while petrol is scarce, such contests should be discouraged."

It was against this vexed background the ACQ Hill Climb went ahead on June 15, 1918, six months before the war ended. Around 2000 spectators gathered on One Tree Hill for the third running at that location. Crowd numbers backed the ACQ's decision to go ahead, although no doubt some others would have frowned on the event. Many people wanted distractions to return some normality in their lives. There was a feeling of, "When will this bloody war end!" (Much the same could as in 2020-21, during the COVID-19 pandemic with football codes forming isolation bubbles to enable games to proceed - without public attendance, but with TV coverage).

Onlookers clambered to the top of One Tree Hill, overlooking the finish line, where there was an elevated paddock: nature's grandstand, similar, but smaller, to that at Bathurst's Mt Panorama circuit, Australia's world-famous racetrack. There were around 200 cars parked beside dusty One Tree Hill Road. They were looking forward to something special. For a few hours, it was if the war did not exist.

Australia's fastest car, AV Dodwell's Studebaker Six, would battle with Fred Eager's Whitey. However, the partnerships between driver and car would this time be different. Jack Walsh, the driving partner of Alec Jewell in the record-breaking Sydney-Brisbane run in January 1917, was steering the Studebaker. Walsh also helped prepare the Studey for the successful assault on the Australian land speed record at Southport. Adding spice to the contest was the legendary Boyd Edkins' appearance, a one-man magnet for hill-climbs. If you wanted a bumper crowd, get Boyd Edkins and his Vauxhall.

Boyd Edkins was unable to bring his Prince Henry 25hp but borrowed another Vauxhall from fellow Sydneysider, Mr Ronald Beale, with whom he had driven north for the competition. This change added even more intrigue as this Vauxhall was an unknown in Queensland.

Since the 1917 event, organisers had improved the track, the dangerous corners now banked, the job done correctly with watering and steam-rollering, to harden the surface. The cambering would ensure faster, and safer, cornering times. At the faster drivers' request - Eager, Walsh and Edkins - the track was shortened by about 30 yards at the finish line. With record speeds expected, drivers passing the finishing line h ad t o contend with an immediate sharp left turn. It was potentially dangerous. This shortening was expected to the lower the race times of the faster cars by around 1.5 seconds.

Private owners' class was first away; however, the four entrants in the open class wanted to see what wear or damage had been done to the track by this earlier class before the fast cars had their turn. As the private racers' heartbeats pumped hard down on the start line, Messrs Eager, Walsh, Edkins and Mr T Reed, driving a Willys Knight, drove sedately to the top. Fred Eager was now managing director of EG Eager & Son after his father's death.

The wait at the top was an opportunity for the speedsters to play spectator before returning to the start line. The Willys Knight was not out to break the One Tree Hill record. It was the car's first public outing since it went on sale in Australia.

"The avowed object in entering this car was to show that it would travel the whole course on top gear under three minutes," stated *The Steering Wheel*.

The purpose was to counter claims about arch-rival, the Studebaker Six, that it had gone up the hill in top gear in standard form, with a reporter aboard from the *Brisbane Courier*. Fred Eager had a long memory. It was a gushing report that irked Eager, and he was keen to set the record straight: Whatever a Studebaker Six could do, a Willys Knight could do as well, or better.

As the faster drivers sat on the grass-covered hill overlooking the finish line, the private owners' race started. The first run was by Mr HS Matchett, in a six-cylinder Buick.

"The crowd sympathy at the top of the hill was undoubtedly with him when, on coming into sight at the flat below the last rise, his engine was heard to be missing in one cylinder," wrote *The Steering Wheel*.

"Even taking this into consideration, Mr Matchett's run was the first made by a private owner to break the even three minutes."

Matchett's run of 2.55 3/5 caused an immediate impact, bringing the crowd to its toes. If a stock Buick, with one cylinder suffering a miss, driven by an amateur, could break three minutes, what would the real speedsters achieve?

The crowd was abuzz in anticipation. Only five cars entered the private section, and Matchett's time was fast enough to take out the event.

When the last private car crossed the finish line, the speedsters picked themselves off the grass and made their way to the vehicles for the inspection run. There was an audible thrill of excitement from the hill crowd when the engines fired up. There is nothing like the throaty burble of a race car's open exhaust as the engine sparks, and the car roars to life. Whitey was always a crank start, and Wally Webb probably performed this. For onlookers, it was theatre at its best. The Vauxhall, Studebaker, Overland and Willys Knight departed for the start line.

"It was generally recognised that the three cars among which would be found the winner were the Studebaker, the Overland and the Vauxhall," stated *The Steering Wheel*.

The drivers drew for starting places with the Studebaker to start, Willys Knight next, Whitey third and the Vauxhall fourth. Eager was pleased with his draw. There were only two cars ahead of him with little chance of causing too much damage to the track. In the Studebaker, Walsh was also happy with his number one position but had the nervous disadvantage of being first away. He was under pressure to perform. Fred Eager beat the same car with Alec Jewell at the helm in 1916.

F. Z. Eager (Overland), fastest time.

Jack Walsh in his Studebaker before the One Tree
Hill climb in 1918, won by Eager's Overland.

Walsh remembered the newspaper saga that ended with the 'sore loser' tag. Jewell redeemed himself at Southport, and then with the recent Sydney-Brisbane record. But the Studebaker was yet to win a hill climb. Today, 2000 people were waiting to see how it would go, and how he would drive.

All the while, AV Dodwell was looking over his shoulder. No pressure! It was Walsh's first ACQ Hill climb. Last year Alec Jewell recorded 2.25 1/5 seconds. Walsh completed the biggest hurdle of a clean launch from the start and delivered a superb first-up performance. He crossed the finish line in 2 minutes 11 seconds, taking 14 1/5 seconds off Jewell's time.

AV Dodwell was reservedly optimistic. At last, his Studey was in with a chance. Next away was the Willys Knight in the hands of Mr T Reed.

"Mr Reed had just come from Sydney, and at his first drive on One Tree Hill, never having seen the course before, took exactly three minutes," reported *The Steering Wheel*.

"His subsequent practice time was 2.57. He surprised even those who knew him best, by covering the distance in 2.33 on the day of the contest, running in high gear all the way.

"This car now has two fine performances to its credit, having come from Sydney in 23 ½ hours running time a fortnight previously."

Next was Fred Eager. He pushed aside the Willys Knight thrill of success and lined Whitey up on the start line. There was more than just a hill climb at stake. AV Dodwell's Studebaker had taken the honours at Southport, then in the inter-city Sydney-Brisbane record. The car was on a roll, but with a new helmsman. It would be unthinkable if it also took out the ACQ Hill climb. Fred Eager shuddered at the thought of the CCM newspaper advertisements if the Studebaker won. He also had a back-up. If he couldn't pilot Whitey to a win, there was always his mate Boyd Edkins to come.

Fred Eager sat calmly focused on the starter as the call to 'go' resounded and the starter's flag dropped. Whitey raced away, engine screaming in low gear, the car's tyres blowing up dust clouds in its path, shrouding tree leaves in fine, thick dust. At the half-way mark, he was taking corners like never before, letting the rear end swing out only to be corrected by the upward camber of the new mounds, and a slight tweak of the steering wheel. Suddenly an official ran out in front of Whitey, waving him down. It was a false start; timekeepers were not ready when the starter waved his flag.

Fred did a three-point turn and Whitey headed back down the hill. Rather than being annoyed with the timekeepers, he treated the false start as a practice run.

His second start was a repeat of the first. Trackside gossip was Fred Eager's practice times had been at least 10 sec. under last year's record and anticipated he would improve this slightly. Some spectators on the hill voiced the opinion that he had the secret of breaking two minutes flat. Others thought this was over-optimistic.

The 'plomp, plomp' of his open exhaust could be heard a long way off and sent a wave of excitement among those at the finish line. As Whitey roared onto the flat at the summit's foot, it looked possible she could break two minutes. As he flashed across the finish line, the hill crowd went wild. They knew they had witnessed something special. When the officials double-checked their time, it was announced Whitey crossed the line in 2 minutes 4 4/5 seconds, smashing his old record by 16 2/5 seconds.

It was not just the slightly shorter track distance or the banked corners that helped Fred Eager create the time. In preparing Whitey, Wally Webb lightened the car in every possible way. Additionally, Webb did not ride in the car with both men now acutely aware of how critical the power-to-weight ratio could be, particularly in hill climbs. Whitey came in 200lb lighter than 1916. The time meant Eager and Whitey had increased the average speed from 38 miles per hour in 1915 to 42mph in 1916 and now 46mph.

The record time spoke volumes for Fred Eager's improved driving skills. He was thrilled by the record time and cared not that his pal Boyd Edkins might come in faster again. After all, Edkins was his speedster mentor. There was little call for Vauxhall sales in Brisbane. American cars, including the Canadian Model T Ford, were all the go in the Queensland capital and he had great hopes for the Willys Knight. Again, he had beaten the time of arch-rival CCM and its Studebaker Six.

The extra pre-race work put into Whitey had its roots back on the Southport sand. They witnessed the difference the streamlined bodywork made to the Studebaker – a factor that possibly cost Whitey the

188

Australian land speed record. There was, after all, precious little in it. It was a 'what-if result' that hurt Eager and Wally Webb. They knew they could, should, do better in preparing Whitey ... tailoring the car to each event, giving the loyal little Overlander every chance of being first across the line.

Boyd Edkins was ready for his pitch at One Tree Hill.

"Boyd Edkins next starter," came the telephone call from the start line. After the Whitey false-start fiasco the timekeepers were now on the ball. Comment among the crowd was: The next three minutes will decide it!.

"The knowledge that the New South Welshmen had brought with them a car of exceptional merit made the feeling of interstate competition even keener", commented *The Steering Wheel*. The State of Origin on wheels. "It was known that in his practice run Mr Edkins had also clipped 10 sec. from Mr Eager's last year's time, and the latter himself had declared before the contest that it was just a matter of a second or so either way ... and good luck to the man who could pick the winner."

Edkins gave the Vauxhall everything. Those on the hill whispered on exhaust roar alone; the Vauxhall could win with a time under two minutes. The roar of the Vauxhall speedster was in contrast to performance.

"But before he neared the foot of the last slope it could be guessed that Mr Eager would have at least three or four seconds to spare."

"When Mr Edkins passed the line the watches registered 2 min. 10 3/5 sec., a bare 3/5 of a second better than Mr Walsh's run in the Studebaker." The hill climb was a triumph for Fred Eager and Whitey. Not only had he taken the Studebaker to the cleaners, he had whipped his good friend, Boyd Edkins, who happened to be not just Australia's, but probably the world's, premier Vauxhall driver. To be fair to Edkins he was not in his car, the highly regarded 1913 Prince Henry 16/40, he affectionately called 'Fifty Bob'.

Fred Eager won the ACQ Hill climb three years in succession, twice against Edkins and twice against CCM's Studebaker speedster. His only regret was his father Edward was not there to witness the event, and able to tell John North Willys how good his car was on his next trip to Toledo. Eagers took out a full-page advertisement in *The Steering Wheel* to at least tell all Queensland motorists. It was headed:

CONCLUSIVE

"Running against the fastest field and keenest competition ever seen in an A.C.Q. Open To-All Hill-climbing contest, the Overland registered its THIRD successive win, won a 12 months' title to the Automobile Club's Hill-climbing Championship Cup, and established a new and brilliant record for the event.

"A 1912 model, with 140,000 miles of strenuous travel behind it, this OVERLAND easily and conclusively defeated a picked field of local and Southern cars -- most of them later models -- and many of them claiming marked superiority in power."

The One Tree Hill victory proved to Fred Eager that both he and Whitey were up to any task. After five years in the car and 140,000 miles under their belt, whenever Fred stepped into the driver's pew, he felt he and the car were as one. He was more than comfortable. The car was an extension of his ability as a driver, of his determined personality, of his father's single-minded goal of taking Willys to the top in Australia and New Zealand. The fact the car had a nickname said it all for the relation-ship between driver and machine. There were still wrongs that required righting in the battle for not just bragging rights, but company pride.

Fred Eager may have forgiven CCM and AV Dodwell for the hurtful *Brisbane Courier* advertisement after his second win the ACQ Hill climb in 1916. But he had not forgotten. It still irked him, despite his response calling Dodwell a 'poor loser'. He was happy Boyd Edkins and Francis Birtles had since eclipsed the Studebaker's Brisbane-Sydney record. His only regret was that it should have been Whitey that beat the Studebaker's time. There was also another, smaller fish to fry, to help set the record straight: The Brisbane-to-Toowoomba inter-city, held by Studebaker.

22

The Roads to Success

By August 1918, the push for improved main roads had gathered momentum. Those passionate about improving roads formed the Main Roads Improvement Association of Queensland and wrote the draft constitution and rules. They outlined the Association's objectives with the aim to represent the public in their capacity as road users.

The objectives were a blueprint for the Queensland road system we see today. That the organisation was serious about improving the state's roads and knew how to go about it, is undoubted. There is also little doubt the formation of this Association, of which Fred Eager was not a member, had his name written all over it. He was, after all, the master marketer. And this was a marketing exercise. Instead of selling cars, he was selling roads: improved roads.

If Queensland had drivable roads, the more cars would sell. People baulked at buying cars because of the roads' poor state, and the primary objection dealers had to contend with when people were looking at buying their first car. The groundwork laid by Fred Eager was paying dividends in one of the two roads he wanted to be improved, and the beneficiary was the South Coast, now known as the Gold Coast.

The State government granted Coolangatta Shire Council a loan of 1000 pounds to build a five-mile-long road from Currumbin to Coolangatta, on condition that the council raises 750 pounds. "The outcome will be a good road … the amount is practically assured," reported *The Steering Wheel*.

"Great improvements have been made of late in the road from Brisbane to Southport and there is now left the stretch from Southport to Currumbin requiring attention. "At present work time is progressing on this stretch, though there is a tremendous amount to be done.

"It was pleasing to hear last week -- unofficially, though aparently reliable -- that Nerang Shire Council proposes to start work at several parts of the road immediately the Currumbin to Coolangatta stretch is commenced."

The exploration, publicity and lobbying by Fred Eager, his cause then taken up by the Automobile Club of Queensland, led directly to the road system we see on the Gold Coast today. For years, the voice piece was Edward Eager's baby, *The Steering Wheel*, while he owned it, and after it passed into independent hands.

The Steering Wheel was changing, evolving to meet its readers' interests and demands. Richard Cobden, who guided the journal through the war years was leaving to become secretary of the ACQ.

He wrote his farewell on the front page: "This is the last issue of this journal to be published under its present editorship, and I think the time is ripe to drop the editorial 'We' and speak for just a moment -- I, to you. Just over four years have elapsed since *The Steering Wheel* was launched by that great-hearted enthusiast -- the late Mr, EG Eager.

"In the first issue were these words, written by my friend, RS Maynard: 'We would publish a magazine of the Out of Doors -- an Australian magazine with the warm sun and the moon and the stars shining on its pages, and the nor'easter blowing through its leaves. We will aim to make *The Steering Wheel* a real expression of the Australian open air. Mr Maynard had much to do with the setting of the course that the '*Wheel*' has followed since 1914.

"The founder of the *Wheel* has 'gone west,' but he lived long enough to see what his dream of what the '*Wheel*' should be, was beginning to materialise. I emphasise that 'beginning', for, speaking with a knowledge of a field of service that lies open to the journal, having glimpsed at the plans of Mr OM Bagot, who follows me, I do not doubt the bright future that lies ahead -- and immediately ahead -- of *The Steering Wheel*."

Cobden asked that people continue to contribute to the magazine. "Stories of trips, paragraphs on phases of motoring, your car troubles, photos -- these have helped," he wrote. "Please continue this friendly assistance. The Editor will appreciate it, and every reader benefit."

23

Brisbane to Toowoomba

A short time after Whitey blew away the field at One Tree Hill there was another record set - this time for the Brisbane-Toowoomba run of 95 miles. Not by a car but a motorcycle. Mr WS Power attempted the record on his Indian bike and shot into Toowoomba in a time of 2 hours and 22 minutes. It was a remarkable record for a bike, given the poor state of many of the roads. Cars handle potholes, bumps, sand, gravel and every other road malaise much better than powered two-wheelers.

The time put up by Power impressed Fred Eager, who was looking for more local success. A shot at the Brisbane-Toowoomba record would not be the logistical nightmare of the Sydney-Brisbane 'road to ruin'. He briefed Wally Webb, who started preparing Whitey for her next challenge.

The record was held by Toowoomba CCM dealer, WA Elvery, in his 1913 four-cylinder Studebaker roadster. On September 9, 1915, he set a new best time of 2 hours 35 minutes. Ads were taken out by CCM Brisbane, under the headline, "A Phenomenal Record" state the run was timed and "verified by Government officials in Brisbane, and Dr AJ McDonnell in Toowoomba." The ad points out closed railway gates delayed the attempt by five minutes.

For reasons unknown, Fred Eager was suspicious of the Elvery record. Something did not ring true about the timing. He was not going to have anyone questioning his time if indeed, he set a record. The former editor of *The Steering Wheel*, Richard Cobden, was now secretary of the Automobile Club of Queensland. Wally Webb probably gave Cobden a call to set the wheels in motion for an officially timed and sanctioned attempt.

On Friday, July 5, 1918, six officials from the ACQ gathered at the starting point. They included Mr J S Badger, President of the ACQ, Mr R Cobden, secretary, Mr H Green of Perdriau Rubber Co, Mr J W White and Mr AJ Leaver of the Motor Traders' Association. At 9.35am Fred Eager was handed a sealed watch by Mr Badger and given the word to go. Wally Webb was already warming the passenger seat.

The trip took them via Ipswich, Rosewood, Calvert, Grandchester, Gatton, Helidon and the long and steep ascent into Toowoomba.

"The hum of the engine could be heard ascending the range, the hum sounding like a bee," reported the *Warwick Gazette*.

The Toowoomba officials were waiting when Whitey came to a halt and included Justice of the Peace, Mr SG Priest, Lieut T Beamish of the Vacuum Oil Co, Mr Reid from Willys Overland, Toledo, US, Mr AE Free, manager Howard Motor Co, and Mr JT Trousdell of the T Cycle and Motor Co.

Whitey and Fred Eager had another record to their credit: Brisbane-to-Toowoomba in 2 hours and seven-and-a-half minutes, cutting a whopping 27 1/2 minutes from WA Elvery's 1915 time.

"A large crowd were at the finishing point and much admiration was expressed for the plucky driver and his wonderful Overland," the *Gazette* reported. Warwick is a Queensland city, south of Toowoomba and the *Gazette* circulated in both cities.

The following passages from the story would have ruffled the feathers of CCM Toowoomba, the Studebaker dealer. After all, this was their backyard. The reporter gave a glowing report of Whitey's history; the ACQ Hill climb wins, the model number, the fact the engine was the original one fitted, likewise the gearbox and how much horsepower ... the story read more like an Edward Eager ad than an independent report. The clincher, though, was yet to come:

"This car is a tribute to the wonderful materials and workmanship of the Overland car and goes to prove their strength and reliability."

The reporter then got down to the only exciting part of an otherwise routine, but fast, trip between the two cities.

"Mr Eager had a rather thrilling experience at Helidon, as the road gang had started to take up the bridge decking and when Mr Eager arrived the gap was about two feet. Mr Eager wanted to jump the gap but the bridge builders would not allow him to take the risk."

Eager reversed up a hill and then crossed the river, running with around two feet of water in it. Whitey, as usual, came through with flying colours and they lost about three minutes.

Fred Eager and Wally Webb returned to Brisbane at a much more sedate pace. Eager picked up the *Brisbane Courier* on Monday morning, and a page 4 story jumped out at him.

Brisbane Toowoomba Record:

"Mr WA Elvery, of Toowoomba, points out in reference to the splendid performance of Mr Eager on Friday that his (Mr Elvery's) record run between Brisbane and Toowoomba of 2 hours and 35 minutes was over a good deal longer road, as owing to the direct road over the Liverpool Plains, having been closed to traffic, he had to make a detour."

For Fred, this was Deja Vu. Another Studebaker complainer AFTER the event, in this case, a record lost. He was furious and penned a response to the *Courier's* Editor:

"On reading the *Courier's* issue of this morning I notice a small article on page four, headed Brisbane - Toowoomba record. I beg to advise you in regard to the record claimed to have been made by Mr Elvery, of Toowoomba, that first, this record was in no sense of the word official: second, that over the route traversed by Mr Elvery the time he claimed worked out at an average of 38 miles per hour, according to his own statements. Against this, permit me to state my record was in every way official, and that my time over the route I travelled works out at just in excess of 40 miles per hour. Fred Z Eager."

Fred Eager probably believed that would be the end of it. He was mistaken.

The following Thursday, July 11, the ACQ wrote to the *Courier* raising Fred Eager's letter and was signed by the Club president, JS Badger and Honorary Secretary of the Motor Traders' Association Queensland AJ Leaver. Both were present at the official start of Eager's attempt at a new Brisbane - Toowoomba record. Badger handed Fred Eager the sealed box containing the timing watch.

For Fred Eager, the letter's content was startling.

"We notice in the *Courier* of this morning a letter from Mr Eager referring to his trip from Brisbane to Toowoomba, in which it is stated the the 'record was in every way official.' The undersigned, representing the greater interests in Queensland, while not wishing to the least to detract from the credit due Mr Eager for the splendid performance, or to cast any doubt upon the genuiness of the record, think it only fair to motorists, and the public generally, to say that in no way was the record official, and it would not be recognised as such by any responsible motoring body in the country.

The fact that several officials of the two organisations were present at the start (in individual capacity only) does not make it an official event." Eager smelled a rat. He did not claim the event was official. He claimed his time was official. He had gone to extremes to make sure no one could deny whatever time he managed in the run.

He insisted six credible people be at the start, and the finish, to guarantee there was no conspiracy suggestion in his time. He was concerned by the fall-out from the publicity and concluded it was better to put his pen away - or keep his correspondence private. The issue was not finished.

Nine days later ACQ President JS Badger again wrote a letter to Brisbane *Courier's* Editor.

"At a meeting of the Council of the Automobile Club held on Tuesday, July 16, matters in connection with Mr Eager's remarkable record of 2 hours and 7 1/2 minutes between Brisbane and Toowoomba on July 5 were considered, and the Council were of the opinion that the record was in every way genuine, and great credit was due Mr Eager for the fine time made."

"The following resolution was passed unanimously by the Council: - (1) On the evidence the Council is of the opinion that the record is not official. (2) Further that the Council is of opinion that Mr Eager acted perfectly sincerely in good faith and undoubtedly believed the record to be official, the secretary (Cobden) acting also in good faith, having given it as his opinion that it was so."

"To make better provision in the future for the conduct of all trials or records for which the recognition of the Club is sought, the following resolutions were passed unanimously."

(A) Seven full days notice, or other such reasonable notice as may be given in writing to the secretary of the Club, setting out the nature of the trial or record, the exact starting and finishing for points, and course over which the trial will be made, and such other detailed information as may be required by the Council of the Club.

(B) The meeting shall consider the application for official supervision, and, if favourable, determine the number and personnel of officials necessary for the proper conduct of the trial or record.

(C) The applicant shall, in making his application, sign an agreement not to use the result of the record or trial, nor permit same to be used for purposes of advertising without first submitting to the Club a copy of the advertising matter proposed to be used, and obtaining a declaration signed by the President (or his deputy) and the secretary, or his deputy, to the effect that the facts as set out in the proposed advertisement are correct. Signed JS Badger."

The ACQ stated that its secretary did not have the power to authorise the event as an official record attempt between Brisbane and Toowoomba. It appears the ACQ had no rules in place at all for motorists who wanted to conduct trials or races and expected ACQ timing to give their records official recognition.

So, how did this impact on the Sydney-Brisbane records and previous Brisbane-Toowoomba records? They stood. So, what took place that changed the goalposts for Eager's record between Brisbane and Toowoomba?

There appear to be two issues. One, Eagers *Brisbane Courier* ad on Monday, July 8, - three days after Eager set the record - in which Eager detailed those who were at the start to witness his departure and those at the finish to do the same there. Above their names, he wrote: The times were certified by the following officials. There was nothing new in that - newspapers had already reported the officials names and why they were there.

The ad also stated the win not only establishes an official intercity record but exceeds the average speed of travel any previously reported trip by any means over any route between the cities.

It was old news by then and also takes in the motorcycle record set only weeks before. Eager then went on with what was a common theme in all ads that featured Whitey - and there were plenty - stating it was the same car which won the recent ACQ Hill-climbing contest, "a 1912 model with over 140,000 miles to its credit. The only alterations since the Hill Climb for this run were strengthened springs and a return to a standard gear ratio."

Now to point (C) in what the ACQ wanted motorists to do. "Sign an agreement not to use the result of the record, or trial, nor permit same to be used for purposes of advertising without first submitting to the Club a copy of the advertising matter proposed to be used, and obtaining a declaration signed by the President (or his deputy) and the secretary, or his deputy, to the effect that the facts as set out in the proposed advertisement are correct."

Fred Eager's *Courier* ad three days after the Brisbane-Toowoomba run, was the target of this point. The implication was that Eager lied in the ad and the ACQ wanted to vet ads before they were published. Simply, an outrageous demand aimed at stifling Eager's advertising after he attempted new records.

It is clear someone was pulling the ACQ's strings, particularly those of its President, JS Badger. It is said people act for two reasons: To gain a benefit or avoid a loss. The only identity that had something lose, or gain, was Eager's old foe, Studebaker dealer, CCM with branches in Brisbane and Toowoomba.

Fred Eager continued to run ads featuring Whitey and detailing the car's many achievements, including the Brisbane-Toowoomba record. As far as Fred was concerned the record stood, the ACQ even stated the "record was genuine", even though they would not recognise it.

Fred Eager let the matter die locally, but behind the scenes briefed the *Adelaide Register's* motoring editor. Without comment, he sent all documents to the journalist. Eager wanted an independent view on the

ACQ comment that any "responsible motoring organistion in the country would not recognise the record."

On December 28, 1918, five months after the record, the *Brisbane Courier* ran a story headlined:

The Position Cleared Up --- Mr Eager's Time not Disallowed.

The motoring editor of the *Adelaide Register* concluded from Eager's documents no conditions were governing official races in Queensland before the Brisbane-Toowoomba attempt. He said the ACQ secretary "gave permission and made arrangements for the trial, and the times checked by recognisable persons."

"The subsequent trouble seems to lie in the fact that the president and other officers of the club did not know of the arrangement made by the secretary, or, if they did, they imperfectly understood them."

Even this is a polite excuse for what went on. ACQ President JS Badger was invited to attend the start of the attempt, which he did, and gave Eager and Webb the official box containing the official clock to time Eager's run.

Were these the actions of someone who was there as an 'individual' as claimed after the event, and he was not aware it was an official send-off? It beggars belief Badger was not aware this was an officially timed event, along with Motor Traders Association President AJ Leaver

The politics of the Brisbane car game were alive and well.

Fred Eager's record stood for the next 15 years until a Chevrolet driven by Mr DD Lupton, who owned a motor garage at Laidley, covered the distance in one hour and 45 minutes at an average speed of 52mph.

24

Whitey: Sydney to Brisbane

FRED Eager was not a vindictive man. But he did have a long memory.

With business commitments under control, Fred Eager asked Wally Webb to prepare Whitey for the most challenging drive of her life, the Sydney-Brisbane record. The car was six years old and an integral part of the Eager family.

Fred talked of Whitey as though she was a living animal, like the family pet dog or cat. There was Fred, Audrey, son Edward and Whitey. She was his daily driver. Eager and Webb drove Whitey to Sydney on precisely the reverse of the route they would attempt to set a new Sydney-Brisbane record. In the back of Fred Eager's mind was one issue: If he did not create a record, that was fine. But he had to beat the time set by Alec Jewell in the Studebaker Six. That was critical.

Webb took notes as they drove, recording distances, route markings, the state of roads and dangerous corners. They arrived in Sydney with no fanfare on Friday, October 18. There was no publicity. No newspapers. The trip down was uneventful. Webb went over the car, checking and double-checking every part.

The 'road to ruin' didn't get its infamous reputation for no reason. Early Saturday afternoon Howard Hunter, Bob Lee, JG Braillard and Frank Smith left Sydney to oversee Wiseman's Ferry and the O'Donnell River punt arrangements. They organised a midnight snack and took hot cocoa and Sydney rock oysters on ice for the arrival of Whitey and her two-man crew.

Eager drove Whitey to the Sydney GPO at 9pm on Saturday, October 19, 1918, after a restful afternoon. Sanctioned by the Automobile Club of Queensland the attempt was way overdue for Whitey. There to see the car away were ACQ representatives, Boyd Edkins, Ronald Beale and AV Guyler. Hardy Bros Sydney supplied not one, but two watches. The ACQ reps synchronised the timepieces with the Post Office tower clock, then sealed them in separate boxes.

Wally Webb stored the precious cargo in an already overcrowded Whitey, packed to the hilt with fuel and spares. Despite an absence of publicity, a small crowd gathered at the Post Office. The send-off was the opposite of that enjoyed by Alec Jewell in his bid. Cars were a common site in Sydney, but the white speedster was something else.

At the first stroke of 10pm on the Post Office clock, Fred Eager was ready, the engine warmed up and first gear engaged. Webb hung on as they tore away. A group of enthusiasts motored to Gladesville Hill to witness Whitey speed past.

"The run out to Wiseman's was made in 1 hour 35 minutes, and the winding, mountainous roads, between the Hawkesbury and Singleton, were covered in just under three hours -- the latter town being passed at 2.34 in the morning," reported *The Steering Wheel*.

"At this point Mr Eager was running 25 minutes ahead of schedule, but this was compensated for almost immediately because six railway gates in rapid succession were shut, and 18 minutes lost."

Near Murrurundi, one of the cylinders started missing, and Wally Webb pinpointed a faulty spark plug, another five-minute delay. A second plug failed between Willow Tree and Wallabadah, so Eager pulled the car over, and Webb fitted four new plugs, that gave no more trouble.

"From this point to Tamworth, no more involuntary stops occurred, and the Central Northern Garage was reached at 6.05am., exactly on schedule."

Inter-city racing captured the Australian populace's imagination much like the modern Bathurst 1000 races at Mt. Panorama. Even if you are not interested in motorsport, most blokes, and a few females, take at least a passing interest in what happens on The Mountain in the first week of October. People in the Australian bush towns who had not had the same exposure to cars as their city cousins, were, in 1918, fascinated by the automobile. And when a speedster came through town -- or the paddocks -- they would do anything they could to help the car on its way.

"It is worth noting here that through the enthusiasm of Mr AV Le Queene, a party of his employees went through Goonoo Goonoo station at five o'clock in the morning and had the seven gates open, saving precious minutes," *The Steering Wheel* reported.

"An extra five minutes was spent in Tamworth as the breakfast provided was appreciated -- a start made at 6.30. "Between Tamworth and Armidale the delay was cut -- the latter town passed at 8.15 --- exactly on time."

Midway between Armidale and Glen Innes, as Fred Eager pushed the car to its limit, a loud explosion came from under the car, and the exhaust note thundered through the hills. Wally Webb gave this description to Whitey historian David Crisp in 1979.

"We were travelling up the hill at high-speed flat out in second gear," he said. "There was a bend to our left just a few yards from the top of the hill. I could not understand why Fred did not ease up, because no one could take the bend at the speed at which we were moving when suddenly he screamed 'accelerator stuck'.

"I yelled 'switch off'. When he did that the power had gone, the car slowed with a jerk, but it enabled us to negotiate the bend okay. The clutch and gears were still engaged, and the motor turning over at high revs, and of course pumping unburnt gas through the muffler, and the atmosphere," he said.

"When we had successfully negotiated the bend, to save a second or so he thought he could cut in the motor before the top of the hill -- a wrong move.

"When he switched on the motor the muffler exploded wide open with a large flame which also set a lot of previously unburnt gas that had been expelled through the muffler on fire in a huge flash.

"Fortunately, neither of us was burnt from the blast. The car's momentum took it to the top of the hill. Fred applied the brakes and the pair alighted. I got out and had a quick look at the damage, then picked up some cutting pliers, went over to the wire fence alongside the road and cut out three lengths to tie around the muffler, as soon as I could.

"I burnt my hands on the hot metal while endeavouring to get it back into shape, but I did not let Fred help, because he might burn his hands also."

The pair drove on, but with the damaged muffler the 'noise was deafening.' Webb was one of those laconic types. "We carried on okay until we got to Brisbane."

The delay cost 19 minutes, and by the time they roared into Glen Innes, they were just eight minutes behind schedule.

"From Glen Innes to Tenterfield another four minutes were lost, but from the town that was home to the Tenterfield saddler to the Queensland border, we picked up six minutes. Between the State border and Warwick, another 12 minutes gain and Warwick reached six minutes ahead of time."

Fred Eager had now been at the wheel for 14 hours and 21 minutes. With Wally Webb's burnt hands, he would drive the full distance. In all Fred Eager's explorations, he probably knew the road between Warwick and Brisbane better than anyone apart from Dave Ezzy, the Warwick Overland agent. If anyone could push Whitey ahead of schedule on this part of the road, Fred Eager could.

"Leaving Warwick at 2.21pm., the run to Brisbane was made in 3 hours 17½ minutes, including a stop of 10 minutes at Spicer's Gap for some fruit and a cup of tea, (to keep the pair alert). "This brought the arrival time at the north end of Brisbane's Victoria Bridge to 5.38½ pm on Sunday, October 20."

Meeting Eager and Webb were members of the ACQ, Messrs AE Hill, MV Corbett, WM Nelson and Richard Cobden. Webb, his hands bandaged, retrieved the sealed boxes and presented them to the officials.

The official time was 19 hours 38½ minutes, showing an average speed of 31½ miles per hour for the distance. Eager smashed Boyd Edkins record by 6½ hours.

Eager relinquished the steering wheel at no stage, in one of the most remarkable feats of driving in Australian motorsport history. Today, it would be considered madness. The actual driving time was 17 hours, 40 minutes. The road to ruin proved to be the road to redemption for Webb and Whitey after coming second at Southport.

Looking at all previous attempts at the Sydney-Brisbane record, one thing stands out with this one: planning. Other attempts had more of a 'let's give it a go' approach. This one didn't. Webb and Eager planned for a drier part of the year, and they had a clinical schedule to stick with between towns. At any given time, they knew if they were ahead, or behind where they were supposed to be, allowing Fred to make up time by pushing Whitey harder where the roads were suitable.

Since the Southport Speed Trials, the white speedster had taken all before it; the ACQ Hill Climb in record time, a record for the Brisbane-Toowoomba intercity run and now the Sydney-Brisbane record by a blistering amount of time. As a sport in this era, road racing took precedence over speed trials and hill-climbs. They were the Bathurst 1000 of their time; A marathon with every car and crew facing adversity, trauma and drama. Eager, Webb and Whitey together conquered the crown jewel of Australian road-racing. The Sydney-Brisbane intercity held more respect than the Sydney-Melbourne, as it was more difficult.

They beat the times of Australia's great long-distance driver, Francis Birtles in his Maxwell, legendary Vauxhall fanatic, Boyd Edkins, in his Prince Henry 35hp, and Alec Jewell in the arch-rival Studebaker Six.

It was a record of epic proportions. Eager's good friend Boyd Edkins conceded his Vauxhall could not compete with Whitey. That did not mean Edkins would not try again, and again, and again. Edkins' car was one of the world's fastest and most successful Vauxhalls. And Boyd Edkins was as stubborn as they came.

25

Never, ever give up.

The 'Road to Ruin' takes up the Edkins response to the drive of Fred Eager's life. "Edkins knew his Vauxhall was not good enough to run under Eager's time. He simmered quietly until the war was finished and Britain was producing better cars."

Before WWI, the British carmaker built thirteen 30/98 model Vauxhalls, destined for thirteen hand-picked owners. These cars were highly developed versions of the Prince Henry C10 model similar to Edkins much loved 25hp racer, nicknamed 'Fifty Bob'.

The 3-litre engine was enlarged to 4525cc for the 30/98 and produced 90bhp at 3000rpm. Vauxhall sent several prototype 30/98s to Australia - one, a gift to Edkins from Vauxhall, to help break the Sydney-Melbourne and Sydney-Brisbane records. Production of the 30/98 did not start until after the war, in 1919.

"The Vauxhall 30/98, then just about the fastest thing on the road, looked the best bet. Edkins stripped it, did a survey, and roared off on his attempt. Mechanical failure put him out after a few hours. It was the start of a series of bad luck and disaster unequalled in Australian record-breaking," recorded the Road to Ruin.

"Edkins tried again ... and failed once more. But with each try, he got closer. He determinedly set off for Brisbane for the sixth try and marked the stretch between Uralla and Armidale as the best.

"But he missed the road gang that descended on it with picks and shovels the next day. What happened next was one of the great Houdini acts of Australian motorsport. Friends in Armidale sent out a man with a red flag to warn Edkins of the newly dug culvert. The man took his position, listened, and heard in the distance the rising howl of the speeding 30/98.

"The sight of the roaring monster, lurching from one side of the track to the other, was too much for the flag holder. His nervous hands gripped the flag tightly, but his legs carried him at a gallop into the scrub."

"Edkins 30/98 slammed into the culvert at 80 miles per hour, somersaulted five times and crashed to rest a mangled heap." Remarkably, neither Edkins nor navigator was hurt. Edkins ordered the wreck to be taken to Sydney and thus ended his sixth attempt to break Fred Eager's record.

"Edkins seventh try was better," states the Road to Ruin. "There were no culverts, and the rebuilt 30/98 never missed a beat. He was 30 minutes under Eager's time at Wiseman's Ferry, gained more on McGrath's Hill. But, like the previous six attempts, this one too was doomed to failure. Then the lights of his speeding Vauxhall picked out a repair sign. Edkins slowed for the first of many detours. The rain had made it greasy, and the Vauxhall slithered uneasily. The next detour was worse, and so was the one after it.

"Then the Vauxhall slid badly and plunged axle-deep in a bog. Edkins and his mechanic worked frantically to free the heavy car. But it was immovable. The precious seconds became minutes ... and the lead of just a few minutes over Eager's soon frittered away. With the Vauxhall still axle deep in mud Edkins again conceded defeat."

Eager's record stood. Boyd Edkins was nothing else if persistent. By mid-1922 --- almost four years since Fred Eager and Whitey set the record --- Edkins again rolled out the 30/98 for his eighth attempt. For this attempt Edkins called in a favour from Fred Eager. Could he borrow Wally Webb?

If anyone could help get Edkins over the line, Wally Webb could. Fred Eager's reliable mechanic, navigator and loyal sidekick. The run was fast and uneventful, taking 18 hours and 58 minutes, some 40 minutes ahead of Fred Eager's record.

Eager was happy for Edkins, the friend who had helped him become one of Australia's premier speedsters. Eager could think of no-one better than Boyd Edkins to break his Sydney-Brisbane record. Records are created to be broken. That he helped Edkins win by 'lending' his reliable sidekick, Wally Webb, gave Eager an immense sense of pride. He had re-paid the debt to Edkins for mentoring him when he first started as a speedster. It was how good friends looked after each other.

In Brisbane, Vauxhall sales were no threat to Willys Overland. What Wally Webb added to Edkins attempt was no doubt the organisational and planning skills. After all, he had been-there-and-done-that before with the ultimate success.

While the Australian speedsters had to rely on intercity racing to make the headlines, their American counterparts had moved on to pur-pose-built race tracks. In August 1918 Ralph de Palma, driving his 12-cyl-inder Packard racing car, lowered the world record for four distances, 2, 10, 30 and 50 miles. Nearly 50,000 people packed the circuit where the prize money was a massive 5000 pounds.

In Australia, attempts at speed records confined to the beach. And that's just what happened before Christmas 1918, in scenes that could well have come from the movie, *The World's Fastest Indian*, the story of eccentric motorcycle genius, New Zealand's Burt Munro.

It was Queensland's first attempt at a world speed record. Bert Munro's exploits would not take place for several decades, when the Queensland Motor-Cycle Club decided to hold speed trials on the Southport beach in December 1918.

It took place on the same stretch of sand where Alec Jewell and Fred Eager set Australian land speed records two years earlier. Officials from the club measured off a mile stretch of beach amid persistent rain.

"The well-known motor cyclist, Ernest Odlum, decided to attempt to lower the world's record for a flying mile on his Indian motorcycle and side car, accompanied by D Penfold as passenger," reported *The Steering Wheel* on January 2, 1919.

"Odlum states that the ride was made under considerable difficulties, as the rain beating in his face made the use of goggles impractical; however, despite this and the extremely difficult nature of the beach, due to recent rough weather, the record was secured in the extraordinarily fast time of 54sec, this being the world record for a mile with motorcycle and side car."

"EE Ferguson made the next best performance at Sellicks Beach, Adelaide, on October 9, 1918, also on an Indian motorcycle and sidecar in 55 2/5 seconds.

"The record secured by Odlum is the first world record secured in Queensland, and this plucky rider decided immediately to attempt the flying mile record on a solo Indian, which he accomplished in 44 4/5 seconds, or over 80 miles per hour."

Odlum worked at Canada Cycle and Motor Agency (Qld) for AV Dodwell. It is much to the credit of AV Dodwell that he had a dream of making Southport Beach another Daytona.

By April 1919 Fred and Audrey Eager relocated to Sydney, Fred wearing his hat as the importer of Willys vehicles, with a national network of agencies to service. Sydney was the hub of business in Australia and more central than Brisbane. He settled into life in Sydney and another senior and respected member of the Queensland motoring fraternity, RS Lough, of Dunlop Rubber Company, elevated to Willys Melbourne. Both were consuls of the Automobile Club of Queensland in their respective southern capitals, giving Queensland local representation to the motoring clubs known as the NRMA and the RACV.

Intercity racing was also the leading motorsport in Europe, but the French had seen what was taking place in the United States. They too saw the possibilities for making money out of motorsport. You could not charge spectators for entry to intercity racing, but you could for admission to a closed racetrack.

"Apparently the French motor manufacturers are going in for motor racing speedways along Amercian lines," reported *The Steering Wheel* on April 1, 1919.

"In the past, all motor car speed events were conducted on the roads in France, but the latest files now bring word that 3000 workmen are already engaged in erecting a very fine motor track at Strassburg, where it is hoped to hold motor racing on a grand scale in the near future." Despite the war being over, Australian sentiments were still anti-German.

The fledgling nation gave up almost 60,000 of her youngest and best. German industry was trying to get back on its feet, much like it would after WW II. The car industry was one place where the Germans were quick to try and re-start world trade. But, if they thought it would be easy, they were in for a shock. *The Steering Wheel,* June 1, 1919:

ALLIED OR GERMAN MADE TYRES

When Herr Rantzau replied to the Peace Terms; he insulted the Allies by remaining seated. Decent minded Britishers all over the World, boiled with anger. When Australians--our sons and brothers--first appeared in France's trench line, the Germans greeted them with placards bearing filthy insults. The World was struck with horror when Nurse Cavell was murdered. Every British bayonet sank home with the hissed reminder, "Remember Louvain" for a month after Louvain.

"The 'Lusitania' remains as the victim of the World's greatest murder. Whenever the first the cables told of the German cruelties to Australian prisoners of war, Australian Mothers and Fathers suffered agonies in silence. Fifty-eight thousand of Australia's Best gave up their lives to lay the German low --For what? --- Was it for Australian Motorists at home to promptly raise the Hun again by helping him rebuild his industries? Every German-made Tyre bought by Australians is an insult to the Price paid for Victory.

"The one thing Germany now most desires is to recapture her lost trade. MOTORISTS --- See to it that she does not recapture her lost Trade in Australia. Therefore, buy only Allied Tyres.

"By Authority, Queensland Motor Tyre Association."

The Dunlop Rubber Company took a more positive approach. DUNLOP TYRES THE DAWN OF BRIGHT DAYS The War is over --- Long Live Peace! National rejoicing signalises the Victory we celebrate --- the triumph of Right over Might. Glorious deeds and saddened memories are Australia's heritage.

Still, brighter days are ahead, and the time has come when motorists are justified in again enjoying the many benefits and pleasures that the motor bestows. So fill up the tanks --- pump up the tyres --- and answer the Call of the Road --- where lies Health and Happiness.

And that's just what Jack Walsh did with the record-breaking Studebaker owned by CCM. as he prepared for the 1919 Automobile Club of Queensland Hill climb. In June he took the big Studebaker Six to Sydney to compete at racing events and put up a record for the fastest lap of one mile, one-furlong circuit. But the record CCM and AV Dodwell craved was the One Tree Hill hill-climb.

Ironically, the Studebaker with Jack Walsh at the wheel caused the speedster event's cancellation on November 1, 1919. "Much of the interest and excitement generally associated with the ACQ Hill Climbing contest was missing this year owing to the absence of the speed cars," reported *The Steering Wheel* on December 1, 1919.

"An accident to the Studebaker car when practising over the course was an undoubted factor in the elimination of the particular contest in which several vehicles were to have competed, including Studebaker, Chandler and Overland makes.

"When travelling at high speed up the hill the Studebaker struck some loose metal on the track, and the car's stability, combined with a magnificent feat of driving on the part of Jack Walsh, averted a serious accident."

The car was severely damaged -- as was Walsh's pride -- and was returned to CCM. workshops. The chassis was twisted beyond repair. As a result of the crash, the ACQ abandoned the speedster event. Fred Eager returned in Whitey to Brisbane to defend his three-year crown, with Whitey, like himself, confined to being a spectator.

David L Crisp of the Willys-Overland Club of Victoria Inc wrote a five-page, unpublished, history of Whitey. He described Fred Eager's departure from competitive motorsport in a matter-of-fact way. "Fred Eager retired from competition after the 1919 Automobile Club of Queensland hill climb at Mt.Cootha (sic), now in suburban Brisbane, when one of his friends, Charlie Holloway, was killed taking part."

Fred won this event three years in a row. Holloway's death came on top of Jack Walsh's close called during practice. It also came after his father, Edward G. Eager, lost his life 18 months after his Toledo crash while testing Overlands in 1916. Frederick Zina Eager called it a day. He had a large company to run and was the Willys Overland importer in Australasia; He had a lovely wife, Audrey and young son Edward. Audrey would be recognised for her selfless work for the Red Cross in WW2, a cause close to Fred's heart.

Fred would no longer sit in his favourite seat -- the driver's pew in Whitey. Whitey too was 'retired' to Eagers Brisbane head office, rarely used, until Fred Eager passed away 30 years later. He could not bear to part with Whitey, the car that was such an integral part of his life.

'Whitey' fitted with V8 Knight engine, 1918 (top).
'Whitey' in 1970 with Graham Crittenden at the wheel after purchasing the car from the Guthrie family.

26

The Legacy

THIS book is not only about the father and son Eagers, but there is little doubt the legacies that live on as a result of the events of 1911 - 1918 in the Brisbane business and motorsport scene belong largely to these two American motoring pioneers.

The obvious benefit of their time in Australia lives on in the car industry itself - the largest car retailing business in Australia-New Zealand, Eagers Automotive, still based in Brisbane and with more than 8000 staff across Australia and New Zealand. The company name EG Eager & Son Limited is still a registered company under the Eagers Automotive banner.

Edward and Fred Eager conducted business in a way that lifted the game across the board for all those seeking success. If you wanted to compete with Eagers, you needed to re-think your business model. You needed to be entreprenurial and at the same time "see the customer right."

Edward and Fred Eager, along with their rival, AV Dodwell from CCM, lead the way in guiding their businesses into the new era of motorised transport. They practised vertical integration before the term was invented with after sales service, car repairs, developing bespoke trailers, small trucks and customised body shapes for commercial uses.

When Queensland had no motoring media in mainstream newspapers, Edward Eager started *The Steering Wheel,* and promised all rival dealers they would be able to have their say and have articles published in the bi-monthly journal. He was as good as his word and competing makes to Willys, if they put the effort in, made the magazine's pages.

Edward Eager's *Steering Wheel* was so popular it forced the *Brisbane Courier* to appoint their first dedicated motoring writer. At a time when the Automobile Club of Queensland, now the RACQ, had no public voice *The Steering Wheel* in 1918 became the official organ of that Club, a role it had until 1935 when the RACQ launched it's own journal, the *Queensland Motorist* (now the *Road Ahead*).

The Steering Wheel became a vehicle of change: it championed better roads for Queensland, signage for all roads, not just the Brisbane CBD, took up issues concerning motorists including speeding, speed limits, drink driving, car repairs, what to look for in a new car, tips on tyres - the entire gambit of questions that confronted would-be buyers more accustomed to dealing with horse-feed and buggies.

When, after just 14 months, *The Steering Wheel* was a profitable going-concern, Edward Eager stepped back from the magazine, launched it as a limited liability company allowing interested parties, the car industry, businessmen and medicos, to own and run the journal.

With Edward Eager's untimely death at an early age in 1917, Fred Z Eager stepped up as managing Director of EA Eager & Son Limited. FredZed, as he was affectionately known, took the reins and lead the company for the next 14 years as a Willys importer and dealer. It was no easy gig and saw Fred relocating to Sydney to oversee the importing business. He then made the tough decision to change from Willys to General Motors in 1930 - a decision that laid a second solid foundation for the company. Edward Eager started the company, set the standards, and Fred built it until his passing in 1949.

Fred Eager's motorsport career was short, but explosive. It could be argued that he was Queensland's top racing driver in the first 50 years of the 19th century, which also happens to be the first 50 years of cars in Australia. Anyone who wins at the Bathurst 1000 is an icon and Queenslander's Allan Grice, Craig Lowndes, Tony Longhurst, Greg Hansford, Paul Morris and Dick Johnson have that honour. In the early days Bathurst was a dirt circuit with drivers needing the skills of a hill-climb wizard and the endurance of an intercity demon. Exactly the skills that took FredZed to the top in his era.

That places Fred Eager's three successive wins at the One Tree Hill in 1916 - 18, against the likes of Boyd Edkins, Munro and Alec Jewell in a true context. The man could steer. Add to that his Sydney - Brisbane record that stood for years, with Fred driving the entire 17 hours 40 minutes, and his exploits behind the wheel in my view add up to one thing: This unassuming businessman, whose achievements have never been recognised outside Queensland, is arguably one of the northern state's greatest race drivers. Unfortunately, until now, his record has been lost in time. It is simply not possible to compare records a century or so apart. His record does, however, speak for itself in the era covered by this book.

27

WHAT happened to...

FREDERICK ZINA EAGER died on August 17, 1949, at age 62, a year after his wife, Audrey (nee Worth), passed away. Following Audrey's passing, Fred suffered from a heart condition and died at home in Brisbane. At the time, he was Chairman of Directors of EG Eager and Son Pty Ltd. He had lived in Australia for 38 years. They had one son, Edward (see below).

Fred Eager was a keen big game fisherman and held the Queensland record with the 1941 catch of a Great White shark weighing 1324lb. He was also a yachtsman and motor sailer. Fred was a member of the Brisbane Club, the Royal Queensland Yacht Club, the Royal Queensland Golf Club, and Tattersalls Club. Later in life, he took up breeding Jersey cattle and owned Grasmere stud which had some of the best jersey bloodstock available.

His luxury boat, Tangalooma, was commandeered by the RAN in World War II, later bought by Hayles Ferry Cruises in Townsville, and used on the Magnetic Island run. More than 450 people attended his funeral at St Augustine's Church of England, Hamilton.

EDWARD McMAKEN EAGER, his son, died in 1964, aged 53, of lung cancer. He attended Harvard University but dropped out to pursue a writing career. Edward made a distinct contribution to children's literature by introducing a theme of magic into children's ordinary lives.

Sound familiar? So it should. Critics have said that children who want more 'Harry Potter' would enjoy Edward McMaken Eager's books. He was also a well-known lyricist and playwright.

Edward McMaken Eager had one son, Fritz, who graduated from Harvard and passed away at a young age, ending this line of the high-achieving Eager family. Harvard holds an art scholarship for Fritz Eager and a creative writing scholarship for Edward Eager.

WHITEY remained at Eagers until Fred Eager died in 1949. As part of the estate, Whitey was sold to Harry Evans, converted into a utility, and used it on his Brisbane farm for chores, including pulling stumps.

After about a year, Sid Butwell bought the utility and used it to haul produce from the markets to his shop and general carrying. At this time, the old 61 Model started showing signs of wear and tear with the wire wheels collapsing. Smaller wheels replaced them. A horse ate some of the upholstery, and one of the unique racing pistons collapsed. Mr Butwell replaced it with a heavy cast iron piston from a stationary engine. Despite having three pistons that weighed 2lb and one weighing 4lb, Whitey continued to function, though not as smoothly as in her heyday.

In the late 1950s, Whitey moved on to Cyril Picton, who owned a garage and service station in the Brisbane suburb of Grovelly. In 1965 it was found at the back of the garage by car collector, Ross Guthrie who bought Whitey for 50 pounds. He, and his brother Rob, replaced the wire wheels with large disc-type wheels, rebuilt the speedster body, and replaced the radiator with a brass one from a Model 60 Willys Overland.

Whitey then got the retirement she deserved and was used in veteran car events and in 1966 passed to the current owner, Graham Crittenden of Kingaroy, two hours drive north-west of Brisbane.

Graham had the engine rebuilt, using a matching set of standard pistons. He also replaced the badly twisted axle shafts --- it is unknown whether Fred Eager's heavy right foot or stump-pulling caused this. Graham has built new wheels almost identical to the ones Whitey had in retirement at Eagers. Whitey is now in the custody of Graham's daughter, Sally York, currently president of the Veteran Car Club of Queensland.

In 2022 Whitey will celebrate her 110th birthday, a remarkable feat for any car, let alone one that spent four years as a 'speedster.' In 2019, Mr Crittenden returned Whitey to road use.

ALEC FRASER JEWELL continued his love affair with police when he was again in court on June 17, 1921, and pleaded not guilty to a charge of reckless driving in Brisbane's Stanley Street. Engine driver Christian Neden told the court he was riding his bike home to Coorparoo when he saw a car coming towards him, doing around 30 to 40mph. The vehicle crashed into the bike, and Neden was thrown into the nearby gutter while the car kept going and careered into the fence. Neden was not seriously injured.

Jewell, who gave his occupation as a motor salesman and repairer, said he was driving along Stanley Street. There was a great deal of traffic, so he moved to the centre of the street, and there was a cart pulled diagonally across the tarmac and other vehicles pulling to the centre of the road, so he drove to the wrong side and then saw a bike coming towards him.

Jewell told the court the rider was swerving from left to right, and he could not tell which way he was going to go, so he drove his car off the road and onto the footpath "to avoid an accident", hitting the brakes and pulling up in 20 yards.

Jewell's attempt to blame other drivers and the bike rider for the accident did not sit well with the magistrate.

"The charge here is reckless driving and I am compelled to find the evidence that, whatever this other party might have done, you have been guilty of reckless driving," he said. The crash cost Jewell four pounds and 1 shilling.

Alec Jewell was driving three passengers home along Geelong road after a day at the Kerang races when his car was involved in a head-on collision about seven miles on the Melbourne side of Werribee. It was late at night on February 7, 1929. Depending on who you believe, the crash took place around 11pm, according to Jewell, and 1am the following day, according to the other driver.

It could have been a disaster with four passengers in one car and three in the other, but only one person was transferred to the hospital, the second driver, John Charles King. King was a cook in the RAAF and was returning to the base at Laverton.

The court case was interesting, not because of the crash itself but Alec Fraser Jewell's evidence. On June 13, 1929, the case came before Cr EJ Coates, chairman, and Mr J McMurray, JP, in the Werribee Court of Petty Sessions.

Jewell faced court charged with having driven an unregistered car along Geelong Road and not having lights on the front of his vehicle. He pleaded not guilty to both charges. King also charged with not having lights burning on his car. So late at night, two cars, both without lights, are heading towards each other.

Both drivers told the court the other car did not have lights on. The local newspaper, the *Werribee Shire Banner*, reported the case.

"Another car loomed up about 50 yards away and the inevitable crash happened," said King, dazed by the crash, was dragged from the car by his passengers and placed on the side of the road.

Giving evidence, Jewell contended that the onus was on police to prove that the car was without lights and whether he was driving. He said his vehicle, a Berleit, was running with lights on, and he then turned them to 'dim' just before the crash. He said the car was unregistered, being on a trial demonstration for one of his car passengers.

Police told the court the car's number plates did not match the Berleit and belonged to an Austin car since 1921 owned by a Mr Lamb.

Jewell said he was Australia's "first and original driver", and he held a clean record.

"This is the first occasion on which I have been charged with any offence against the motor regulations," he said.

Police visited Jewell at his home in North Melbourne after the crash, and he refused an interview.

"I did not make any statement to the police who visited my home as I considered it unnecessary", he said.

Jewell was fined 10 pounds for driving an unregistered car and three pounds for driving at night without lights. King was also fined three pounds for driving without lights.

AV Dodwell was incredibly loyal to his staff, but the 1921 incident in Brisbane probably pushed the envelope to breaking point. Through Jewell's high-profile wins in the Studebaker, everyone knew who he was and where he worked.

Jewell returned to Melbourne in 1922 or 23 and became the proprietor of the Ritz Hotel in St Kilda, described at the time as the finest pub in

Australia. His wife, Elsie, was the licensee. It was a new hotel with 146 rooms, each with hot and cold water and a telephone. The dining room seated 350 people, adding to its reputation as a luxurious hotel in this era, particularly in St Kilda, where fine hotels were scarce.

While at the hotel, Alec continued his love of motoring and started a business taking tours to Victorian holiday spots such as Warrnambool, Ballarat, Bendigo, and Gippsland. Nothing but the best for his guests, a Rolls-Royce, no less. Alec told friends on 'good roads' he would sit the Roller on 80 to 90mph, but on lesser roads, slowed down to 50 or 60mph. Elsie Jewell sold the Ritz licence in 1925.

In April that year, Alec boarded a ship, the Esperance Bay, for England, via Fremantle, and told friends he wanted to visit Brooklands speedway. Two years later, he revealed he had called into the iconic British racetrack and competed in an event, topping 115mph in his car. Unfortunately, this was not quick enough to win the race. While he brought back great memories of Brooklands, he also imported an idea that surfaced two years later, in 1927.

Alec announced he had formed a syndicate to establish a speedway after Brooklands' style, "away in a remote part of the Dandenong Ranges." He said the location was close to Melbourne, but far enough away, so it could not disturb the "peaceful slumbers" of Squizzy Taylor and others. Taylor was a Melbourne gangster, gunned down and killed a few years earlier. Like Squizzy, the proposal for a speedway in the Dandenongs also died.

Never short on ideas, Alec, with two others, Patrick Quinlan and John Gerald Hopkins, formed a new company on November 14, 1930. That company was Melbourne Motor Auctioneers Pty Ltd, a business that took cars on consignment and sold them for the owners. By May 1931, it was in dire financial trouble. The three shareholders called an extraordinary meeting and decided the business could not continue with its liabilities and went into voluntary liquidation.

The liquidator, Edward Smail, reported to the Practice Court in August that the company had a nominal capital of 2000 pounds, divided into one-pound shares. The company filed no records in the Office of Registrar General. These records were to show the allotment of shares, as required by the Companies Act. Records showed Jewell, Quinlan, and Hopkins held one share each.

The company failed to record details of directors appointed. The only document that gave any information showed A Jewell was the governing director and public officer of the company.

The liquidator said records he found indicated more than 27 people to whom money was owed for cars at the company's garage in Elizabeth Street, Melbourne. The amount involved was 747 pounds and 14 shillings.

All three men attended the hearing under judicial orders, and Jewell was about to drop a few bombshells. The men had no money when the company started, and they set up with borrowed capital. Jewell said Hopkins was the managing director and Quinlan a director and secretary. They had borrowed 100 pounds from the New South Wales Monte de Piete (Similar to a pawn shop). The men raised the money on an endorsed bill, signed by Quinlan's sister and made by the three men.

When asked if he was aware of a bank account held in North Melbourne into which someone had paid 18,000 pounds, Jewell said he was not aware of the account. Adding further intrigue was that Jewell thought the company had one bank account, while it had five. He did not know who opened a trust account just three days before liquidation. Alec Jewell passed away in Melbourne on May 9, 1937, aged 57. He had suffered from double pneumonia.

ALEXANDER VAUGHAN DODWELL, the proprietor of CCM, passed away in May 1945, aged in his early 70s. He was a pioneer of car sales in Brisbane, importing his first car in 1906. He was the first to bring Studebakers into Australia and sell a Ford Model T in Brisbane. As a youth, he won a scholarship to attend Brisbane Grammar School and was keen on cycling, rugby union, and sailing. He was captain of the original Brisbane Bicycling Club and designed the first cycling track around Brisbane's Cricket Grounds. (The Gabba) He captained a rugby union club to a premiership.

He was an agent for Massey Harris bicycles and opened the cycling manufacturers' business in Queensland. Massey Harris was a Canadian company, and in 1898 several similar companies in Canada came together to form Canada Cycle and Motor (CCM). This move was the uniting of bicycles and cars under one roof, which became common in the automobile's early years.

CCM Brisbane folded in 1930, a victim of the Great Depression, but AV Dodwell could not be held back and became managing director of Champion Automobile Pty Ltd, Adelaide Street, Brisbane. His reputation was untarnished by the CCM. Brisbane collapse and Dodwell continued to import Studebaker cars into Australia, along with Triumph.

The naming of his new company, Champion, is fascinating. From 1939, Studebaker released a new line of vehicles - the Studebaker Champion. This use of the name reveals how entrenched Dodwell was in the Studebaker company. The Champion was a lightweight auto, powered by a straight-six engine, and was a five-generation car, coming to a halt in 1958. Studebaker used this engine until 1964. The Lark took over from Champion.

Dodwell was a president of the Motor Traders Association of Queensland and a life member of Brisbane Cricket Club, Royal Queensland Golf Club, and the Lawn Tennis Association. He left a considerable legacy in Brisbane as a supporter of various charities. Almost half of his CCM staff during WW I enlisted, and he would hold farewell parties for those staff. He was a big supporter of the war effort and supplied car transport for returning servicemen, as did Eagers.

STUDEBAKER produced electric vehicles from 1902 and petrol vehicles from 1904. The company built coaches, carriages and buggies from around the 1860s. Even after it started motorised vehicle production it continued to manufacture horse-drawn vehicles until 1920. This timeline shows just how long the transition from horse and cart took to motorised vehicles. Even then, genuine horsepower was still prevalent, and relevant, for many decades in many rural communities across the world. The company suffered from cash flow problems after WW II and in 1954 merged with Packard. This did not work out and in 1966 the last Studebaker rolled off the production line.

CCM's STUDEBAKER SIX that set the first Australian land speed record and broke the Sydney-Brisbane record suffered a fate common to many race cars; severely damaged in a crash during the 1919 hill climb at One Tree Hill. However, a faithful reconstruction of that vehicle, built by Brisbane's Gavin Mutton, in the body style used in Alec Jewell's record-breaking Sydney-to-Brisbane run. Even the bonnet's rough writing describing the Southport Speed Trials' feats adorns the car. This big Studebaker is an impressive vehicle that does full justice to the CCM. original. Mr. Mutton placed the car on display at RACQ headquarters in Brisbane in 2019. Some parts of the car's mechanicals may be from the same vehicle that took all before it in 1916 -17.

BOYD ROBERTSON HUEY EDKINS, born in 1884 in Muttaburra, near Longreach, Queensland, died in 1930 at 46. He developed chronic Nephritis – a kidney disease – and passed away on January 23, 1930. He was probably the best New South Wales race driver of the early days of motorsport. Edkins twice broke the speed record from Melbourne to Sydney (in 1914 and 1916) and held hill-climb records in New South Wales and Brisbane.

In a Royal Automobile Club hill climb in 1921, Edkins entered both cars, the Prince Henry in the handicap event, and the 30/98 in the speed event. He won both. In December 1922, he broke the record from Sydney to Brisbane.

His business record is no less impressive than his driving record. He was President of the Motor Traders' Association of New South Wales for four years. In 1920 chaired the National Roads Association's inaugural meeting, was chairman of its provisional committee and became one of the first vice-presidents. He negotiated for amalgamation with the Victorian Roads Association and was a councilor of the Association until 1929.

NSW Police consulted him frequently on traffic policy. He was still driving a 30/98 Vauxhall in competitions at the time of his demise. Like Edward and Fred Eager, he left a legacy to Australian motoring, Boyded Holden in Sydney.

WALLY WEBB worked at Eagers for four decades. After Fred Eager retired from competitive racing in 1919, Wally Webb took over the role of 'race driver' for various events. He was highly regarded as a driver and won, and was placed, on many occasions, keeping the Willys Overland name to the fore in newspaper publicity. Webb said tuning cars was his hobby and liked nothing better to be under the bonnet of the Willys Knight and the Overland replacement, the Whippet.

PROFESSOR STARLIGHT

Professor Starlight also had a fondness for the ladies. During the visit to New Zealand in 1896, he met and married Eveline Fanny Rollins. The couple lived together for six months after tying the knot on August 17, 1895. According to Starlight, he needed to go back to Melbourne to get a job. However, as we know, he hopped on a ship and went to London. In a 1902 District Court divorce hearing in Melbourne, Eveline Rollins stated Starlight left, with her blessing, to find work. However, despite repeated letters to him, she only received one reply. She was now petitioning for a divorce on the grounds of desertion. Starlight did not appear at the court hearing. Rollins said she worked as a domestic servant in New Zealand.

She said she bumped into Starlight in Bourke Street, Melbourne, and they arranged to meet the next day, but he failed to make the appointment.

"I traced him to a boat at the wharf," she said. "He was about to leave for Sydney to take part in a fight," she said.

"Evidence was forthcoming that respondent (Starlight) had lived with another woman in Fitzroy, who passed as his wife," the court was told by Mrs Rollins' lawyer Mr LH Woolf.

The Judge granted Mrs Rollins a *decree nisi* with costs against Starlight.

The court again highlighted a Starlight marriage - this time, Vera Rollins charged with assault in the Melbourne District Court, with the same charge alleged against her by Walter Edwards, stage manager of the Gaiety Theatre Melbourne.

The three-tier heading was alluring:

Hotel Bar Quarrel

Stage Manager and Barmaid

Glasses and Bottles Fly

Starlight was a regular on the boxing card at the Gaiety Theatre and would have known Edwards well. Mrs Rollins was a barmaid employed in the American Bar at the Palace Hotel, next door to the Gaiety. Its name correctly implies a vaudeville theatre that staged musicals, plays, and a fight program. The Palace, opened in 1899, was a luxurious, 7-storey hotel on Bourke Street featuring 260 rooms, a public billiard hall with 20 tables, bars, 300-seat dining room, two Otis lifts, a skating rink on the roof, refrigeration, massive kitchen. On grand opening night, guests sipped on Moet & Chandon. So Mrs Rollins was not working in some dive. Lavish was a word often used to describe the Palace.

Mrs Rollins said on the night in question, and she was serving drinks when Mr Edwards entered the bar with two friends. On previous visits, she had lent Edwards money and given him drinks, adding up to around two pounds. She asked Edwards for the money.

"He started throwing off at me," she said, " referring to my black husband, Starlight."

The magistrate, Mr Dwyer, queried Starlight name and asked: isn't your name Rollins?

Her lawyer replied: "Starlight is her husband's *non-de-boxe*" (laughter) "I threw the contents of a glass over Edwards and he 'hauled off' and struck me in the eye." As she said this, she raised a veil and revealed a black eye.

Edwards then gave evidence. He said Rollins emptied a glass over him and then hurled a water bottle at him, hitting him on the head. Rollins came from the bar with another bottle in her hand, he pushed her, and she fell over a table.

Archie Olera, a vaudeville artist, said he was leaving the bar when he just missed a glass of whisky.

Mr Dwyer: You just 'missed' it? (laughter)

Olera: Edwards got it! (laughter) "I turned around in time to see a water bottle or decanter strike him on the back of the head. Later on glasses started to fly and I got out."

Next to give evidence was Thomas Armstrong, who told the court he was " a theatrical."

Mr Dwyer: "What are you?"

Witness: "I am supposed to be a comedian! (laughter)

Armstrong confirmed previous evidence and said he was the one that held Mrs Rollins, and then he let go and she tried to go for Edwards, who pushed her among the tables.

Mr Doria (acting for Rollins) asked Armstrong, "Did Edwards push her with his left or right?

Armstrong: "I don't know."

Mr Dwyer: Did he push her in the eye? (laughter)

Both cases were dismissed.

In July 1926 Starlight was working as a cook on the coastal passenger steamer, the Cooma. She was heading from Brisbane to Cairns on July 7, when the ship ran aground and was wrecked on North Reef, 50 miles NE of Rockhampton. There were 174 passengers and 84 crew aboard when the ship struck the reef with a 'grinding, crunching' noise. This was at high tide and as the tide went out waves crashed over the decks. Everyone aboard was rescued by passing ships the next day.

Professor Starlight passed away in 1939 – the last months of his life in a Melbourne nursing home comforted by his old foe and great friend, Dan Creedon.

Professor Starlight's legacy lives on with a high-profile Australian song-stress. The Professor married Kate Pratt, the daughter of Afro-American parents. Their daughter, Majorie Duguid, is the grandmother of Australian pop singer Colleen Hewitt and the Professor, her great grandfather.

EG EAGER & SON Ltd., the forerunner of today's Eagers Automotive, between 1925 and 1930, held the record of Willys Overland sales to total market sales of any country in the world. General Motors-Holden approached Fred Eager, and on November 1, 1930, a profound change came when Eagers took over the distribution of GM Vehicles and car parts for Queensland and northern New South Wales. They ceased to be Australia's Willys importer.

In 1934 GMH. reopened its Brisbane manufacturing plant, and by 1936 more than 10,000 vehicles rolled off the production line, mostly Chevrolet. Those vehicles passed through Eagers hands as the distributor for Queensland and the northern rivers of NSW, via their 200 dealerships. At this time, Eagers employed 356 staff and had an annual wages bill of 66,469 pounds.

Today, Eagers has a portfolio of automotive brands including all of the top 20 selling car brands in Australia and nine of the top 10 selling luxury car brands. In total, it represents 33 car brands and 12 truck and bus brands. Its operations are provided through strategically clustered dealerships, many of which are situated on properties it owns, with the balance leased. It holds $267 million of prime real estate in Brisbane, Sydney, Melbourne, and Adelaide.

The company is currently in the advanced design phase of an automotive retailing and mobility hub, set on 64,124m² of land in Brisbane Airport's new $300 million BNE Auto Mall. Eagers Automotive has paid a dividend to shareholders every year since 1957.

Since 2000, sales revenue from continuing operations, which excludes operations, either divested or held for sale, has increased from $500 million to $5.8 billion in 2019. The number of employees has increased from 600 to 8432. It is the largest operator of motor vehicle dealerships in Australia.

THE history of Willys-Overland and John North Willys is one of producing great cars and great debt. His factories were highly leveraged meaning hiccups in the US economy sent tremors through his businesses. Not only that he borrowed to buy other businesses such as the Moline Plough Company in 1918 which made the "Universal" farm tractor range and then a year later the Duesenberg company, mainly for their factory in New Jersey, where he planned to build a new range of six-cylinder cars.

At the same time his workers at the Toledo plant were restless over industrial issues and violent strikes happened, closing the plant for many months. Willys brought in General Motors' vice-president Walter Chrysler, (on a salary of $US1 million a year) to sort out the mess. However, when Chrysler tried to get rid of Willys, shareholders blocked the move and he left to start his own business, the Chrysler company.

Willys sold two businesses, including the New Jersey plant to pay down debt and the company's finances were again stable. Politically a Republican, Willys was appointed the first US ambassador to Poland in 1930. That posting ended in 1932 and Willys returned to the US to find his company again deep in debt. Willys-Overland went into bankruptcy in 1933 and John Willys worked hard to get the company through the Great Depression, an event that claimed many car makers. He died in 1935 of a stroke.

Willys-Overland was reorganised in 1936 and became Willys Overland Motors. In 1941 the Willys MB, better known as the Willys Jeep, started production and more than 653,000 were produced by Willys, Ford and American Bantam for the war effort. A fitting tribute for John North Willys, even though he did not have a hand in its creation.

SPEED TABLES

mph	Km/h
10	16.09
15	24.1
20	32.18
30	48.2
40	64.36
50	80.46
60	96.56
70	112.6
80	128.7
85	136.7
90	144.8

The lightweight piston used in 'Whitey'.

Acknowledgements

Many thanks to the following individuals and organisations for their assistance in my research.

David L. Crisp from The Willys-Overland Club of Victoria Inc. for use of his document, WHITEY.

Whitey owner, Graham Crittenden and Whitey's custodian, Graham's daughter, Sally York and Studebaker Six replica owner, Gavin Mutton.

George Gilltrap for giving me rare original photographs of Whitey when briefly fitted with a Knight V8 engine in 1916.

The RACQ, The State Library of Victoria, The State Library of Queensland. The book, The Road to Ruin.

The digitised newspaper web site, Trove, was invaluable for research of key figures in this book: Fred Z. Eager, Edward Eager, A.V.Dodwell, Alec Fraser Jewell and Professor Starlight.

I would like to acknowledge my wonderful wife Shelly for supporting me while I launched into a third research and writing bender.

To the many unkown newspaper photographers and one known snapper, George Jackman, *Brisbane Courier* and *Brisbane Mail* correspondent, for his 1916 images taken on Southport Beach.

Lastly, many thanks to my good friend, and motoring journalist, Derek Ogden who read the manuscript and corrected my mistakes. Any errors that remain are mine alone.

INDEX

Australian states as follows: NSW - New South Wales; Qld - Queensland;
SA - South Australia; Vic - Victoria; Tas - Tasmania; WA - Western Australia.

Cartoon from *The Steering Wheel* September 1916 showing Fred Eager in 'Whitey' struggling with the Queensland roads system.

www.ingramcontent.com/pod-product-compliance
Lightning Source LLC
Chambersburg PA
CBHW021225090426
42740CB00006B/379